Partition and the Practice of Memory

Churnjeet Mahn · Anne Murphy
Editors

Partition and the Practice of Memory

Editors
Churnjeet Mahn
Department of English
University of Strathclyde
Glasgow, UK

Anne Murphy
Department of Asian Studies
University of British Columbia
Vancouver, BC, Canada

ISBN 978-3-319-64515-5   ISBN 978-3-319-64516-2   (eBook)
https://doi.org/10.1007/978-3-319-64516-2

Library of Congress Control Number: 2017948718

Cover image: © Raghavendra Rao K.V.

Printed on acid-free paper

This Palgrave Macmillan imprint is published by Springer Nature
The registered company is Springer International Publishing AG
The registered company address is: Gewerbestrasse 11, 6330 Cham, Switzerland

For Kabir, who draws the world with a careful eye, named for someone who crossed borders of all kinds.

Acknowledgements

This book emerges out of a multi-session panel that was convened by the editors at the 24th European Conference on South Asian Studies in Warsaw, Poland 27–30 July 2016, under the auspices of the European Association for South Asian Studies. We are grateful to all the participants in the panel for the conversations that emerged and lead to the volume, and for their quick turnaround on the essays, as well as to the Conference for providing us the location to undertake them. Sincere thanks are also due to Palgrave for undertaking this publication and making it possible to publish it in 2017, the 70th anniversary of Partition; thank you particularly to Molly Beck and Oliver Dyer for shepherding us through the process. Anne Murphy's participation in the conference was made possible by a Dean of Arts Travel grant from the University of British Columbia, with the additional support of the Wall Scholars program of the Peter Wall Institute for Advanced Studies at UBC; Murphy was a Wall Scholar for the 2016-7 academic year. She would also like to thank author Zubair Ahmed for his generosity in sharing his work and ideas. Churnjeet Mahn would like to thank the University of Strathclyde and the AHRC (AH/L503587/1 & AH/N004094/1) for supporting her research in Punjab and would like to give a special acknowledgement to collaborative work with Gurmeet S Rai. Special thanks to artist Raghavendra Rao K.V. for engaging with the idea for the volume to produce an original cover image within a narrow timeframe. And, as always, thanks are due to Aidan and Kabir for their patience with their mother's scholarly work; they were sorely missed during the trip to Warsaw.

CONTENTS

Editors and Contributors

About the Editors

Churnjeet Mahn is a Chancellor's Fellow and Senior Lecturer in English Literature at the University of Strathclyde. Her research falls into the areas of heritage and memory in conflict, and travel studies, with a special interest in race and sexuality. Her first monograph, *British Women's Travel to Greece, 1840–1914* (Ashgate 2012) analysed the interplay between discourses of Hellenism and Orientalism in nineteenth-century British women's writing. She is currently working on a large three-year AHRC project which provides a comparative approach to understanding Partition. She has edited special journal editions, serves on editorial boards and has published in journals including *Victorian Studies* and *Annals of Tourism Research*.

Anne Murphy is Associate Professor in the Department of Asian Studies at the University of British Columbia. Dr. Murphy's research interests focus on early modern and modern cultural representation in Punjab and within the Punjabi Diaspora, as well as more broadly in South Asia, with particular attention to the historical formation of religious communities and special but not exclusive attention to the Sikh tradition. Her monograph, *The Materiality of the Past: History and Representation in Sikh Tradition* (Oxford University Press 2012), explored the construction of Sikh memory and historical consciousness in textual forms and in relation to material representations and religious sites from the eighteenth century to the present. She edited a thematically related volume entitled *Time, History and the Religious Imaginary in South Asia* (Routledge 2011). She has published articles in *History and Theory*, *Studies in Canadian Literature*, *South Asian History and Culture*, *the Journal of the American Academy of Religion*, and other journals.

Contributors

Heba Ahmed completed her MPhil at the Centre for Political Studies, Jawaharlal Nehru University in 2016. Her M.Phil. Dissertation is titled "Remembering Gujarat 2002: Contending Memories and the Politics of Violence". Her research interests focus on minority rights and anti-Muslim violence in India, feminism and the place of Muslim women in India, and the politics of memory and majoritarianism.

Michel Boivin is Director of Research at the National Centre for Scientific Research (CNRS) and is a member of the Centre for South Asian Studies (CEIAS). His work focusses on the historical anthropology of South Asian societies in colonial and postcolonial periods. His teaching at the School of Advanced Studies in Social Sciences (EHESS) covers a wide scope of topics from social hierarchy and the construction of new elites to material religious culture, including iconography, with a focus on the Sindhicate area. He has authored or edited 13 books, and numerous papers published in academic journals.

Anne Castaing is a senior researcher at CNRS–CEIAS (Centre for South Asian Studies, Paris) and a former research fellow at IIAS (Leiden). Her main research topics include: South Asian literatures, postcolonial and gender studies, and subaltern studies. Her publications include *Ecrire et penser le genre en contexte postcolonial* (2017); *La Modernité Littéraire Indienne: Perspectives Postcoloniales* (2009); *Ragmala: Une anthologie* (2005), and several articles on South Asian literatures and subaltern studies. She is currently editing a volume on the representation of Partition in the arts in South Asia. She heads two research programmes: DELI (Encyclopaedic Dictionary of Indian Literatures, 2015–2018); and Gender and Divided Nations (2017–2018).

Pallavi Chakravarty teaches history at the School of Liberal Studies, Ambedkar University Delhi, New Delhi, India. She completed her Ph.D. from the Department of History, University of Delhi in 2013. Her thesis looked at the rehabilitation of the "Partition-refugee" in India from a comparative perspective, focussing on Punjabi refugees in Delhi and Bengali refugees in Calcutta. Her thesis is soon to be published by Primus Publications: *Rehabilitating the Refugee: An East–West Story* (1947–1971).

Sanchari De is a doctoral student at the department of Film Studies, Jadavpur University, India, and an Erasmus Mundus fellow at the department of Communication and Media, Lund University, Sweden. She studied English literature at the University of Calcutta and film studies at Jadavpur University. Her research interests include digital media, memory and political mobilisations. Apart from her research and academic interests, she enjoys teaching her mother-tongue language, Bengali in schools in Sweden.

Radha Kapuria is a Commonwealth Scholar currently completing her Ph.D., "Music in Colonial Punjab: A Social History", at King's College London. She completed her MPhil in Modern Indian History at the Centre for Historical Studies, Jawaharlal Nehru University in New Delhi. She has a bachelor's degree in history from Delhi's Lady Shri Ram College and a master's degree from St Stephen's College. She has taught history at Delhi's Indraprastha College for Women.

Siobhan Lambert-Hurley is Reader in International History at the University of Sheffield. Her research focusses on women, gender and Islam in South Asia. Her recent publications include *Speaking of the Self: Gender, Performance, and Autobiography in South Asia* (co-edited with Anshu Malhotra) (2015). Currently, she is completing a book on women's autobiography in Muslim South Asia, while leading a project on Muslim women travellers from Asia and the Middle East. She also curates the website, "Accessing Muslim Lives" http://www.accessing-muslimlives.org.

Bhavna Rajpal is a doctoral candidate working on the subject of Sindhi cinema at the University of Westminster. She was the curator and the director of the first-ever Sindhi Film Festival in London (December 2015–January 2016), which screened Sindhi films from both Pakistan and India. More recently, in December 2016, with Prof. Michel Boivin, Rajpal co-organised the Sindhi devotional conference and the Sindhi Film Festival 2.0 in Paris at the Centre for South Asian Studies (CEIAS), CNRS-EHESS. She will be making her acting debut in the upcoming Sindhi film *Oh Muhinji Soni* (Oh My Darling). To commemorate the Partition, Rajpal will be presenting papers and delivering lectures at various international conferences in 2017.

Daniela Vitolo is a Ph.D. candidate at the Department of Literary, Linguistic and Comparative Studies of the University of Naples "L'Orientale". Her research focus is the representation of national identity in Pakistani Anglophone literature. Her study analyses contemporary fiction focussing on how the authors represent the relationship between physical or symbolic border-crossings and the processes of personal and collective identity formation. Her works have appeared in *Transnational Literature*, *Anglistica* and *Quaderni della ricerca*.

Philipp Zehmisch is Postdoctoral Research Fellow at the Center for Advanced Studies, LMU Munich. His research in political anthropology, postcolonial studies, and migration studies has a regional focus on South Asia. Philipp's current project, "Dichotomous Sovereignty: Cultures of Remembrance, Historiography and Nation-Building in South Asia". examines contemporary legacies of Partition from an ethnographic perspective. His monograph *Mini-India: The Politics of Migration and Subalternity in the Andaman Islands* was published in 2017 by Oxford University Press.

LIST OF FIGURES

CHAPTER 1

Introduction: Partition and the Practice of Memory

Churnjeet Mahn and Anne Murphy

In October 2016, the Partition Museum opened in Amritsar, Punjab with the aim of delivering "a world class, physical museum, dedicated to the memory of the Partition of the subcontinent in 1947—its victims, its survivors and its lasting legacy."[1] Claiming to be the first museum of its kind, the museum sits in Amritsar's Town Hall and is part of the city's "Heritage Mile" linking the Town Hall to the Golden Temple. The museum contains a representation of a well to signify honour killings and suicide, and contains extracts of oral histories from a spectrum of witnesses ranging from significant players in the execution of Partition to ordinary refugees. Red and white are dominant colours through the

---

[1] For further details see the Partition Museum http://www.partitionmuseum.org/about-us/. Accessed 13 May 2017.

C. Mahn (✉)
University of Strathclyde, Glasgow, UK
e-mail: churnjeet.mahn@strath.ac.uk

A. Murphy
University of British Columbia, Vancouver, Canada
e-mail: anne.murphy@ubc.ca

© The Author(s) 2018
C. Mahn and A. Murphy (eds.), *Partition and the Practice of Memory*,
https://doi.org/10.1007/978-3-319-64516-2_1

1

exhibition space and several maps illustrate the borders and boundaries of the emergent nations. Alongside the 1947 Partition Archive, which collects oral histories from across South Asia on an online platform, the museum represents a significant step towards bringing memories of Partition into contact with the present and making them available to a broad public.[2] Restoring and conserving memories of Partition, and housing and displaying them in a museum, frames such memories in the context of heritage and its management. The conservation of these memories becomes an act of restorative justice, although their caretaking by the state or institutions can complicate the way in which they can be used to interrogate the ongoing effects and legacies of Partition. Across Amritsar, new statues to Maharaja Ranjit Singh and the architect of the Indian constitution, Dr. B.R. Ambedkar, have been erected alongside the augmentation of existing sites of commemoration, such as Jallianwala Bagh. Histories of nation, empire, decolonisation and violence have thus been simultaneously renovated in Amritsar, a kind of cacophony of memory inscribed in the built environment. Heritage can be understood as a practice of memory: a process whereby the past is selectively used for contemporary cultural and ideological imperatives, often to create national, ethnic, religious, or cultural belonging. Memory can be institutionalised, and through this process it can lose its vital character.

An example of this can be seen in the area surrounding the Partition Museum, which has undergone significant renovation, with pedestrianised walkways alongside the imposition of a standardised architectural style, more Jaipuri than Punjabi.[3] As one commentator put it:

> The facades of all buildings are blushing pink in Kota stone tiles and trellis screens and this includes the market places and shops selling the city's famous 'pappar-warhian', Punjabi 'juttis', religious artefacts and much

---

[2] Digital innovations have transformed the available archive of Partition accounts available to the general public and scholars. The 1947 Partition Archive runs a series of internships for the purpose of gathering new oral histories, to grow an online interactive database which aims to document the range and diversity of experiences, recorded across languages. It also crowdsources personal stories of Partition thereby offering a route for the South Asian diaspora to contribute their own accounts. See the Partition Archive http://www.1947partitionarchive.org/. Accessed 13 May 2017.

[3] The name of the architectural firm leading this work, Sincere Architects, betrays its own stance on representing heritage in Amritsar.

more. It is disbelief for a moment that one is perhaps a trespasser into a cinema studio all painted and unreal waiting for directors to call the shots. Even shopkeepers look like some junior artistes who do not know how to play their part and what lines to say. The grimy Dharam Singh Market on the Golden Temple road has been turned into pretty pink, and right in front is a rectangular block on which life-size bhangra dancers, carved out of black marble, are jeering and striking poses.[4]

Amritsar's markets already contained examples of intangible heritage from the region, all of which have significant histories, from the areas selling *juttis* (traditional shoes) to ornate metal work used in temples across northern India and local delicacies such as *kulche* (a type of fried bread). Pink plaster, marble and trellis have become ways of covering over, reorganising and displacing some of these shopkeepers, artisans and families, who have carried with them generations of skills and craft embodied in the objects, foods and services they provide. The simulacra represented above are modelled on a homogenous, more recognisably "Indian", architecture which works to erase the authentic layered "grime" of the past.[5] The levelling of the past in the face of the present and the former's reanimation through a programme of heritage management represents how memories, history and the past can be recycled and refashioned by the present in a way that evacuates them of real or visceral connections to the past. Memory is not an inert archive to be organised and collected, nor is it something that can simply be recorded or restored. It is a dynamic process and sits in larger contexts that define, delineate and can ultimately limit its character.

---

[4] See Nirupama Dutt, "Amritsar's Makeover: Golden Grandeur with a Heritage Tinge," *Hindustan Times*, 24 October 2016 http://www.hindustantimes.com/punjab/ht-special-amritsar-gets-a-majestic-makeover-golden-grandeur-with-a-heritage-tinge/story-0GisnbT-7dbOtJj4l6fG2aI.html. Accessed 13 May 2017.

[5] A range of press articles have addressed the admixture of older Indian architectural styles that are not indigenous or apparently sympathetic to the region but which nonetheless impart a sense of authenticity through historicity. For example, see the use of "vintage" in Gautam Dheer, "Vintage Look for Amritsar City," *Deccan Herald*, 27 November 2016 http://www.deccanherald.com/content/583306/vintage-look-amritsar-city.html. Accessed 13 May 17.

Partition has been described as "not a static event of the past, but an evolving moment in history."[6] But the moment of Partition does not evolve in a straight line with clearly delineated cause and effect. Instead, it is marked fundamentally by moments of interruption and breakage (in both cause and effect), hiccups in time and unpredictable repercussions and impacts. The inability to come to terms with that past, and the repeated recurrence of sectarian violence since, may reflect, Tarun Saint has argued, the "belated psychological after-effects of the rupture of Partition."[7] In this way of thinking, Partition then is a set of events, but also a series of material and psychological effects that move forward (and some might even say backward, retrospectively) in time from the event— Bhaskar Sarkar argues that Partition functions across time, forward and backward, as an originary site of a larger history of violence; he thus includes 1905 in his Partition chronology.[8] Indeed, one of the important recent observations of new scholarly work on Partition has been attention to the "long Partition", which in the words of Vazira Zamindar is the unfinished "post-colonial burden of this political Partition" and a history that "unsettles ... [the] national closure given to Partition's displacements."[9] The years 1971, 1984 and 2002 can thus be added to a list of dates which have their own specificity, but whose rupture opens a route into, and is often named as a repeat of, the past. Memory does not simply move forward or accrue more wisdom in its accumulation: it is a process anchored in the present, reaching into the past.

This edited collection attends to the locations of memory along and about the Indo-Pakistan and Indo-Bangladesh borders and the complex ways in which such memories are both allowed for and erased in the present. The collection is situated at the intersection of memory and commemoration in order to ask how memories have been formed and

---

[6] Amritjit Singh, Nalini Iyer, and Rahul K. Gairola, "Introduction," in *Revisiting India's Partition* (Lenham: Lexington Books, 2016), 15–35: 28.

[7] Tarun Saint, "The Long Shadow of Manto's Partition Narratives: 'Fictive' Testimony to Historical Trauma," *Social Scientist* 40, no. 11/12 (2012): 53–62; see 53.

[8] Sarkar Bhaskar, *Mourning the Nation: Indian Cinema in the Wake of Partition* (Durham: Duke University Press, 2009), 15.

[9] Vazira Fazila-Yacoobali Zamindar, *The Long Partition and the Making of Modern South Asia: Refugees, Boundaries, Histories* (New York: Columbia University Press, 2007), 7. See also: Tai Yong Tan and Gyanesh Kudaisya, *The Aftermath of Partition in South Asia* (London: Routledge, 2000).

perpetuated across the imposition of these borders as kinds of intentional practice. This allows us to explore how national boundaries both silence memories and can be subverted in important ways, which we will address through a consideration of (a) physical sites and cultural practices on both sides of the India–Pakistan–Bangladesh borders that gesture towards that which has been lost—that is, the cultural whole that was (and as is shown here, still *is*) South Asia, and particularly the cultural regions of Punjab and Bengal, before Partition; (b) broader cultural "wholes" across South Asia, across religious and linguistic lines; alongside (c) forces that deny such connections. The chapters contained herein address issues of heritage and memory through specific case studies on present-day memorial, museological or commemorative and creative practices, through which sometimes competing memorial landscapes have been constructed and memories of past traumas and histories have become inscribed into diverse forms of cultural heritage (the built landscape, literature, film).

Memory has constituted a significant locus of work on Partition, exemplified by the field-defining work of Gyanendra Pandey, such as his 2001 *Remembering Partition: Violence, Nationalism, and History in India*; Ritu Menon and Kamla Bhasin's *Borders and Boundaries: Women in India's Partition* from 1998; and Urvashi Butalia's 1999 *The Other Side of Silence: Voices from the Partition of India*.[10] These works aimed to augment the (then typical) focus of scholarship on elite political perspectives on independence in the subcontinent with personal narratives by individuals who experienced Partition violence and its aftermath. Discussion of the history of the Partition of the Indian subcontinent up until that point had largely involved a process of disavowal, described by Gyanendra Pandey as "justifying, or eliding, what is seen in the main as ... an illegitimate outbreak of violence, and at making a case about how this goes against the fundamentals of Indian (or Pakistani) tradition and history: how it is, to that extent, not our history at all."[11] Nationalist historical narratives then, in Alex Padamsee's apt phrasing,

---

[10] Urvashi Butalia, *The Other Side of Silence: Voices from the Partition of India* (Karachi: Oxford, 1999); Ritu Menon and Kamla Bhasin, *Borders and Boundaries: Women in India's Partition* (New Delhi: Kali for Women, 1998); Gyanendra Pandey, *Remembering Partition: Violence, Nationalism, and History in India* (Cambridge: Cambridge University Press, 2001).

[11] Pandey, *Remembering*, 4.

"fled the scene for the onward progress of the newborn state" (more appropriately, states).[12] This non-history also recurs: Ritu Menon, Kamla Bhasin and Urvashi Butalia pointed out in ground-breaking articles in 1993 (and in larger bodies of work) that a then new accounting of the history of Partition was brought into being by the experience of anti-Sikh violence in Delhi in 1984, which made the Partition vividly present for a new generation of researchers. With such recurrence, according to Menon and Bhasin, "the question of how such events are recorded, and by whom, returns to haunt us and acquires greater urgency with each subsequent episode."[13] The emergence of this memory work thus emerged roughly in response to the 1984 violence against Sikhs in Delhi and other north Indian urban centres, and conjoined strikingly with the fiftieth anniversary of the Partition of the subcontinent, in 1997. The recurrence of Partition violence and the commemoration of it were thus marked within scholarly accounts, part of an ongoing understanding of Partition as an idea and experience marked by repetition and reiteration.

In the decade following, creative production came to occupy a particularly important locus for investigation of how memory has been construed across the Partition border, both in specific genres (such as Tarun Saint's important 2010 monograph entitled *Witnessing Partition: Memory, History, Fiction*, Sarkar Bhaskar's 2009 work *Mourning the Nation: Indian Cinema in the Wake of Partition*, and Jisha Menon's more recent exploration of both public and theatrical performance, *The Performance of Nationalism: India, Pakistan, and the Memory of Partition* in 2013) and in broader terms (such as in the essays found in Anjali Gera-Roy and Nandi Bhatia's 2008 edited volume, *Partitioned Lives: Narratives of Home, Displacement, and Resettlement*, which combined work on film and literature with work on personal narratives [and such narratives themselves], alongside historical accounts of Partition).[14]

---

[12] Alex Padamsee, "Uncertain Partitions: 'Undecidability' and the Urdu Short Story," *Wasafiri* 23, no. 1 (2008): 1–5; see 1.

[13] Ritu Menon and Kamla Bhasin. "Recovery, Rupture, Resistance: Indian State and Abduction of Women during Partition," *Economic and Political Weekly* 38, no. 17 (April 24, 1993): WS2–WS11; see WS2. See also: Urvashi Butalia, "Community, State and Gender: On Women's Agency during Partition," *Economic and Political Weekly* 28, no. 17 (April 24, 1993): WS12–WS21 + WS24; see WS12.

[14] Bhaskar, *Mourning the Nation*; Jisha Menon, *The Performance of Nationalism: India, Pakistan, and the Memory of Partition* (Cambridge: Cambridge University Press, 2013); Anjali Gera-Roy and Nandi Bhatia, *Partitioned Lives: Narratives of Home, Displacement,*

Ian Talbot's *The Independence of India and Pakistan: New Approaches and Reflections* and Amritjit Singh, Nalini Iyer and Rahul Gairola's *Revisiting India's Partition: New Essays on Memory, Culture and Politics* from 2013 and 2016, respectively, are two more recent collections that demonstrate the range of current thinking in Partition studies.[15] Talbot's work weaves in material that interrogates the British role in Partition while Singh et al. focus on a demonstration of a range of case studies from across India, moving across time. To this we can also add Ishtiaq Ahmed's *The Punjab Bloodied, Partitioned and Cleansed: Unravelling the 1947 Tragedy through Secret British Reports and First-person Accounts*, which constructs a history of Partition from a wide range of archival and oral sources, simultaneously seeking to explore historical causality and to theorize based on this case.[16] With the publication of volumes such as Nandita Bhavani's 2014 *The Making of Partition: Sindhi Hindus and the Partition of India* and Debjani Sengupta's 2016 *The Partition of Bengal: Fragile Histories and New Borders,* Partition studies has expanded to produce accounts of a range of borders, communities and experiences, providing a needed counterpoint to a prior emphasis on Punjab.[17] In terms of disciplinary range, such works evidence how the integration of methodologies such as oral history, theorisation of memory (predominantly from Holocaust studies), and the study of intersectionality has radically diversified the range of evidentiary material.

A good example of this is Ananya Jahanara Kabir's 2013 monograph, *Partition's Post-Amnesias: 1947, 1971 and Modern South Asia,* which explicitly addresses the limitations of using models of memory and

and Resettlement (New Delhi: Pearson Longman, 2008); Tarun Saint, *Witnessing Partition: Memory, History, Fiction* (New Delhi: Routledge, 2010).

[15] Ian Talbot, *The Independence of India and Pakistan: New Approaches and Reflections* (Oxford: Oxford University Press, 2013); Singh, Iyer, and Gairola, *Revisiting India's Partition.*

[16] Ishtiaq Ahmed, *The Punjab Bloodied, Partitioned and Cleansed: Unravelling the 1947 Tragedy through Secret British Reports and First-person Accounts* (Karachi: Oxford University Press, 2012).

[17] Nandita Bhavani, *The Making of Partition: Sindhi Hindus and the Partition of India* (New Delhi: Tranqubar Press, 2014); Debjani Sengupta, *The Partition of Bengal: Fragile Histories and New Borders* (Cambridge: Cambridge University Press, 2016).

trauma taken from Holocaust studies.[18] Work such as Kabir's focusses on the development of new theoretical paradigms not only for addressing the temporality of Partition, but also how affect and narrative can be understood as intersecting forces. This moves *beyond* readings of art in terms of historical realism into a consideration of sensation and embodied emotion.[19] Studies of cultural production around Partition have been particularly significant in this respect, as the impossibility of definitively capturing or describing Partition has been inscribed in the experimental writing of figures such as Amitav Ghosh and Salman Rushdie. While literature can be a way of imagining representations missing from the archives, this reductive reading of the literary misses the politics behind creative interrogations of truth-making and authenticity in accounts of Partition. Debali Mookerjea-Leonard's 2017 *Literature, Gender and the Trauma of Partition: The Paradox of Independence* and Rini Bhattacharya Mehta and Debali Mookerjea-Leonard's 2015 edited collection, *The Indian Partition in Literature and Films: History, Politics and Aesthetics* offer important interrogations of discussions around trauma, gender and memory through creative examples whose loosened ties to historical veracity open complex discursive planes; these can demonstrate how the figuration of "silence" or "multi-directional memory" can be seen in the metaphorical space and narrative dexterity of Partition literature, which configures lives and societies in the processes of becoming.[20]

This volume constitutes a fitting addition to this existing body of scholarship on Partition, timed to coincide with its seventieth anniversary in 2017, while making several specific interventions: (1) it updates and extends scholarship that is now a decade or more old, integrating the current understanding of commemorative practices and cultural representation with our understanding of the ongoing transnational dominance

---

[18] Ananya Jahanara Kabir, *Partition's Post-Amnesias: 1947, 1971 and Modern South Asia* (New Delhi: Women's Unlimited, 2013).

[19] A recent example of this work can be seen in Rituparna Mitra, "Affective Histories and Partition in Postcolonial South Asia: Qurratulain Hyder's *Sita Betrayed*," in *The Postcolonial World*, ed. Jyotsna G. Singh and David D. Kim (London: Routledge, 2017), 68–85.

[20] Debali Mookerjea-Leonard, *Literature, Gender and the Trauma of Partition: The Paradox of Independence* (London: Routledge, 2017); Rini Bhattacharya Mehta and Debali Mookerjea-Leonard, eds., *The Indian Partition in Literature and Films: History, Politics and Aesthetics* (London: Routledge, 2015). See Butalia, *Other Side of Silence* for one seminal discussion of silence, and Michael Rothberg, *Multidirectional Memory: Remembering the Holocaust in the Age of Decolonization* (Stanford: Stanford University Press, 2009).

of memory as a cultural form today in general, and specifically with reference to Partition; (2) it focusses on cultural representation and the representation of the past (rather than merging personal experiential narratives with such representations) while maintaining a commitment to a range of genres and forms: film, literature, site/the built landscape, cultural practice/ritual and historical narrative; and (3) we extend our understanding of Partition beyond the traditional temporal boundaries that have previously dominated work on the subject, to examine the contemporary production of references to Partition and commemorative practices, in relation to recent and ongoing events. This latter point is of particular importance to us. Partition in this view is not only a set of temporally ordered events, but also acts as a series of material and psychological effects and representations that move in time from the event. This draws on the already mentioned insights of Menon, Bhasin and Butalia that a then new accounting of the history of Partition was brought into being by the experience of anti-Sikh violence in Delhi in 1984, which made Partition (and Partition-like violence) vividly present for a new generation of researchers. Our work pushes this envelope, inviting readers to consider Partition not as past, but as a continually unfolding present; not in terms of nostalgia, but as reference point and frame, functioning to structure experience through a past that continues to change the present in terms of how it is narrated, commemorated and referred to.

Structure of the Volume

This volume is divided into three parts. The first of these, entitled "Commemoration in the Everyday", explores everyday lived practices of memory-making among communities impacted by the cultural and religious divisions that accompanied the imposition of the 1947 border. We begin with a chapter by Radha Kapuria (King's College London, PhD candidate), "Music and its Many Memories: Complicating 1947 for the Punjab", which provides an entry into the impact of Partition "on the quotidian lives of the subcontinent's musicians."[21] Through examination of the experiences of exemplary classical musicians active in Punjab, Kapuria complicates our understanding of both the divisions and continuing connections that accompanied Partition, demanding that we interrogate and historicise the pre-Partition period independently

---

[21] This volume, 19.

from Partition and post-Partition experience, moving beyond nostalgia towards a critical engagement with cultural practices and historical change. This paper is well positioned in relation to the joint work of Michel Boivin (Director of Research at National Centre for Scientific Research (CNRS) and Member, Centre for South Asian Studies [CEIAS]) and Bhavna Rajpal (University of Westminster, PhD candidate), "From Udero Lal in Sindh to Ulhasnagar in Maharashtra: Partition and Memories across Borders in the Tradition of Jhulelal", which explores the continuities that persist across the Indian/Pakistani border within Jhulelal worship traditions. Through this essay we see the intimate connection between physical objects and sites and the project of remembrance in multiple terms: with reference to the charismatic figure of Jhulelal, as an object of devotion, as well as to a region, language and culture that has become distant and unavailable (for some members of the tradition) and fractured for all. This can remind us of the ways in which commemorative sites function across cultural contexts, both within and outside of the heritage discourses that predominate in our understanding of the production of sites of memory in modern regimes of remembrance. Along parallel lines, the paper by Philipp Zehmisch (Center for Advanced Studies, Munich, Research Fellow), "Between Mini-India and Sonar Bangla: Memorialisation and Place-Making Practices of East Bengal Hindu Refugees in the Andaman Islands" explores the multiple layers of identitarian discourse production for Bengali Hindu refugees in the Andaman Islands, who simultaneously appropriate nationalising discourses while celebrating a regional identity that entails a specific experience of deprivation that is particular to the experience of Partition. We can see such practices along a continuum with the practices explored in Part III, where contemporary commemorative practices are explored in relation to a past imagined to serve a present.

Part II of this volume explores the intersection of the archive and the literary. In her essay "The Story of Partition at the Intersection of the Official and the Alternate Archives", Pallavi Chakravarty (Assistant Professor, Ambedkar University Delhi) offers insight into the ways in which the archive that Partition Studies draws on has changed and expanded. Charting the changing shape of the Partition archive from official contemporary documents to historiography and more contemporary feminist interventions, Chakravarty offers a reminder of how the limits of the archive mark the limit of our own understanding of 1947 and its moment. The archive becomes another practice of memory, collecting, collating and organising its narratives, at dynamic exchange with archives constructed out of the personal and the narrative. This focus on narrative remains in the following essay. With her contribution, entitled "Narrating Trauma, Constructing Binaries, Affirming Agency: Partition in Muslim Women's Autobiographical Writing", Siobhan Lambert-Hurley (University of Sheffield, Reader in International History) continues important work on women's writing around Partition by addressing the relative absence of Muslim women's memoirs from existing feminist criticism. By using gender and religion as analytical categories for discussing trauma, Lambert-Hurley is able to show how "widening the corpus to include autobiographical writing by Muslim women—not just from Bangladesh, but India and Pakistan too—can establish new parameters and possibilities for our understanding of Partition."[22]

In "Relocating the Memory of the Partition in Bapsi Sidhwa's *Defend Yourself Against Me*", Daniela Vitolo (University 'L'Orientale—Naples, PhD candidate) offers an analysis of Bapsi Sidhwa's short story "Defend Yourself Against Me" to question some of the ways in which the trauma resulting from Partition echoes through the South Asian diaspora. How does the memory and the associated guilt or trauma of that moment transmit itself across different borders, to North America? How do narratives of pain and shame work in communities which are not partitioned and have not experienced it in their own diasporic communities? Vitolo offers a route into thinking about the effect of Partition across territories, and what dislocation can, in some sense, *enable*, through the experience of distance. "Poetics of Pain: Writing the Memory of Partition" by Anne Castaing (CNRS, Paris, Research Fellow) draws on the major developments and innovations in feminist approaches to Partition studies to question the way in which literature can be used to give voice to embodied violence and its attendant emotions, especially in the context of women's writing. By drawing on a range of literary case studies, she considers how violence is inscribed in the text and in memory.

In Part III of the volume, essays explore a diverse array of locations where the spectre of Partition haunts the lived present, and the ways this spectre has served to provide the grounds for understanding a present marked by loss and violence that evoke Partition as a foundational moment. "The Gulbarg Memorial and the Problem of Memory" by Heba Ahmed (Jawaharlal Nehru University, New Delhi, PhD candidate) explores the genocidal violence against Muslims in Gujarat in 2002 and the effort required to remember this violence within political

---

[22]This volume, 134

circumstances that insist upon its erasure. Here we see the way politics in the present impinge on memory and memorialisation, where the commemoration of trauma becomes itself a political act within a politics of forgetting. The trope of Partition functions here to name violence, but perhaps falsely so: perhaps there is the need to break that tie, to allow us to see the violence of 2002 for what it is, not as a spectre of another violence. Or, if it is connected, as the founding violence of the nation that undergirds both experiences of violence, perhaps we need to account for the specificity of the politics associated with this connection, such that it is the violence of the national project that we see enacted again and again? We see similar tensions in the essay "The Shahbag Protest and Imagining an 'Ideal' Bangladesh", by Sanchari De (Jadavpur University, Kolkata/Lund University, Sweden PhD candidate/EMINTE scholar), where the author explores individual accounts of national belonging that received a platform for expression in Bangladesh in the Shabhag protest there, articulating new ideas of an "ideal" Bangladesh grounded in the founding ideals of Bangladeshi independence.

In "Remembering a Lost Presence: The Spectre of Partition in the Stories of Lahore-Based Punjabi-Language Author Zubair Ahmed" by Anne Murphy (University of British Columbia, Canada, Associate Professor), we see exploration of Partition as a spectre—as the underlying ground that constitutes the present for a contemporary writer living in Lahore today. Here memory as an intentional practice is foregrounded, as constituting the very ground of life today. With 'Memory in Ruins: "Past Presents" in the Aam Khas Bagh, Churnjeet Mahn (University of Strathclyde, Senior Lecturer) offers a summary of a collaborative heritage project in Sirhind, Indian Punjab, which focussed on Mughal-era buildings and monuments left largely abandoned in the wake of Partition. With the evacuation of Sirhind's Muslim population to Pakistan, the emptiness and gradual ruination of key heritage sites, such as the sixteenth-century Aam Khas Bagh, marks how signs from Sirhind's diverse past fail to be sustainable or fully realisable in the present.

In sum, these essays suggest the ways in which a set of intentional practices inform our production of an understanding of Partition today, complicating our interpretation of the "memory" of Partition and extending the broad relevance of "heritage" to this foundational violence. The politics of commemoration are imbedded within both nationalising and international discursive regimes. Here in these essays we see the ways in which Partition as a form of founding national violence eludes conventional nationalising representational discourses and persists to haunt the present, both in creative and memorial forms, as the outside that is always already there.

Works Cited

Ahmed, Ishtiaq. *The Punjab Bloodied, Partitioned and Cleansed: Unravelling the 1947 Tragedy through Secret British Reports and First-person Accounts*. Karachi: Oxford University Press, 2012.

Bhaskar, Sarkar. *Mourning the Nation: Indian Cinema in the Wake of Partition*. Durham: Duke University Press, 2009.

Bhavani, Nandita. *The Making of Partition: Sindhi Hindus and the Partition of India*. New Delhi: Tranqubar Press, 2014.

Butalia, Urvashi. "Community, State and Gender: On Women's Agency during Partition." *Economic and Political Weekly* 28, no. 17 (April 24, 1993): WS12–WS21 + WS24.

——. *The Other Side of Silence: Voices from the Partition of India*. Karachi: Oxford, 1999.

Dheer, Gautam. "Vintage Look for Amritsar City." *Deccan Herald*, 27 Nov 2016 http://www.deccanherald.com/content/583306/vintage-look-amritsar-city.html. Accessed 13 May 2017.

Dutt, Nirupama. "Amritsar's Makeover: Golden Grandeur with a Heritage Tinge." *Hindustan Times*, 24 Oct 2016 http://www.hindustantimes.com/punjab/ht-special-amritsar-gets-a-majestic-makeover-golden-grandeur-with-a-heritage-tinge/story-0GisnbT7dbOtJj4l6fG2aI.html. Accessed 13 May 2017.

Kabir, Ananya Jahanara. *Partition's Post-Amnesias: 1947, 1971 and Modern South Asia*. New Delhi: Women's Unlimited, 2013.

Mehta, Rini Bhattacharya, and Debali Mookerjea-Leonard, eds. *The Indian Partition in Literature and Films: History, Politics and Aesthetics*. London: Routledge, 2015.

Menon, Jisha. *The Performance of Nationalism: India, Pakistan, and the Memory of Partition*. Cambridge: Cambridge University Press, 2013.

Menon, Ritu, and Kamla Bhasin. "Recovery, Rupture, Resistance: Indian State and Abduction of Women During Partition." *Economic and Political Weekly* 38, no. 17 (24 April 1993): WS2–WS11.

——. *Borders and Boundaries: Women in India's Partition*. New Delhi: Kali for Women, 1998.

Mitra, Rituparna. "Affective Histories and Partition in Postcolonial South Asia: Qurratulain Hyder's *Sita Betrayed*." In *The Postcolonial World*, edited by Jyotsna G. Singh and David D. Kim, 68–85. London: Routledge, 2017.

Mookerjea-Leonard, Debali. *Literature, Gender and the Trauma of Partition: The Paradox of Independence.* London: Routledge, 2017.

Padamsee, Alex. "Uncertain Partitions: 'Undecidability' and the Urdu Short Story." *Wasafiri* 23, no. 1 (2008): 1–5.

Pandey, Gyanendra. *Remembering Partition: Violence, Nationalism, and History in India.* Cambridge: Cambridge University Press, 2001.

Rothberg, Michael. *Multidirectional Memory: Remembering the Holocaust in the Age of Decolonization.* Stanford: Stanford University Press, 2009.

Roy, Anjali Gera and Nandi Bhatia. *Partitioned Lives: Narratives of Home, Displacement, and Resettlement.* New Delhi: Pearson Longman, 2008.

Saint, Tarun. *Witnessing Partition: Memory, History, Fiction.* New Delhi: Routledge, 2010.

———. "The Long Shadow of Manto's Partition Narratives: 'Fictive' Testimony to Historical Trauma." *Social Scientist* 40, no. 11/12 (2012): 53–62.

Sengupta, Debjani. *The Partition of Bengal: Fragile Histories and New Borders.* Cambridge: Cambridge University Press, 2016.

Singh, Amritjit, Nalini Iyer, and Rahul K. Gairola. "Introduction." In *Revisiting India's Partition*, 15–35. Lenham: Lexington Books, 2016.

Talbot, Ian. *The Independence of India and Pakistan: New Approaches and Reflections.* Oxford: Oxford University Press, 2013.

Tan, Tai Yong, and Gyanesh Kudaisya. *The Aftermath of Partition in South Asia.* London: Routledge, 2000.

The Partition Archive. http://www.1947Partitionarchive.org/. Accessed 13 May 2017.

Zamindar, Vazira Fazila-Yacoobali. *The Long Partition and the Making of Modern South Asia: Refugees, Boundaries, Histories.* NY: Columbia University Press, 2007.

PART I

Commemoration in the Everyday

CHAPTER 2

Music and its Many Memories: Complicating 1947 for the Punjab

Radha Kapuria

Music is often invoked as the "glue" that unites people, acting as a perennial symbol of a historically composite culture disrupted by the rupture of Partition.[1] This view posits a kind of pluralistic and decentred South Asian "musical citizenship" that counters the narrow, antagonistic and populist definition of citizenship tied exclusively to either India

---

[1] For a representative example, see Varun Soni, "India, Pakistan and the Musical Gurus of Peace," *Huffington Post*, 14 June 2010, http://www.huffingtonpost.com/varun-soni/india-pakistan-and-the-mu_b_606870.html. Accessed 2 May 2017.

R. Kapuria (✉)
King's College London, London, England, UK
e-mail: radhakapuria@gmail.com

© The Author(s) 2018
C. Mahn and A. Murphy (eds.), *Partition and the Practice of Memory*,
https://doi.org/10.1007/978-3-319-64516-2_2

17

or Pakistan.[2] However, we cannot easily transpose such views of cultural citizenship back in time, as doing so leads to a gravely presentist reading of our musical pasts, and rides roughshod over the complex trajectories musicians' lives took post-1947. At the same time, there is no doubt that the division of the subcontinent on the basis of religion instituted changes in the way music was conceptualised, patronised and understood in the fledgling twin states of Pakistan and India. As demonstrated by Michael Nijhawan, Partition "led to a redistribution of performative styles and repertoires", with a greater emphasis on religious content.[3] Virinder Kalra's recent work on Punjab also demonstrates the overlapping boundaries between *kirtan* and *qawwali* music, and how over the course of the twentieth century, and particularly in the wake of Partition, the two "became Sikh and Muslim music, respectively ... despite similarity in audibility and performer overlap."[4] He thus remarks how, as a result of Partition, "musicians with broad repertoires began to restrict themselves in the face of a narrowing patronage."[5]

In Pakistan, as noted by Pakistani scholar Saeed Malik and Indian documentary filmmaker Yousuf Saeed alike, there was a proactive attempt to Islamicise music, by ridding it of any Hindu referents.[6] In a parallel way,

---

[2] This idea is derived from the IMR Distinguished Lecture Series on "The Musical Citizen" delivered by Martin Stokes, especially the first lecture on "How Musical is the Citizen?," at the Senate House, University of London, 4th May 2017. See http://www.the-imr.uk/distinguished-lecture-series/. Accessed 1 May 2017. Stokes focussed on the debates around citizenship which music has been meshed with, building on scholarship across disciplines such as sociology, philosophy, anthropology and ethnomusicology; ranging from Aihwa Ong's concept of "flexible citizenship" (1999) in globalised, transnational times, to Hannah Arendt's critique of citizenship under totalitarian regimes (1951). See Aihwa Ong, *Flexible Citizenship: The Cultural Logics of Transnationality* (Durham, NC: Duke University Press, 1999); Hannah Arendt, *The Origins of Totalitarianism* (New York: Harcourt Brace and Company, 1951).

[3] Michael Nijhawan, "Punjab's *Dhadi* Tradition: Genre and Community in the Aftermath of Partition," *Indian Folklife* 3, no. 4 (October 2004): 5–7; see 7.

[4] Virinder Kalra, *Sacred and Secular Musics: A Postcolonial Approach* (London: Bloomsbury, 2014), 16.

[5] Ibid., 137. He also notes that, mainly on account of their ascriptive identity as Muslims, the "remaining *rababis* in East Punjab no longer found patronage in *gurdwaras* and had to engage in the emerging state-sponsored folk art, with an emphasis on Sufi texts that were seen as part of a distant folk culture." Ibid.

[6] Saeed Malik, *The Musical Heritage of Pakistan* (Islamabad: Idara Saqafat-e-Pakistan, 1983); Yousuf Saeed, "Fled Is That Music," *India International Centre* Quarterly 35, no. 3/4, the Great Divide (Winter 2008–Spring 2009): 238–249.

in India there was a strengthening of the trends of Hinduisation, begun in the nineteenth century by Pandit Paluskar, the man who spearheaded the nationalisation and standardisation of Indian classical music, as well as a more conscious packaging of music as an "ancient" cultural symbol that could represent the new India to the rest of the world.[7] Yet, while we know of these broader changes in the musical landscape, the impact of Partition on the lives of musicians and artists has been little studied, scattered as it has been across disparate accounts of music, and different biographies of musicians.[8] As a result, we lack a comprehensive account of the repercussions of this cataclysm on the quotidian lives of the sub-continent's musicians, relying instead on superficial celebrations of music as a means of building unity and on assumptions about what came before Partition.[9] However, if we closely examine the life stories and views of a handful of musicians, we find that examples of "Punjabiyat"[10] accompany instances of prejudice. The relationship of musicians to Partition

[7] For more on Paluskar, see Janaki Bakhle, *Two Men and Music: Nationalism in the Making of an Indian Classical Tradition* (New Delhi: Oxford University Press, 2005). With the assertion of a monolithic Sikh identity in the late nineteenth century, music was also defined anew. See Bob van der Linden, *Music and Empire in Britain and India: Identity, Internationalism, and Cross-Cultural Communication* (New York, NY: Palgrave Macmillan, 2013), Chap. 5 on "Sikh Sacred Music: Identity, Aesthetics, and Historical Change," 129–156.

[8] Barring the work of Yousuf Saeed, there has been little scholarly or sustained engagement on this theme. In 2008, along with Prof. Lakshmi Subramanian, Saeed co-organised a 2-day workshop in August 2008, on "Hindustani Music and Partition" at New Delhi's Jamia Millia Islamia, where musicians and musicologists from India, Pakistan and beyond participated. For details see http://ektara.org/workshop08.html. Accessed 14 May 2017.

[9] In contrast, there is a vast and proliferating literature detailing the impact of Partition on the literature, cinema and intellectual life of South Asia. For a representative and concise example, see Meenakshi Mukherjee, "Dissimilar Twins: Residue of 1947 in the Twenty-First Century," *Social Semiotics* 19, no. 4 (December 2009): 441–451.

[10] Madan Gopal Singh has recounted to the author his early childhood memories of growing up in Amritsar, being able to tune in and listen to Radio Lahore, evoking how the idea of "Punjabiyat" in a broader "radio republic," as it were, that integrates and subverts the border, re-connecting people. On Punjabiyat, see Alyssa Ayres, "Language, the Nation, and Symbolic Capital: The Case of Punjab," *The Journal of Asian Studies* 67, no. 3 (August 2008): 917–946; Pritam Singh, "The idea of Punjabiyat." *Himal Southasian* 23, no. 5 (2010): 55–57; and "Introduction: Punjab in History and Historiography," in *Punjab Reconsidered: History, Culture, and Practice*, ed. Anshu Malhotra and Farina Mir (New Delhi: Oxford University Press, 2012), xv–lviii.

and to religious difference, therefore, is complex and at times contradictory, and eludes simple characterisation, positive or negative.

In this chapter, I wish to examine, in preliminary terms, the impact of India's partition on practitioners of Hindustani classical music, in particular those belonging to the region of Punjab. Punjab provides an interesting case study, for three reasons. First, as Nijhawan, Kalra and Anjali Gera-Roy have established, the post-Partition restructuring of performance styles has blinded us to the more amorphous performative world of pre-1947 Punjab.[11] This is so, even as the shared cultural matrix of ideas and aesthetic sensibilities that characterised the undivided Punjab continues to resonate across the borders today in the many songs and traditions shared by people in West (Pakistan) and East (India) Punjab. Second, in Punjab the degree of personal rupture was more thorough, and achieved in a shorter period of time, given the "genocidal proportions" of the 1947 mass killings, which were in contrast to the lesser degree of violence on the Bengal side (which, thanks to its more porous riverine borders, among other factors, experienced a slower process of population exchange).[12] Third, while the work of Kalra and Nijhawan has addressed folk musicians, *dhadhis* and performers of Sikh *kirtan* like the Ragis and Rababis, classical musicians have been neglected in these and other scholarly accounts of music in Punjab.[13] Kalra briefly examines the discourse of colonial commentators and native elites, to conclude that "colonial modernity shaped and crafted designs" of both folk and classical music: while the latter "was able to service the new nation", the former "remained the local residual and thus steeped in

---

[11] See Anjali Gera-Roy, *Bhangra Moves: Bhangra Moves: From Ludhiana to London and Beyond* (London: Ashgate, 2010), 22, 55, 72–75.

[12] Joya Chatterji, *The Spoils of Partition: Bengal and India, 1947–1967* (Cambridge: Cambridge University Press, 2007), 111. On the nature of Partition-induced migrations in Bengal, see chap. 3, "Partition and Migration: Refugees in West Bengal, 1947–1967," 105–158. Chatterji demonstrates how the bulk of East Bengali Hindu peasants migrated much later, in the wake of communal conflagrations beginning in 1949.

[13] Kalra notes the connections between folk and classical in post-1947 Punjab, while noting the almost exclusive patronage of folk music in the Indian Punjab. Kalra, *Sacred*, 134–146.

colonial terminology."[14] However, he doesn't sufficiently account for the marginalisation of the classical from discourses on Punjabi culture.[15] In contrast, I wish to portray the importance of hereditary Hindustani/art musicians for the regional Punjab context, to reveal how classical training had a relevance outside, and beyond, the paradigm of the nation in a more local milieu.[16] I thus wish to challenge the symbolic alienation of the "classical" from Punjab's culture in both popular and scholarly discourse. While doing so, I am mindful of the paradoxical locations that "classical" music has historically had in the Punjab context, within spaces associated with "folk", *qawwali*, or *gurbani* music—such as *melas* (fairs), or shrines of Sufi saints. The celebration (both lay and academic) of genres of music performed *only* in these "popular" spaces, symbolised semiotically by either a bucolic conviviality or a martial vigour, has obscured the important role played by classically trained, *gharana*-based musicians in the sociocultural history of Punjab. By focussing on classical musicians in Punjab, whilst simultaneously being attentive to their connections with folk, *gurbani*, or *qawwali* music, I hope to offer a distinctive perspective within work on culture in modern South Asia.

---

[14] Ibid., 134–135.

[15] While colonialism surely changed the ways in which Hindustani art (or Classical) music was perceived and organised in South Asia, it would be erroneous to assume that the binary between Classical and Folk, or *Margi* and *Desi* music was thoroughly a product of colonial modernity, as the assumption seems to be in Kalra. For a good summary of these debates, see Katherine Butler Schofield, "Reviving the Golden Age again: 'Classicization', Hindustani Music, and the Mughals," *Ethnomusicology* 54 (2010): 484–517.

[16] See my in-progress PhD thesis (expected June 2018). I wish to build on recent literature on the social histories of music in other regions, e.g. the recent PhD theses of Richard D. Williams and Sharmadip Basu on Bengal. For Rajasthan, see Daniel Neuman, Shubha Chadhuri, and Komal Kothari, *Bards, Ballads, and Boundaries: An Ethnographic Atlas of Music Traditions in West Rajasthan* (Oxford: Seagull Books, 2006); and more recently, Shalini Ayyagiri, "Spaces Betwixt and Between: Musical Borderlands and the Manganiyar Musicians of Rajasthan," *Asian Music* 43, no. 1 (Winter/Spring 2012): 3–33.

The Shared Space of Music[17]

Undivided Punjab has historically been a site of communally amorphous culture-making. Ustad Badar-uz-Zaman of Lahore has described to Yousuf Saeed the "Zinda-dilan-e Lahaur" (lit., "Cheerful folk of Lahore"), an informal club of music lovers, constituted of cloth merchants and vegetable and meat sellers, who hosted evenings of classical music.[18] In this, Punjab was not unusual; as Heidi Pauwels' recent work demonstrates, musical and literary milieus in Delhi, what is now Rajasthan and elsewhere have long provided a location for dynamic and diverse forms of cultural exchange.[19] In the colonial context, research on culture in Bengal (particularly Sumanta Banerjee's earlier monograph, and Anindita Ghosh's more recent one) has also noted the permeable boundaries between elite and popular cultures in South Asia, albeit focussing on patterns of circulations between these two domains.[20]

The question animating this paper is part of a larger project to explore the several ways in which people from Punjab have been viscerally connected through their shared poetry, music and literature, despite the rigidity of borders. It is fitting that the panel leading up to this book, "Imagining a Lost Present: Situating Memory across/beyond Partition", was organised in 2016, coinciding with the two hundred and fiftieth anniversary of the birth of renowned Punjabi poet Waris Shah, whose classic composition of the folk tale of Heer-Ranjha has continued

---

[17] I borrow this term from Farina Mir's idea of Punjabi *qisse* reflecting the existence of "shared notions of piety." She posits this in opposition to the notion of "syncretism," which presupposes a fixed, "pre-existing religious identity," which was not representative for most of colonial Punjab. See Farina Mir, "Genre and Devotion in Punjabi Popular Narratives: Rethinking Cultural and Religious Syncretism," *Comparative Studies in Society and History* 48, no. 3 (July 2006): 727–758.

[18] Yousuf Saeed, "Jugalbandi: Divided Scores," *Himal SouthAsian*, February 2011, http://old.himalmag.com/component/content/article/3607-divided-scores.html. Accessed 30 June 2016.

[19] Heidi Pauwels, *Cultural Exchange in Eighteenth-Century India: Poetry and Paintings from Kishangarh* (Berlin: EB Verlag, 2015).

[20] Sumanta Banerjee, *The Parlour and the Streets: Elite and Popular Culture in Nineteenth Century Calcutta* (Calcutta: Seagull Books, 1989); Anindita Ghosh, *Power and Print: Popular Publishing and the Politics of Language and Culture in a Colonial Society, 1778–1905* (Oxford: Oxford University Press, 2006).

to unite scores of Punjabis across the border for the past 65 years.[21] However, while the subversive power of music is well recognised, it would be hazardous to impose any kind of simplistic "syncretism" on the musicians themselves. What musicians—then and now—thought of different circumstances, and of borders themselves, is not very easily categorised. Instead, musicians responded in ways that reflect their specific personal circumstances, just as other humans and agents do. A focus on the musicians of Punjab during the 1940s and 1950s, and indeed, even in the present, sensitises us to how the hard borders (including visa regimes, and passport issuance, etc.) engendered by 1947 did not appear overnight, but instead, materialised over what Vazira Zamindar has called the "Long Partition" of the subcontinent.[22]

At one level, musicians are a group for whom borders are consistently envisaged as fluid, if not entirely irrelevant, given their historic tendency to be perennially on the move, in search of patronage and audiences. This physical mobility is also tied to their institutional mobility, as liminal border-crossers, with their musical prowess helping them overcome the traditionally negative ascription of musicianship as a profession.[23] Perhaps it was in recognition of this tendency that the most famous classical musician produced by twentieth-century Punjab, Ustad Bade Ghulam Ali Khan, said with a ringing certainty that if one child in every family across the subcontinent had learnt classical music, Partition and the violence accompanying it could have been avoided. Unfortunately, this was not the case, and Partition did take place, with calamitous, unintended and sometimes surprising consequences for the subcontinent's musicians. Bade Ghulam Ali's somewhat rhetorical statements about the power of classical music are important at a deeper level too. One can read in his statement a celebration of the virtues of patience, the many

---

[21] See the commemorative event held at SOAS, London on 6 Sept 2016, titled "250 Years of Waris Shah's Heer," where speakers included Amarjit Chandan, Mahmood Awan, Madan Gopal Singh, Nur Sobers-Khan, and Navtej Purewal: https://www.soas. ac.uk/south-asia-institute/events/heritage-and-history-in-south-asia/06sep2016-250-years-of-waris-shahs-heer.html. Accessed 11 May 2017.

[22] Vazira Zamindar, *The Long Partition and the Making of Modern South Asia* (New York: Columbia University Press, 2007).

[23] Katherine Butler Brown, "The Social Liminality of Musicians: Case Studies from Mughal India and Beyond," *Twentieth-Century Music* 3 (2007): 13–49.

years of rigorous practice required to become even a merely competent classical musician; this is in contrast to the immense speed with which Partition was achieved and the havoc it created in its wake.[24] Regardless of his precise meaning, Bade Ghulam Ali recognised the power of music in preventing violence, and building peace; this is an area that demands critical research in the context of South Asia.[25]

In what follows, I explore the consequences of Partition for the musicians of the Punjab through the life-trajectories of two well-known musicians, Roshanara Begum and Ustad Bade Ghulam Ali Khan, and the views of two lesser-known ones, Muhammad Hafeez Khan Talwandiwale and Pt. Ramakant Sharma. I utilise the moment of Partition, and the divergent views it precipitated amongst musicians, to shed light on a more chequered social history of the musicians in the region. Section 1 of the paper explores the material changes and shifts in the lives of classical musicians in Punjab, as well as attempts at subverting and traversing the Radcliffe line made by musicians and their patrons. Section 2, on the other hand, examines how musicians view the particular character of this divide; I illustrate that views around the *mirasi*, Punjab's caste of hereditary musician-genealogists, became especially central to it. While a Pakistani musician attributes the decline in patronage to the loss of patrons, and consistently defined the *mirasi*s as a plague and a negative force to be reckoned with, an Indian counterpart patronisingly appropriates to India the status of "saviour" of the *mirasi*. In both cases, views regarding these two contradictory groups—the *mirasi* at the low end of the spectrum, and elite, state-supported patrons on the other—are at the heart of understanding the differences in the life of music between India and Pakistan. Finally, Sect. 3 takes a step back to consider the recurring trope of nostalgia, delineating its centrality for musicians in South Asia. In the case of musicians affected by Partition, I argue for the existence of a "double nostalgia": one for a better time of musical patronage, performance and audience appreciation, as well as for the undivided space that existed in the pre-Partition times. Throughout the paper, my concern is with how musicians viewed: (a) the shared past; (b) their musical worlds

---

[24] I am grateful to Anne Murphy for this insight.

[25] In the western context, see Morag Josephine Grant, "Music and Human Rights," in *The Sage Handbook of Human Rights*, ed. Anja Mihr and Mark Gibney, vol. 1 (Los Angeles/London/New Delhi/Singapore/Washington, DC: Sage, 2014).

and communities of musicians across borders; and (c) differences in state patronage in India and Pakistan.

MUSICIANS AND THE MATERIALITY OF PARTITION

Khalid Basra's excellent and intensive ethnography of the Talwandi *gharana*, now based in Lahore, sheds light on the attitudes of musicians towards sociopolitical developments. Ustad Muhammad Hafeez Khan Talwandiwale came from a long lineage of *dhrupad* musicians, whose family moved from East Punjab to the newly set-up canal colony of Lyallpur (now Faisalabad) in West Punjab in the early twentieth century when his grandfather Mian Maula Bakhsh (1845–1930) accepted the invitation of wealthy Sikh landlords. For the family of Hafeez Khan Talwandiwale, Partition meant the loss of their family's patron, Sardar Harcharan Singh, who had to move to India in the wake of the violence of 1947. Basra's interviews with Hafeez Khan abound in nostalgia for the abundance of pre-Partition Faisalabad. At one point he tells Basra of the family's pre-Partition wealth, albeit with a hint of exaggeration,

> Before partition our circumstances were such that father used to bring fruit and it used to be packed in neat boxes wrapped in cotton—grapes, citrus, litchis—such top quality fruit. His income in those days was at least Rs. 500/- per day … *Our financial position was such that we used to play hockey with fruit*. Mother also used to have three changes of clothes a day … of course after Partition conditions went from bad to worse …[26]

This evocation of an abundance of quality food in pre-Partition Punjab is of course a common nostalgic trope across Partition narratives, and is noted by Basra elsewhere as well.[27]

---

[26] Khalid Basra, "'A Garland of razors': The Life of a Traditional Musician in Contemporary Pakistan" (unpublished PhD dissertation, SOAS, January 1996), 320, Emphasis added.

[27] "The Sikh patron Sardar Harcharan Singh provided the family with a large house, and was also responsible for supplying them with grain, vegetables, milk, etc. Other pupils like the Hindu barrister Amarnath were also *lavish patrons* of the family." Ibid.

The life-trajectory and career of another Punjabi musician, who hailed from west Punjab, and migrated eastwards to India a few years after Partition, provides one of our case studies. Ustad Bade Ghulam Ali Khan, the iconic and legendary vocalist of the Kasur-Patiala *gharana*, faced a problem of patronage in the fledgling state of Pakistan. Recognising greater avenues for survival in India, and disgruntled with the Islamicisation of music in Pakistan,[28] Bade Ghulam Ali migrated to India, lured by the offer of Indian citizenship made by Jawaharlal Nehru, and the encouragement of music-loving politicians like Morarji Desai.[29] This was also a result of Bade Ghulam Ali's famous tiff with the famous and powerful Director of Radio Pakistan, Z.A. Bokhari, when the latter apparently dismissed Bade Ghulam Ali's singing as "below the level of acceptability."[30]

Yet, despite the official narrative of the positive reception afforded to Bade Ghulam Ali by representatives of the so-called "secular" Indian nation, and its more open-minded patrons, India posed other problems. A brief example from the Harballabh music festival of Jalandhar (on which more below) during the 1950s bears this out. Harballabh has been feted as a place where musicians performed for a minimal fee, given its status as a space of devotionalism, where musicians performed for more mystical reasons. I have described elsewhere how the festival, which started in 1875, had its origins in a tradition of cosmopolitan devotionalism (with *dhrupad* music as the primary genre performed), which had shifted by the turn of the twentieth century to a more Hindu devotional sphere, thanks to the efforts of Pt. Paluskar, who also popularised *khayal*

---

[28] See Basra, "A Garland," 128–129, for an account of this. He quotes from the Public Relations Directorate Radio Pakistan which goaded Pakistani musicians to "draw inspiration from the music of other Muslim countries," and lauded the efforts of those composers who created "compositions based on Arabic and Iranian music forms."

[29] Malti Gilani and Qurratulain Haidar, *Ustad Bade Ghulam Ali Khan "Sabrang": His Life and Music* (New Delhi: Harman Publishing House, 2003).

[30] Basra, "A Garland," 325.

across India, and especially at the Harballabh.[31] However, the turn to greater professionalisation ushered in under Mr. Ashwini Kumar, who was charged with the organisation of the festival (on whom more below), was seen as a negative development by many old Harballabh hands, like Jagannath Parti, one of the founder members of the Sangeet Mahasabha in 1922. The finger of blame was unequivocally pointed in the direction of Ustad Bade Ghulam Ali's insisting that he be paid a performance fee; he was contrasted with the more pious (and unsurprisingly, Hindu) performers of the past[32]—mostly students of Pt. Paluskar, who himself had inaugurated the era of a nationalised, Hindu devotional avatar for Indian classical music, coupled with a suspicion of dancing girls and Muslim performers.[33]

This example illustrates the hidden hostility exhibited by upper-caste Hindu music patrons and audience members towards even the most accomplished of Punjabi Muslim musicians. It is no wonder then that not all Punjabi Muslim musicians felt as secure staying on in India as Khan *saheb*: to counterweigh the substantial presence of a sole Bade Ghulam Ali Khan (who chose to migrate to India only late in the day), there was a greater outflow of legendary classical musicians from eastern Punjab to Pakistan. These included Patiala *gharana* doyens like Fateh

---

[31] Radha Kapuria, "Rethinking Musical Pasts: The Harballabh Music Festival of Punjab," *Social Scientist* 43, no. 5–6 (May–June 2015): 77–91. In his otherwise valuable book, Virinder Kalra erroneously claims that the Harballabh had undergone a process of nationalisation and religious revival *prior* to the arrival of Paluskar, when, in fact, the evidence points to the contrary. Kalra, *Sacred*, 61. As I have demonstrated in my MPhil thesis, Paluskar's visits to the Harballabh (among other reasons) were the prime motivating factor that impelled the organisers to change the character of the festival from a fair to a concert resembling those organised in *metropoli* like Lahore, Bombay and Calcutta.

[32] Kapuria, "Muse for Music," 99–103.

[33] For a more detailed account of Paluskar's reception in Punjab, see James Kippen, *Gurudev's Drumming Legacy* (London: Ashgate, 2006), 24–26. For a more general account on Paluskar, apart from Bakhle's seminal work, see Michael David Rosse, "The Movement for the Revitalization of 'Hindu' Music in Northern India, 1860–1930: The Role of Associations and Institutions" (unpublished PhD dissertation, University of Pennsylvania, 1995).

Ali-Amanat Ali[34] and the brothers Salamat-Nazakat Ali, exponents of the Sham Chaurasi *gharana*, amongst many others.

Ashwini Kumar, the man responsible for the modernisation of the Harballabh classical music festival in Jalandhar in the Indian Punjab, represents a mature form of nationalism, not grounded in cultural exclusivism. One of India's most highly decorated policemen, he went on to become the Director General of the Border Security Force, one of the high points of his illustrious career. He retired from the latter position and was awarded the Padma Bhushan in 1972 for his outstanding service in the Indo-Pak War of 1965. In the 1950s he also modernised the Harballabh festival, which he had attended since childhood. His favourite vocalist was Calcutta-born Roshanara Begum, a cousin of the legendary Ustad Abdul Karim Khan who went on to become one of Pakistan's most accomplished female classical musicians. She migrated to Pakistan in 1948 with her husband, who hailed from Lala Musa of the Gujrat region in West Punjab. In a 2011 interview, Kumar recounted the story of surreptitiously collaborating with Roshanara Begum's husband (who, like him, was a policeman) to enable her to cross the border, so that she could perform at Harballabh.

> People were ready to pay 10 lakhs for (her to sing) a 10-minute raga in Bombay. They would say, please just do the 'aaa' of an 'alaap'; she still didn't come. Her husband was a policeman, so that's how I got to her. He used to be in the police in Bombay, then in Pakistan.

> When I went to Lahore, I called her husband. I said: Please ask your wife to come and perform at Jalandhar. She sang … and I tell you, (even) Bhimsen Joshi couldn't control the crowd that night, it was so rowdy. I said (to her), you go and sit. She sang, the moment she said 'aaaa', the whole crowd, must have been about 15–20,000 people, it was raining outside, winter, 27th of December, they wanted to listen to her. With one hour, she captured the audience, and stilled the entire crowd.[35]

---

[34] Fateh Ali-Amanat Ali made their first spectacular debut in Lahore in 1945, thanks to the sponsorship of Pt. Jeevan Lal Matto, Program Executive of the All India Radio in the city. Matto was also the man responsible for spotting the musical talent in a young Mohammed Rafi, who was working at a barber's shop in Lahore, and encouraging him to sing on Radio.

[35] Interview with Ashwini Kumar dated 2 Feb 2013.

This example demonstrates how Kumar utilised his precolonial professional ties in the police bureaucracy to actually subvert the Radcliffe line, so that an Indian audience could revel in the unparalleled artistry of a Pakistani musician. His musical zeal thus existed simultaneously with his status as an Indian policeman at the forefront of a war against Pakistan, revealing the complications and contradictions in the postcolonial middle-class patronage of music in India.

These narratives of migration across the border came together in real time when the organisers of the Harballabh festival in 2011 scaled immense bureaucratic hurdles to ensure the performance of Lahore-based *dhrupad* musicians of the Talwandi *gharana*. Exponents of this *gharana* were performing in Jalandhar for the first time in almost 135 years, when their forebear Miyan Qalandar Bakhsh was first offered a *nazrana* (homage) of one and a half rupees by the *mahant* of the Devi Talab *sakti peeth* site and festival founder Baba Harballabh, as an invitation to come and perform there.

Although Partition impeded musicians from performing across the 1947 borders, there exist numerous instances indicating how these boundaries did not daunt all musicians. In a version of the Roshanara Begum anecdote, Ustad Nusrat Fateh Ali Khan's father and uncle, who migrated to Pakistan in 1947 (but were originally based in Jalandhar's Pathan *basti*s or settlements), made the journey back to their home town in 1952 as a kind of pilgrimage—to perform at the annual *urs mela* (fair) held at the shrine of Sufi saint Hazrat Imam Nasr. Jalandhar's Hindu and Sikh inhabitants apparently turned out in vast numbers to listen to their former co-residents perform at the legendary fair for the first time in more than five years.[36] Thus, the very real boundaries that existed were also subverted at times, allowing for performance opportunities across the border. At the same time, however, older caste prejudices continued to create *internal* borders, within individual national contexts.

---

[36] Anecdote narrated by Jalandhar-based musician Mohan Malsiani in an interview dated 19 Oct 2011. Malsiani recounted listening in rapt attention, as a young man, to the *qawwalis* they performed in the saint's honour.

CLASSICAL MUSICIANS AND THE *MIRASI*

Pt. Ramakant Sharma, tabla maestro, before his retirement the most senior music teacher at the old Kanya Mahavidyalaya of Jalandhar, and the longest-serving performer at the Harballabh, hails from a family, from the Nurmahal district close to Jalandhar, that had participated in the struggle for freedom. He represents the devotional Hindu strain of performers at the Harballabh, who, whilst participating in its Hindu façade and veneer, nonetheless have a somewhat romantic-nostalgic view of the *mirasi*.

> There has been a tradition of having Mirasis in Punjab, even though common people viewed them negatively, yet there was also such a time when *these very* Mirasis nourished music, kept it alive ... To a great extent they kept our classical music alive.
>
> Also, *just look* at the regard in which they are held here, these people don't enjoy the same respect in Pakistan ... Over there 60–70 per cent people don't view the Mirasis from a good perspective. I have seen this: the High Commissioner of India used to say that *the Mirasi who has crossed the Ravi dariya [river], he goes to India and becomes Allah (God)*.
>
> *You see, before Partition, whatever* mehfils *used to take place were primarily run by Hindus*. Nobody used to differentiate (between people) ... (but), for those who used to sing, it was the children of the Hindus who touched their feet, and took their blessings, [even] ate together—there was no differentiation. Because the 'vidya' [knowledge] of music is 'Brahm Vidya'.[37]

After proffering a (somewhat grudging) acknowledgement of the positive role played by the "socially low" *mirasi*, Ramakant thus glorifies India, while at the same time, looking down at Pakistan from a superior, subtly condescending position. We also witness Ramakant's tendency to generalise and attribute all positive patronage of art musicians to "India" and/or Hindus. This positioning is typical: India is often seen—by

---

[37] Interview dated 24 Oct 2011, in Kapuria, "A Muse for Music," 300–320.

musicians on both sides of the border—as a space with greater avenues for the fostering and reproduction of classical music.[38]

Yet, despite an external patronising attitude and the apparent encouragement proffered vis-à-vis the *mirasi* in India, as we see in Ramakant's account, there has been, on the whole, a steady current of censure towards this community. Similarly, according to the world view of Pakistan-based Hafeez Khan, who inherited the majority of his *mirasi* students "from his father, grandfather, and other ancestors through various pupillary linkages",[39] we find a strongly negative stereotype and "Othering" of the *mirasi*. Otherwise praised for their "profound understanding of the *ustad–shagird* [master–student] relationship", they were condemned for their "dangerous" proclivity to "pass off the knowledge learnt from the *ustad* as 'inherited'. They attempt to fabricate identities and use the knowledge, the composition and *rags* as weighty evidence in the politics of pedigree."[40] In the following quote on the *mirasi*, Hafeez Khan sets up a strict dichotomy between them and more accomplished purveyors of classical music, or *gavayyah*s:

So in the villages all the Sikhs and other *dihati* [rural] people etc., got hooked on to their *rags* [throat movement] *avazaan* [peculiar voice culture] and manner and style of singing. When the *riasats* finished and the *gavayyah*s came to these towns and places these '*mirasis*' had already been accepted as *gavayyah*s. Their voices were very different. *Gavayyah*s' voices were polished and cultured whereas their [*mirasis*'] voices were raw and uncouth like *dangaris*; tremulous and thick and loud like the village watchmen who boast of having the capability of being heard across the village. Sikhs used to like these voices a lot as these resembled theirs and [they] accepted them (as *gavayyah*s). This is also a reason for the downfall of classical music.[41]

<hr />

[38] In this regard, the eminent Pakistani musicologist and inventor of the Sagar Veena, Raza Kazim—who migrated in 1947 from Lucknow—argued in a 2009 interview with filmmaker Yousuf Saeed that despite the veneer of state patronage, classical music in India was not doing well either. See Yousuf Saeed, *Khayal Darpan: 'A Mirror of Imagination'* (New Delhi: Ektara, 2007).

[39] Basra, "A Garland," 101.

[40] Ibid.

[41] Ibid., 111–112. More references to the ignominies of being a *mirasi* are found on 113; and 208–211.

Hafeez Khan thus constructs a clear connection between the *mirasi* and the Sikhs—ascribing to them the common qualities of being "uncouth" and "loud", and indeed holding them responsible for the downfall of the classical style in the Punjab.

Ironically, though unsurprisingly, many Sikhs themselves saw the *mirasi* as being extraneous to the Punjab itself. For example, the Sikh Memorandum in [July 1947] to the Boundary Commission argued against the division of Punjab, which they claimed, belonged more to them than other Punjabis. Pointing to the long history of Sikh–Muslim antagonism, the political machinations of the Muslim League and Congress, and mainly to counter the Muslim predominance in the population of Punjab, they singled out the "floating population", which accounted for around 31 per cent of the entire Punjabi Muslim population, comprising, among others, mendicants, cobblers, blacksmiths, potters, bards, and *mirasi*, a group which:

> is not rooted in the soil of the Punjab and is essentially of a floating character. The floating population amongst the Hindus and Sikhs, according to the census returns, is almost nil … .[42]

It is interesting how, on account of their itinerant nature, the *mirasi* and other low-status Punjabi Muslims are seen as being "un-Punjabi" and extraneous to the land by representatives of the Sikh Memorandum to the Commission.[43] In short, on account of their lower-caste status, the *mirasi* were roundly castigated by all middle-class and elite Punjabis, regardless of religious orientation.

To return to the Talwandi *gharana*, a close examination of Hafeez Khan's views helps us see the very real effects of division. His eagerness to reclaim *dhrupad* as an Islamic practice (where the genre's characteristic *alaap gayaki* [singing] is claimed to be a corruption of "Allah Aap" or "God Thyself"[44]), as well as negatively stereotyping Sikhs and *mirasi* as

---

[42] "Sikh Memorandum to the Punjab Boundary Commission," in *Select Documents on the Partition of the Punjab 1947*, ed. Kirpal Singh (New Delhi: National Book Shop, 1991), 226–263.

[43] This was not necessarily the view of all Sikhs in Punjab.

[44] I borrow this translation from Saeed, "Fled Is That Music," 2009, 242.

being cut from the same (musical) cloth, can be situated in the social and ideological attitudes of a Pakistan preoccupied with Islamicisation. This contrasts both with his positive romantic-nostalgic memories of pre-Partition Sikh and Hindu patrons, and his adoption of certain Hindu-Sikh practices (such as not eating beef).

In both India and Pakistan, however we have seen how the *mirasi* function in tropes of self-identification that the more elite *kalawant* musicians narrate and believe about themselves. Lower-caste communities, *mirasi* and *kanjris*—viewed through a derogatory lens—are at the heart of this variety of "Othering". An observation of the opinions of musicians therefore reveals how the "Other" is often not simplistically identified with the enemy nation; rather, older asymmetries (on the lines of caste) persist, are re-enforced, and are common to musicians on both sides of the border. The hostility towards the *mirasi* remains a constant, throughout time and across space.

A DOUBLE NOSTALGIA: IMAGINING ALTERNATIVE PASTS AND FUTURES

There have been attempts to revive Punjabiyat through music, theatre and other cultural forms in recent years. Navtej Purewal, among others, has noted the substantial cultural efforts made in contemporary times to transgress borders.[45] Musicians have been at the forefront of this transgression, for sound is a medium that has relentlessly offered an opportunity to subvert man-made boundaries, and musical memory has always been perpetuated and shared across these hard borders. Throughout South Asia, scenes and settings for music which existed before, and which go beyond national borders, are alive in the memories of music lovers. For example, M.A. Sheikh's reminiscences about a soirée in pre-Partition Lahore at which the teenaged Roshanara Begum supposedly outshone Bade Ghulam Ali Khan belong to a cultural space where the

---

[45] There have been successive attempts, in independent India and Pakistan, at subverting the effects on the cultural life of the nation as created by the borders of 1947. The efforts of the Pakistan India People's Forum for Peace and Democracy (PIPFPD), have, in particular been inspiring. For a more general account of these efforts, see N. Purewal, "The Indo-Pak Border: Displacements, Aggressions and Transgressions," *Contemporary South Asia*, 12, no. 4 (2003): 539–556.

1947 borders are irrelevant, regardless of the fact that those two musicians later became inscribed as citizens of rival nations.[46] Studying the broader cultural "whole" of Hindustani art music that has historically existed across the length and breadth of north India, across religious and linguistic lines, is thus a productive site for tracking subversion of the 1947 borders.

Given the fact that Bade Ghulam Ali Khan's home town was Kasur, in the Pakistani Punjab, and that much of his professional life was spent in Lahore, toward the end of his life, he deeply longed for his place of origin, reminiscing over facets of it including the quality of the land, its water and especially the grain, and other food-related experiences. Svetlana Boym's pithy and humorous words about the conditions in which nostalgia can flourish are rather apt here: "nostalgic love can only survive in a long-distance relationship."[47] We have already noted Hafeez Khan's longing for the flourishing patronage and cultural (even agricultural!) milieu of pre-Partition Lyallpur. In Roshanara Begum's interviews too, we find her professing nostalgic memories and love for her native Calcutta, the cities of Bombay and Lucknow (from where her family hailed) and for the audiences of the first two cities.[48] Hence, we also note a strain of nostalgia for the learned audiences of connoisseurs, who could appreciate the intricacies of the classical.

We thus encounter mirror images of nostalgia for musical forms and cultural milieus on opposite sides of the border. There is a need to distinguish between the temporal nostalgia for a different time, i.e. the time of the past, and the nostalgia for an undivided Punjab, undergirded by visions of Punjabiyat. The first is what Regula Burckhardt Qureshi, in an incisive article on the social location of Begum Akhtar, calls the "nostalgia for the feudal past."[49] In the case of Punjab, the second is the nostalgia for the shared past of pre-Partition times. Nostalgia is important, because

---

[46] M.A. Sheikh, *Great Masters, Great Music* (Bloomington, USA: Xlibris Corporation, 2010).

[47] Svetlana Boym, *The Future of Nostalgia* (New York: Basic Books, 2001), 18.

[48] See Roshanara Begum's PTV "Program Mulaqat" interview by Khalil Ahmad and M. Iqbal: https://www.youtube.com/watch?v=IjstjdxlVhE. Published 12 September 2015; Accessed 14 November 2017.

[49] Regula Burckhardt Qureshi, "In Search of Begum Akhtar: Patriarchy, Poetry, and Twentieth-Century Indian Music," *The World of Music* 43, no. 1, Ethnomusicology and the Individual (2001): 97–137.

"unlike melancholia, which confines itself to the planes of individual consciousness, nostalgia is about the relationship between individual biography and the biography of groups or nations, between personal and collective memory."[50] Boym also cautions us against nostalgia without an eye to the future, because, "fantasies of the past determined by needs of the present have a direct impact on realities of the future.'[51]

We see in these memories, then, a nostalgia for an alternative past that has been lost. This is embodied in physical structures,[52] symbols of a now-forgotten musical past. Pul Kanjri or Tawaifpul (the Bridge of the Dancing Girl) is located between Amritsar and Lahore, near the present-day Wagah border. This abandoned precinct consists primarily of a bridge that included on it, at one point, "a *dharamsala*, a well, a tank, a garden and a *sarai*";[53] it was built for, and on the insistence of, the Muslim courtesan who went on to become Maharaja Ranjit Singh's favourite wife, Moran Sarkar. The structure is located on the present-day border of the two states, and has been briefly conquered in skirmishes by both nations: by Pakistan in 1965, after which it was "reclaimed" by India in 1971. If "consideration of the future makes us take responsibility for our nostalgic tales", as Boym urges us to do, then we must take a newer look at the past, and excavate fresher stories from it about the divergent figures peopling it.[54] The story of Bibi Moran, Ranjit's favourite wife, for whom he braved stiff Sikh orthodoxy, is one such story, pointing to a time of remarkable cosmopolitanism, when many parts of Punjab witnessed a cultural efflorescence, and where religious and/or political ideologies failed to stifle art.[55]

---

[50] Boym, *Future*, 27.

[51] Ibid., 26.

[52] See Churnjeet Mahn's chapter in this volume on the Aam Khas Bagh complex in Sirhind.

[53] Ganesh Das, *Early Nineteenth Century Panjab: From Ganesh Das's "Char Bagh-i-Panjab,"* trans. Grewal and Banga (Amritsar: Guru Nanak Dev University, 1975), 139.

[54] Boym, *Future*, 26.

[55] The Maharaja's marriage with Moran brought his way severe opposition from the orthodoxy: he was summoned to the Akal Takht and awarded the punishment of a hundred lashes, which he apparently went forth to receive valiantly. H.R. Gupta, *History of the Sikhs, Vol. V: The Sikh Lion of Lahore (Maharaja Ranjit Singh, 1799–1839)* (Delhi: Munshiram Manoharlal, 1991), 35. For more, see chap. 1 on "Musicians and Dancers in Pre-Colonial Punjab, with a focus on Maharaja Ranjit Singh's Court," in Radha Kapuria (in-progress PhD, expected June 2018), "Music in Colonial Punjab: A Social History," King's College London.

Conclusion

This chapter has highlighted how the lives of musicians were impacted by 1947. First, the reasons for migration across the borders during and after 1947 have been varied: marriage (Roshanara Begum and Iqbal Bano); career progression and professional recognition (Bade Ghulam Ali Khan); and, of course, the most common factors, fear of violence (the *mirasi* from Pakistan, according to Ramakant; Nusrat's father and uncles; and the Talwandiwale's patron Sardar Harcharan Singh). We have also discussed some important examples of border-crossings post-1947: Ashwini Kumar and Roshanara Begum, Nusrat's father and uncle coming to perform at Jalandhar, plus many more. These border-crossings stand out in sharp relief against the context of increasing intolerance toward cultural expression in South Asia—whether this takes the form of Hindu right-wing activists in India asking for a ban on performances by Pakistani artistes today, or of Islamist groups attacking musicians (as in the brutal assassination of Pakistani *qawwal* Amjad Sabri in 2016).

Second, divisions of caste and community in the eyes of musicians themselves have persisted across the border: practitioners of classical music across the border, have in common an "Othering" of, and distancing from, the *mirasi*. The ambivalent and consistently negative attitude toward the *mirasi*, which has a longer genealogy, perhaps holds a clue to the outlying of the classical in Punjab.[56] Partition, and the exclusions and tensions manifest within it, drew on existing issues and tensions in the social fabric that preceded it—and which adversely impacted practices comprising the shared spaces of Punjab.[57] As we saw, elite *kala-want* musicians such as Pt. Ramakant and Us. Hafeez Khan—regardless of their own social origins—held a common disdain for Punjab's *mirasi*. Whether Indian or Pakistani, therefore, maintaining a strict social distance from the *mirasi* is a crucial marker for the "respectability" of professional, *gharana*-based musicians in both Punjabs.

---

[56] See chap. 2 "A Genealogy of the *Mirasis* and *Kanjris* in Colonial Punjab," in my in-progress PhD.

[57] Anil Sethi's research excavated the shift from the secular to the religious in naming practices in 19th century Punjab, Sethi, "The Creation," 66–71. On the practices, e.g. ritual and public mourning among others, shared by women across religious boundaries in Punjab, see Anshu Malhotra, *Gender, Caste and Religious Boundaries: Restructuring Class in Colonial Punjab* (New Delhi: Oxford University Press, 2002).

Finally, Partition inaugurated a new era: in some cases marked by what I have called a "double nostalgia" for (a) the feudal past comprised of benevolent patrons (as exemplified in Us. Hafeez Khan's discourse) and (b) the shared past of "Punjabiyat" (evident in Bade Ghulam Ali's interviews). We have also witnessed other results: a self-congratulatory nationalism and condescension towards the conditions of musical production in Pakistan (Pt. Ramakant); and an emphasis on *dhrupad*'s Islamic origins, combined with an "Othering" of both the *mirasi* and Sikhs (Us. Hafeez Khan).

The impact of the 1947 borders on the new nation-state dispensations is thus very evident in the minutiae of everyday life, and in quotidian notions about music and musical communities. These beliefs, held by practising classical musicians on both sides of the border, coupled with the troubled legacies of musical genres emerging from a century of socio-religious reform and division, reveal the futility of glibly romanticising musicians as carriers of a "syncretic" phenomenon. Rather, this paper has tried to resituate musicians and patrons as historical agents functioning within complex and diverse historical contexts.

While I have consciously focussed more on views of and around musicians, and less on the music itself, future research needs to map musicians' specific memories of trauma, violence and loss in 1947, employing ethnography and biography. More crucially, it will need to excavate how the primacy of the moment of performance itself may hold the power to transform prejudice or hostility.[58] Roshanara Begum's command over the restless crowds at Harballabh, mentioned in the anecdote related by Ashwini Kumar, is a good example of the power of music. Further, as we know from the extensive literature on the *impact* of Indian music, especially the *ta'sir* (effect on the listener and the supernatural world) of a *raga*,[59] music can also have the opposite result. An anecdote from 1947,

---

[58] For the proactive uses of music in current-day peacebuilding in Palestine, see Yara El-Ghadban and Kiven Strohm, "The Ghosts of Resistance: Dispatches from Palestinian Art and Music," in *Palestinian Music and Song: Expression and Resistance Since 1900*, ed. Moslih Kanaaneh, Stig-Magnus Thorsén, Heather Bursheh, and David A. McDonald (Bloomington: Indiana University Press, 2013), 175–200.

[59] Munshi Muhammad Karam Imam Khan, *Ma'dan al-musiqi* (Lucknow: Hindustani Press, 1925), 111–116; quoted in *Tellings and Texts: Music, Literature and Performance in North India*, ed. Francesca Orsini and Katherine Butler Schofield (Cambridge: Open Book Publishers, 2015), 26–27.

featuring two foremost Delhi-based musicians with significant ties to the Patiala *gharana* and court, captures this:[60]

> At a musical soiree in early 1947 in Delhi, the renowned *sarangi* player Ustad Bundu Khan[61] insisted on playing *Raga Deepak*, a Raga charged with the brilliance and power to create fire. This was despite protestations from his cousin, foremost vocalist of the Delhi *gharana*, Ustad Chand Khan.[62] Later that year, the entire subcontinent was consumed by the fire of mass violence that spread across the land. Chand Khan went on to lay the blame solely on his cousin's shoulders, exclaiming, 'I had told you, hadn't I, not to play this sinister (*manhoos*) *Raga*?'

This anecdote holds a clue as to how at least some musicians made sense of the frenzy, insanity and "fire" of 1947, attempting to understand it through a musical metaphor, squarely outside the rational causes of "high politics" or other explanations. Perhaps this was an attempt to locate a modicum of control (albeit allegorical) within musicians' hands, during an otherwise chaotic and utterly tumultuous time? Ultimately, the anecdote holds a key for metaphorically countering Deepak's fiery impact with the cathartic showers of a raga Megh, in the way Tansen's daughter Saraswati purportedly did at Akbar's sixteenth-century court;[63] a possibility more relevant than ever for South Asia in 2017.

---

[60] I am grateful to Ayyub Auliya, the London-based independent music historian, for sharing with me this anecdote—that he read in an Urdu translation of a collection of essays by B.R. Deodhar.

[61] Ustad Bundu Khan hailed from a Rajasthani family that later settled in Delhi. His uncle and *guru*, Ustad Mamman Khan was connected to the Patiala tradition and court. See Daniel Neuman, *The Life of Music in North India: The Organisation of an Artistic Tradition* (New Delhi: Manohar, 1980), 156; Regula Qureshi, *Master Musicians of India: Hereditary Sarangi Players Speak* (New York: Routledge, 2007), 185.

[62] See Neuman, *Life*, 157. According to Amal Das Sharma, Ustad Chand Khan served as court musician at the Patiala court from 1913–1937. Amal Das Sharma, *Musicians of India* (Calcutta: Noya Prokash, 1993).

[63] Bonnie C. Wade, *Imaging Sound: An Ethnomusicological Study of Music, Art, and Culture in Mughal India* (Chicago: Chicago University Press, 1990), 116–117.

Works Cited

Arendt, Hannah. *The Origins of Totalitarianism*. New York: Harcourt Brace and Company, 1951.

Ayres, Alyssa. "Language, the Nation, and Symbolic Capital: The Case of Punjab." *The Journal of Asian Studies* 67, no. 3 (August 2008): 917–946.

Ayyagiri, Shalini. "Spaces Betwixt and Between: Musical Borderlands and the Manganiyar Musicians of Rajasthan." *Asian Music* 43, no. 1 (Winter/Spring 2012): 3–33.

Bakhle, Janaki. *Two Men and Music: Nationalism in the Making of an Indian Classical Tradition*. New Delhi: Oxford University Press, 2005.

Banerjee, Sumanta. *The Parlour and The Streets: Elite and Popular Culture in Nineteenth Century Calcutta*. Calcutta: Seagull Books, 1989.

Basra, Khalid Manzoor. "'A Garland of razors': The Life of a Traditional Musician in Contemporary Pakistan," Unpublished PhD Dissertation, SOAS, January 1996.

Basu, Sharmadip. "Tuning Modernity: Musical Knowledge and Subjectivities in Colonial India, c. 1780s—c. 1900," unpublished PhD dissertation, Syracuse University, 2011.

Boym, Svetlana. *The Future of Nostalgia*. New York: Basic Books, 2001.

Chatterji, Joya. *The Spoils of Partition: Bengal and India, 1947–1967*. Cambridge: Cambridge University Press, 2007.

El-Ghadban, Yara and Kiven Strohm. "The Ghosts of Resistance: Dispatches from Palestinian Art and Music." In *Palestinian Music and Song: Expression and Resistance Since 1900*, ed. Moslih Kanaaneh, Stig-Magnus Thorsén, Heather Bursheh, and David A. McDonald, 175–200. Bloomington: Indiana University Press, 2013.

Gera-Roy, Anjali. *Bhangra Moves: Bhangra Moves: From Ludhiana to London and Beyond*. London: Ashgate, 2010.

Ghosh, Anindita. *Power and Print: Popular Publishing and the Politics of Language and Culture in a Colonial Society, 1778–1905*. New Delhi: Oxford University Press, 2006.

Gilani, Malti, and Qurratulain Haidar. *Ustad Bade Ghulam Ali Khan "Sabrang": His Life and Music*. New Delhi: Harman Publishing House, 2003.

Grant, Morag Josephine. "Music and Human Rights." In *The Sage Handbook of Human Rights*, Vol. 1, ed. Anja Mihr and Mark Gibney. Los Angeles: Sage, 2014.

Gupta, H.R. *History of the Sikhs, Vol. V: The Sikh Lion of Lahore (Maharaja Ranjit Singh, 1799–1839)*. Delhi: Munshiram Manoharlal, 1991.

Kalra, Virinder Singh. *Sacred and Secular Musics: A Postcolonial Approach*. London: Bloomsbury, 2014.

Kanwal, Balbir Singh. *Panjab Te Parsidh Ragi Te Rababi*. Amritsar: Singh Brothers, 2010.

Kapuria, Radha. "A Muse for Music: The Harballabh Musician's Fair of Punjab, 1947–2003." Unpublished MPhil Dissertation, Jawaharlal Nehru University, 2013.

———. "Rethinking Musical Pasts: The Harballabh Music Festival of Punjab." *Social Scientist*, 43, no. 5–6, (May–June 2015): 77–91.

———. "Unconquerable Nemesis," *Postscript* in *Economic and Political Weekly*. 50, 51 (19 Dec 2015), 91–92.

Kippen, James. *Gurudev's Drumming Legacy*. London: Ashgate, 2006.

Linden, Bob van der. *Music and Empire in Britain and India: Identity, Internationalism, and Cross-Cultural Communication*. New York, NY: Palgrave Macmillan, 2013.

———. "Pre-Twentieth-Century Sikh Sacred Music: The Mughals, Courtly Patronage and Canonisation." *South Asia: Journal of South Asian Studies*, March 2015.

Mahajan, Sucheta, ed. *Towards Freedom: 1947 (Part II)*. New Delhi: Oxford University Press, 2015.

Malhotra, Anshu. *Gender, Caste and Religious Boundaries: Restructuring Class in Colonial Punjab*. New Delhi: Oxford University Press, 2002.

Malhotra, Anshu, and Farina Mir, eds. *Punjab Reconsidered: History, Culture, and Practice*. New Delhi: Oxford University Press, 2012.

Malik, M. Saeed. *The Musical Heritage of Pakistan*. Islamabad: Idara Saqafat-e-Pakistan, 1983.

Mir, Farina. *The Social Space of Language: Vernacular Culture in British Colonial Punjab*. Ranikhet: Permanent Black, 2010.

———. "Genre and Devotion in Punjabi Popular Narratives: Rethinking Cultural and Religious Syncretism." *Comparative Studies in Society and History* 48, no. 3 (July 2006): 727–758.

Mukherjee, Meenakshi. "Dissimilar Twins: Residue of 1947 in the Twenty-First Century." *Social Semiotics* 19, no.4 (December 2009): 441–451.

Neuman, Daniel. *The Life of Music in North India: The Organisation of an Artistic Tradition*. New Delhi: Manohar, 1980.

Neuman, Daniel, and Shubha Chaudhuri with Komal Kothari. *Bards, Ballads and Boundaries: An Ethnographic Atlas of Music Traditions in West Rajasthan*. Oxford: Seagull Books, 2006.

Nijhawan, Michael. "Punjab's *Dhadi* Tradition: Genre and Community in the Aftermath of Partition." *Indian Folklife* 3, no. 4, Serial No. 17 (October 2004): 5–7.

———. *Dhadi Darbar: Religion, Violence, and the Performance of Sikh History*. New Delhi: Oxford University Press, 2006.

Ong, Aihwa. *Flexible Citizenship: The Cultural Logics of Transnationality*. Durham NC: Duke University Press, 1999.

Orsini, Francesca, and Katherine Butler Schofield. *Tellings and Texts: Music, Literature and Performance in North India*. Cambridge: Open Book Publishers, 2015.

Pauwels, Heidi. *Cultural Exchange in Eighteenth-Century India: Poetry and Paintings from Kishangarh*. Berlin: EB Verlag, 2015.

Purewal, Navtej. "The Indo-Pak Border: Displacements, Aggressions and Transgressions." *Contemporary South Asia* 12, no. 4 (2003): 539–556.

Qureshi, Regula Burckhardt. "In Search of Begum Akhtar: Patriarchy, Poetry, and Twentieth-Century Indian Music." *The World of Music* 43, no. 1, Ethnomusicology and the Individual (2001): 97–137.

———. *Master Musicians of India: Hereditary Sarangi Players Speak*. New York: Routledge, 2007.

Rosse, Michael David. "The Movement for the Revitalization of 'Hindu' Music in Northern India, 1860–1930: The Role of Associations and Institutions." Unpublished PhD dissertation, University of Pennsylvania, 1995.

Saeed, Yousuf. "Fled is That Music." *India International Centre Quarterly* 35, no. 3/4, the Great Divide (Winter 2008–Spring 2009): 238–249.

———. "Jugalbandi: Divided Scores." *Himal SouthAsian*, February 2011, http://old.himalmag.com/component/content/article/3607-divided-scores.html. Accessed 30 June 2016.

Schofield (née Brown), Katherine Butler. "The Social Liminality of Musicians: Case Studies from Mughal India and Beyond." *Twentieth Century Music* 3, no. 1 (2007): 13–49.

Schofield, Katherine Butler. "Reviving the Golden Age again: 'Classicization', Hindustani Music, and the Mughals." *Ethnomusicology* 54 (2010): 484–517.

Schreffler, Gibb. "Signs of Separation: Dhol in Punjabi Culture." Unpublished PhD Dissertation, University of California at Santa Barbara, 2010.

———. ed. *Journal of Punjab Studies*, 2012, 18: 1&2: Special Issue on 'Music and Musicians of Punjab.'

Sethi, Anil. "The Creation of Religious Identities in the Punjab. c. 1850–1920." Unpublished PhD Dissertation, University of Cambridge, 1998.

Sharma, Amal Das. *Musicians of India*. Calcutta: Noya Prokash, 1993.

Sheikh, M.A. *Great Masters, Great Music*. 2010.

Singh, Kirpal. ed. *Select Documents on the Partition of the Punjab 1947*. New Delhi: National Book Shop, 1991.

Singh, Pritam. "The Idea of Punjabiyat." *Himal Southasian* 23, no. 5 (2010): 55–57.

Soni, Varun. "India, Pakistan and the Musical Gurus of Peace," *Huffington Post*, 14 June 2010, http://www.huffingtonpost.com/varun-soni/india-pakistan-and-the-mu_b_606870.html. Accessed 2 May 2017.

Vadehra, Ganesh Das. *Char Bagh- yi Punjab* (1849). Translated by J.S. Grewal and Indu Banga, *Early Nineteenth Century Panjab: From Ganesh Das's "Char Bagh-i-Panjab."* Amritsar: Guru Nanak Dev University, 1975.

Wade, Bonnie C. *Imaging Sound: An Ethnomusicological Study of Music, Art, and Culture in Mughal India.* Chicago: Chicago University Press, 1998.

Williams, Richard David. "Hindustani Music Between Awadh and Bengal, c. 1758–1905." Unpublished PhD Dissertation, King's College London, 2014.

Zamindar, Vazira. *The Long Partition and the Making of Modern South Asia.* New York: Columbia University Press, 2007.

Filmography

Ahmad, Khalil, and M. Iqbal, Roshanara Begum's PTV interview in Program Mulaqat: https://www.youtube.com/watch?v=IjstjdxlVhE, Published 12 September 2014; Accessed 15 November 2017.

Saeed, Yousuf. *Khayal Darpan: 'A Mirror of Imagination'* (Classical Music in Pakistan: A Journey by an Indian Filmmaker). New Delhi: Ektara, 2007.

CHAPTER 3

From Udero Lal in Sindh to Ulhasnagar in Maharashtra: Partition and Memories Across Borders in the Tradition of Jhulelal

Michel Boivin and Bhavna Rajpal

In this paper we focus on the physical spaces and ritual objects that support practices of remembrance in Pakistan, and also in India, in order to evaluate the possible impact of the Partition on memories of Jhulelal.[1] Our main purpose is to examine how Jhulelal is remembered

[1] This essay is a part of an ongoing project named the Udero Lal Research Project (ULRP) which is related to Jhulelal, a sacred figure venerated in Pakistan and in India among the Sindhis https://uderolalresearchproject.wordpress.com/. The project is hosted by the Center for South Asian Studies (CEIAS) at the Advanced School of Social Sciences (EHESS) and the French National Center for Scientific Research (CNRS). The best introduction to Jhulelal is Lata Parwani, "Myths of Jhuley Lal: Deconstructing a Sindhi Cultural Icon," in *Interpreting the Sindhi World. Essays on Society and Culture*, ed.

M. Boivin (✉)
National Centre for Scientific Research (CNRS), Paris, France
e-mail: michel.boivin@ehess.fr

B. Rajpal
University of Westminsterm, London, England, UK
e-mail: bhavnarajpal@gmail.com

© The Author(s) 2018
C. Mahn and A. Murphy (eds.), *Partition and the Practice of Memory*,
https://doi.org/10.1007/978-3-319-64516-2_3

in Sindh, presently located in Pakistan, and in India, among the Hindu and the Muslim Sindhis. Through the course of this chapter, we aim to address the following questions: who and what is commemorated in the shrines dedicated to Jhulelal in Pakistan and in India? Are the dynamics of remembrance and the processes of worship similar on both sides of the border 70 years after Partition, or in other words, how did Partition and migration impact the cult (especially regarding its physical spaces and other locations of memories)? Did the complex interplay between these change? Finally, we ask, is the figure which is remembered under the unique name of Jhulelal still the same? We argue that despite the upheavals related to Partition, and the diversity of elements associated with Jhulelal's tradition, it still constitutes a continuum between Pakistan and India.

Two case studies will be taken into account. The first one is the *darbar* (sanctuary) in the Udero Lal village in Sindh, Pakistan, and the second one is the Chaliha Sahib *mandir* in Ulhasnagar in Maharashtra, India. The two sites are diverse in terms of location, size and history. Udero Lal is a small village located about 50 km north of Hyderabad in Sindh. Ulhasnagar, which is about the same distance north of Mumbai, and has around half a million inhabitants, is usually described as the most Sindhi-dominated city in India, as this group accounts for about 90% of the total population of the city. The *darbar* of Udero Lal was built in the seventeenth century, while the *mandir* of Ulhasnagar was constructed after Partition by the Hindu Sindhis who had migrated from Sindh.

This paper is divided into four sections: the first is on Partition in Sindh, shrines and memories, and details the effect of Partition on the Hindu Sindhis and introduces the shrines of Jhulelal. The second section elaborates on the physical spaces of the two temples of Jhulelal, one from India and one from Pakistan, which provide the case studies for this chapter, in order to explore how the memory of Jhulelal is spacialised and materialised in these shrines. The third part analyses how processes

---

Michel Boivin and Matthew Cook (Karachi: Oxford University Press, 2010), 1–27; see also Anita C. Ray, "Varuna, Jhūlelāl and the Hindu Sindhis," *South Asia: Journal of South Asian Studies* 35, no. 2 (2012): 219–238. Jhulelal's worship is of course mentioned in other writings devoted to the Hindu Sindhis, see for example Steven Ramey, *Hindu, Sufi, or Sikh: Contested Practices and Identifications of Sindhi Hindus in India and Beyond* (New York: Palgrave Macmillan, 2008).

of remembrance surrounding Jhulelal are based on universal elements such as light or *jyot*,[2] its virtual presence, and water or *jal*. Finally, the fourth section focusses on a vernacular ritual object, the *bahraano*, whose role is crucial for memories of Jhulelal, but also for other functions connected to the relationship between Jhulelal and his devotees, in Pakistan as well as in India.

Partition in Sindh, Shrines and Memory

Partition was a total upheaval for millions of people living in the Indian subcontinent. While it occurred 70 years ago, its impact is still alive in people's memories, especially because of the massacres which occurred on both sides of the borders of the two new nation states, India and Pakistan. It is commonly understood that two provinces felt the greatest impact of Partition since in both of them, about 50% of the population were Hindu or Sikh, and 50% were Muslim: Punjab and Bengal. The word "partition" itself is especially well adapted for these provinces since they were literally, i.e. geographically, "cut" into two distinct parts, each of them becoming a province or state in a new country.

In Sindh, however the scenario was quite different for a number of reasons. First, the ratio of religious belonging was different: between 20 and 25% of the population there were Hindus or Sikhs, and 75% were Muslim. Second, most Hindu and Sikh Punjabis and Bengalis migrated to the Indian Punjab or Delhi area and Indian Bengal, respectively: thus they largely shared the culture and language of their host area, to at least some degree. Furthermore, Sindh did not suffer from the same degree of violence as Punjab and Bengal did. Although it is difficult, if not impossible, to know how many Hindus and Sikhs left Sindh, most agree on the figure of 1 million. In comparison with the experience of Hindu and Sikh Punjabis and Bengalis, the scenario was different for the Hindu Sindhis. The main difference was that they had to leave their ancestral country entirely to reach a new country, where different languages were spoken, and where the religious culture was different too. And as

---

[2] A number of words are used in Sindhi for light. For convenience, we will use one: *jyot*.

a number of recent works show, they were not always welcomed in their new country.[3]

Why did they migrate to India? This decision resulted from an array of factors. Despite the so-called lack of violence in Sindh, rumours could have played a leading role, especially since dramatic reports about Punjab were reaching the province, leading many people to be "uncertain of the future".[4] There was, therefore, a clear sense of the threat of violence. The role played by politicians, both from the Muslim League and then Pakistan, as well as the Sindh Congress and later the Indian government, is not always obvious, although the official discourse genuinely tried to convince the Hindus to stay. In any case, one event served as a turning point, although Hindus had already started to migrate to India at this point. On 6 January 1948, a crowd of Sindhi Sikhs was attacked by Muslim refugees, and while the number of victims is once again debated, a number of them were killed. Also, the Congress office in Karachi was attacked. The immediate consequence was that on 14 January, the government of India appointed a Director General of Evacuation to formally assist non-Muslims who wanted to migrate from Sindh to India.

Regarding the issue of Jhulelal's tradition, a number of Hindu Sindhi religious figures migrated to India; the transference of Sindhi sanctuaries followed the migration of its *gaddi nashins*. Hence, a number of important sanctuaries of Sindh were recreated in India by the *gaddi nashins* who had migrated. The sanctuaries in Sindh were always protected, but with varying arrangements regarding their management. But with increasing frequency, the now-Indian *gaddi nashins* or his/her followers began to provide money to the caretakers in charge of maintaining the initial shrines, now located in Pakistan. Furthermore, despite the fluctuating diplomatic relations between Pakistan and India, it was always possible to travel across the border, especially before the 1971 war.

---

[3] See in particular Rita Kothari, *The Burden of Refuge: The Sindhi Hindus of Gujarat* (Hyderabad: India Orient Longman, 2007); Nandita Bhavnani, *The Making of Exile: Sindhi Hindus and the Partition of India* (London: Westland and Tranquebar Press, 2014).

[4] Vazira Fazila-Yacoobali Zamindar, *The Long Partition and the Making of Modern South Asia* (Karachi: Oxford University Press, 2008), 66. On Sindh and partition, see also the recent issue edited by Priya Kumar and Rita Kothari, "Sindh, 1947 and Beyond," *South Asia: Journal of South Asian Studies* 39, no. 4 (2016): 773–789; see in particular the Introduction.

For example, the sanctuary of Sadh Belo was transferred from Sukkur to Mumbai (Maharashtra), Halani Darbar from Halani (between Nausharo Firuz and Khairpur) to Ajmer (Rajasthan) and Khatwaro Darbar from Shikarpur to Nagpur (Madhya Pradesh). In Ulhasnagar, there is the sanctuary of Sain Vasan Shah, whose original sanctuary is in Rohri. The *gaddi nashin* of this shrine is usually the direct descendant of Vasan Shah (1848–1928), the founder of the tradition in Sindh. Beyond this inherited legitimacy, other forms of legitimation are implemented through narratives that are usually published in books written both in Devanagari and in Perso-Arabic Sindhi scripts. The iconography of these sites also provides a sense of continuity, contrary to their architecture. In the Mumbai Sadh Belo sanctuary for example, it is difficult to see any architectural continuity with the Sadh Belo site on the island in the Indus River, in Sukkur. Continuity is, however, provided through the spiritual genealogical chart which is exhibited in the main entrance. It starts with the name of Baba Bankhandi (d. 1863), the Udasi who founded the sanctuary of Sadh Belo in Sindh in 1823.

In the case of Jhulelal's tradition, the situation is far more complex, as there was no single authority responsible for it. Before Partition, there were many communities of Jhulelal's followers scattered all across Sindh. Since the nineteenth century, Jhulelal's Hindu followers have been said to form a *panth* or community known in Sindhi as the Daryapanth, or "the path of the River". Interestingly, the Daryapanth was an oral tradition up to the very end of the nineteenth century. When books in this tradition first appeared, they were mostly of the *janam sakhi* genre,[5] but later on they were dedicated to devotional poetry, used as prayers; particularly the *panjra*s, or five-line poems, but also *madahun, munajatun, bhajan*s[6] and so on, devoted to the different figures of Jhulelal.[7]

All of the remembrance mechanisms discussed in this essay are rooted in a narrative: thus it is through narrative that the past is brought into

---

[5] Possibly borrowed from the Sikhs as a literary genre, the *janam sakhi* is a hagiographical narrative of Jhulelal's life.

[6] All these terms refer to different genres of devotional literature in Sindhi, some of which are shared with Muslims, such as the *madahun* and *munajatun*.

[7] The expression "different figures" here refers to the different names given to him, such as Amar Lal, Darya Lal and so on.

the present.[8] The narrative concerning Jhulelal generally stages relations between Muslims and Hindus in Sindh through a process of pacification, and does not erase interdenominational rivalries. Here the past is chronologically and geographically located, since Jhulelal is said to have been born in 1007 Vikram Samvat (CE 950), and a number of places are associated with him such as Naserpur, Thatta, Jahejan or Bakkar/Rohri. Every place is associated with a significant act performed by Jhulelal: his birth, battles or miracles.

In the *janam sakhi*s, one can distinguish two main parts in the narrative: (1) the persecution of the Hindus under Muslim rule; (2) the reconciliation of the protagonists. Thus Jhulelal is remembered both as a *saviour* for the Hindus, and as a *peacemaker* for the Hindus and the Muslims. Nonetheless today opinions diverge as to the religious affiliation of Jhulelal: was he Muslim or Hindu? According to the Muslims, he was born Hindu but then converted to Islam. According to the Hindus, he always remained Hindu. But beyond this disagreement, the founding narrative is accepted by all the actors, Muslims as well as Hindus. Of course, the religious communities each give a different status to Jhulelal: he is a saint for the Muslims, and a god for the Hindus.

Jhulelal's tradition was first framed in Sindh. Before focussing on the remembrance processes themselves, as they work through a number of media, it is necessary to examine how physical spaces can impact, or not, Jhulelal's tradition, especially in the context of the migration of Hindu Sindhis to India.

PHYSICAL SPACES

The physical spaces of Jhulelal worship play a leading role in articulating Jhulelal's traditions and the community of his followers. When Jhulelal was said to be preparing for his own departure, Muslim and Hindu Sindhis started fighting over structures to remember him by. Jhulelal asked the Muslims to build their own shrine, a *qabr*, and the Hindus to build another one, a *samadhi*. This narrative is reminiscent of that

---

[8] For example Talhiram Asodumal, *Janam sakhi Shri Udero Lal Sahab ji* (Hyderabad: Sindhu, 1926). The book was regularly republished in Pakistan as well as in India, and has circulated between countries. This is the most commonly used source for Jhulelal's tradition in Pakistan and in India, and it is our main reference here. Some variation can be seen in the various oral and written versions.

provided within hagiographical traditions for Kabir and Nanak, who have also been positioned in some later traditions as reconciling Hindu and Muslim communities. The terms that could be used for commemorative shrines for religious worship are: *than*, an old Sindhi word now out of use, *mandir* and *darbar*, the latter of which is only used for a complex hosting several temples, as at Udero Lal in Sindh. However, it must be noted here that the Chaliha Sahib *mandir* in Ulhasnagar also houses several temples within its complex but it is termed Jhulelal Mandir and not a *darbar*.[9] Initially, the *darbar* at Udero Lal was probably built near the River Indus, but the original site was abandoned some centuries ago. Furthermore, there is a hierarchy in Sindh regarding the physical spaces of Jhulelal's worship: the highest level includes those places where Jhulelal is supposed to have been present in his human form (there are four of these, in Naserpur, Thatta, Udero Lal and Rohri); the others are locations where the most common legitimising discourse claims that a devotee was asked by Jhulelal in a dream to build a temple.

The oldest buildings of Jhulelal worship that have survived in present-day Pakistan present a similar architectural pattern to each other: a simple structure made of a single-square room with a dome. The oldest surviving sanctuary is from the late seventeenth century, and features the architectural style for mausoleums used by the Kalhora dynasty, which ruled Sindh from that period through the eighteenth century. The basic structure can be seen in the oldest temples, even though they have been deserted, such as the one in Naserpur, which was built to commemorate the birthplace of Jhulelal.

In the town of Uderolal in Pakistan, there is only one sanctuary devoted to Jhulelal, but it is the largest of all those dedicated to him. It is located in the north of the village, in close proximity to the Shia Muslim *imambara*.[10] Nonetheless, there are other Jhulelal temples in neighbouring towns such as Tando Adam or Shahdadpur, visited only by the Hindus. Though several architectural elements can be seen at Udero Lal, the central focus is the *darbar*—which is a complex building

---

[9] In India, the use of the word *darbar* is common within Sikh shrines.

[10] The *imambara* is a sacred building among the Shia community, where the ritual objects are put when they are not used for the celebration of Moharram, the first ten days, commemorating the martyrdom of Imam Husayn and his family in 680 in Kerbala, Iraq. It is also used during Moharram for the preachers who delivered their sermons facing the crowd of devotees.

with several poles of sanctity. There are two main divisions separated by a narrow lane. The first part is like a fort, whose shape is an irregular rectangle of 70 metres long and 50 metres wide. It hosts a number of elements, Muslim as well as Hindu, distributed around a huge courtyard. Across the road, there is another compound containing only Hindu religious buildings. A third space was built recently for hosting the *samadhi*s of the *mata*s or "mothers"—this is the name given to the Hindu *gaddi nashin* of Udero Lal, presently Mata Bina; on the Muslim side, the tomb is looked after by a *sajjada nashin*, Ghulam Abbas Shaykh—but no regular ritual is performed there.

In the fort, all the rooms are oriented toward the west and most of them are managed by Muslims. On the far side of the building, as the visitor comes to the end of their journey, they find one single room: it is called the *mandir*. This having been said, the Hindus circulate in all the rooms, as part of their visit to the *darbar*. Some rooms can be tagged as neutral, since no iconographical or architectural element can be identified. Examples of these include the room hosting the *chakri*s, the wooden sandals, or the sacred tree resulting from a miracle performed by Jhulelal. The other part of the fort, across the lane, is usually named Balanbo Sahib; this name was arrived at through a metonymic process since it is the name of the well or *khooh* that is the most sacred place in the compound. However, other rooms are also sacred, especially the one hosting a large equestrian statue of Jhulelal. Consequently, at Udero Lal, space has been made to facilitate the different processes of commemoration performed by Muslims, in their own part of the complex, and the Hindus, mostly in their specific parts, but after having paid respect to the Muslim rooms. Hence distinct processes of commemoration come into play.

On the other side of the border, in the city of Ulhasnagar in India, there are several Hindu temples, including some specific to Jhulelal. However, the two main Jhulelal temples in the city are Jhulelal *mandir*s in Ulhasnagar's Camp No. 2 and Camp No. 5, Bhau Parsram Jhulelal *mandir* and the Puj Chaliha Sahib Puj Jhulelal *mandir*, respectively. Popularly referred to as the *chaliha mandir*s, these two Jhulelal temples do not share any affiliation and are run by separate organisations. Although the rituals of Jhulelal worship performed in both these temples are similar, this paper shall take the Jhulelal *mandir* situated in Ulhasnagar's Camp No. 5 as a case study.

The Chaliha Sahib *mandir*, in the initial years after Partition, was a small *pathharon jo mandir* (temple made of stones). When the *akhand jyot* (eternal light) was brought over from Sindh to India, it formed the basis for this Jhulelal *mandir*. According to the interviews conducted with temple authorities, because of the lack of funds and of a dedicated space for religious observances by the Sindhi community, the *mandir* was small. The military *talaav* (pond) that remained was used by the worshippers to perform their rituals involving water, as part of the Jhulelal worship. However, over the years, with Ulhasnagar coming to host a significant Sindhi population, the *mandir* is now comprised of a huge complex which houses several *mandir*s, a *sarovar* (a tank, in Sindhi), and is also used as a space to conduct social events and public awareness seminars.

Remembrance Process Through Universal Symbols: Light (*Jyot*) and Water (*Jal*)

The Jyot

In the town of Udero Lal, the worship of Jhulelal is performed in the *darbar* with iconic representations, as well as with an aniconic representation: the light, or, in Sindhi, *jot* or *jyot*. The concept of light is universal in devotion, but in this case, it also serves as a representation of Jhulelal. According to the built structure of the old temples, one can surmise there were no *murti*s or sculptural/material representations, but only the *jyot*, or by metonymy the *diyo*, the lamp. Sometimes, the core of the temple is still the *jyot* instead of a figurative representation. In Pakistan, more recent temples, such as the ones in Mol Sharif, Mirpur Khas or those in Karachi (Varun Dev and Darya Lal) are made of several rooms, and other sacred figures are portrayed in association with Jhulelal, either Hindu divinities such as Hanuman, or mostly sacred Sikh figures such as Guru Nanak, or his son Shri Chand. However, in all the cases, the *sanctum sanctorum* is the room where the *jyot* lies. According to the narrative, Jhulelal gave the spiritual leadership of the Daryapanth to his cousin Pugar along with several symbols, among which the most important was the *jyot*, the eternal lighted candle which symbolises the Almighty.

At Udero Lal, the issue of the location of the *jyot* is complex. This is due to the fact that the Hindu shrine has two parts: one is inside the fort, but most of the rooms in the shrine are Muslim-oriented. And on the other side of the lane, there is the Balanbo Sahib, another complex which is completely Hindu, with a well or *khooh*, Mata Bina's room, a large equestrian statue, and so on. Amazingly, there is no permanent *jyot* in this part of the shrine. The only permanent *jyot* is to be found in the *mandir* which is located in the fort. Notwithstanding, many *jyots* are lit and put in different spaces of the Balanbo Sahib side when Mata arrives, or where there is a celebration, such as Chand, the new moon, for instance. When Mata is present, the devotees should pray before the *jyot* before being graced by *Mata*'s blessings, which are materialised by the gift of a sacred thread (*dhago*). Consequently, the physical spaces despite their diversity allow for the enactment of a remembrance process in prayer, through the worshipper facing the *jyot*, the very symbol of Jhulelal. For all celebrations, be they daily ones or during the main festivals such as Chetichand, commemorating Jhulelal's birthday as well as the Sindhi New Year, rituals and prayers centre on the *jyot*. These are similar in ways to those conducted in other Hindu *panths*: the gesture is comparable, for example, to the waving of the oil lamp during the *aarti* (a central ritual in the Hindu worship when a lamp is taken for broad circle around the deity). In this context, the prayers contribute to the remembrance of Jhulelal, naming him explicitly.

On the Indian side of the border, in Ulhasnagar, at the Chaliha Sahib *mandir*, the *akhand jyot* is located in the main *mandir* of the complex. While the *jyot* is kept securely in a caged metal structure, the lamp itself forms the central part of this dome-shaped *mandir*. Above the lamp is the statue of Jhulelal and these two objects are placed in an enclosed transparent glass structure. On the left side of this structure is a *jhoola* or a cradle, another symbol of Jhulelal, which is swayed gently by all the devotees during their trip to the temple. This structure housing the Jhulelal statue and the *jyot* stands in the centre of a series of statues of gods and goddesses. After the *jhoola*, this series goes on with Hanuman, Ram-Sita, Radhe Krishna, Saraswati, Lakshmi, to name a few. The main hall of the *mandir*, however, just forms one part of the Chaliha *mandir* complex. The *akhand jyot*, which forms the crux of the *mandir*, was brought over from the Jhulelal temple in "Peergoath" during Partition.[11] Thus, as a symbol of their continued connection to their homeland Sindh, and by extension, to its people, the *jyot* is an element that symbolises the inability of material borders to separate the Sindhi community from its homeland.

---

[11] Probably Pir jo goth, the village of the *pir*, an element which is common in Sindh place names. However, this location was probably close to Rohri, in the northern part of Sindh.

This *jyot* then becomes an integral part of the remembrance process of the motherland Sindh for the Sindhis of India. With its presence amidst the deities from the Hindu pantheon, on the one hand it depicts the national integration of the Sindhis into the Indian ethos; on the other, it also signifies their unbroken bond to their community in Sindh and their community religious practices. Further on, the Chaliha *mandir* not only continues to protect and preserve the flame, and thus its metaphorical umbilical cord with Sindh, but it also becomes a means to connect the Sindhis worldwide through their virtual presence. The *jyot* and the *mandir* serve as the medium to connect the diasporic and the Non-Resident Indian Sindhis, to help them stay connected to their motherland, and thus, Jhulelal.

An Alternative Space

The Chaliha temple of Ulhasnagar 5 has a virtual presence as well: that is, the Puj Chaliha Sahib Jhulelal *mandir* on the internet. In the virtual space too, placed at the centre of the temple website's homepage, the *jyot* occupies the same central focus as it does in the physical structure of the temple space in Ulhasnagar. On the first visit to the temple's website, the viewer is greeted with a thumbnail image of the *jyot* in an embedded YouTube video titled, "*Akhand Jyot—Puj Chaliha Sahib Jhulelal Mandir*". The *darshan* (visualisation) of the *jyot* provided by this thumbnail image continues further when one clicks on the video (Fig. 3.1).

Fig. 3.1 *The* jyot: *left Udero Lal, Pakistan, April 2016; right Chaliha Sahib, from* www.chalinhasahib.com. Accessed 15 June 2017

The video starts with a quick glimpse of the main hall of the *mandir*. After the text of the title credits *"Puj Chaliha Sahib, Darshan of Akhand Jyot"* have rolled on the screen, a full-frame visual appears of the *jyot* housed in the lamp. The lamp, placed in a metal open cage structure, is decorated with flower garlands and the video of the *jyot* is accompanied by the soundtrack of the Jhulelal *aarti*. The *aarti* chorus and the male-voice chanting of "o jai jhulelal muhinjo, jai amarlal" along with the visual *darshan* of the *jyot* continues for three-quarters of the total video length. Then, the video transitions into information on the *jyot*, which appears on the screen as written text. While the details and the description of the *akhand jyot* in English roll across the screen, the soundtrack that accompanies this information is that of a Sindhi song called "Sabhin jyun sad-haayeen jhulan aasun pujayeen laalan, aasun pujaayeen" (Jhulelal always fulfils everyone's wishes), sung by a female voice. The video ends with the words "Ayo lal sabhai chavo Jai Jhulelal" (Let us all say in unison— "Jai Jhulelal").

Thus, the two-minute-long video on the homepage of the temple website focusses on the *jyot* in its entirety for about the first minute and a half, followed by information on the *jyot* via a textual description. Through the *darshan* of the sacred *jyot*, the viewers of the video are directly connected to the sacred *jyot* for what can be termed a personal divine experience, albeit virtually. An all-encompassing *darshan* of the *jyot* coupled with the Jhulelal *aarti* and information on the *jyot* enables the video to not only serve as a medium to the divine but also provide information about the *jyot* and the Partition. The soundtrack in the Sindhi language further connects Sindhi viewers to the temple and the rituals of Jhulelal worship. All at once, the viewer/devotee accesses the *jyot* and experiences its *darshan*, an experience which would otherwise require him/her to go to the temple situated in Ulhasnagar. Simultaneously he/she feels an immediate connection to the original Jhulelal temple in "Peergoath" and, by extension, the homeland/motherland of the Sindh.

For the Sindhis across the world who cannot visit Pakistan, then, this physically inaccessible (temple) space in Sindh then not only becomes accessible via the internet, but also becomes manifest through the experience of the Jhulelal temple in India, which has its roots in pre-partitioned Sindh. The temple's virtual space surpasses national borders. The *akhand jyot* video on the website gives a complete *darshan* of the *jyot* along with the visual and the auditory experience of being present in the Jhulelal *aarti* in the Chaliha Sahib temple, all at the click of a mouse. To the Jhulelal devotees, this process, it can be argued, serves as the thread connecting the Indian Sindhis to their motherland Sindh through an alternate virtual location on the internet.

Furthermore, the web address of the temple website—'chalihasahib. com'—ends with the domain suffix '.com'. While '.com' is generally used by commercial organisations worldwide, the usage of the '.com' here by the temple authorities could further testify to efforts to erase differences based on borders and country-code suffixes. Transcending the borders dividing the two countries, and thus Sindhi Hindus from Sindhi Muslims, this virtual *darshan* on the Chaliha temple website serves to make it easier for Sindhis to seek Jhulelal's blessings and pray for the fulfilment of their wishes in the Chaliha temple of Ulhasnagar. Finally, with its informative text about the *jyot* in English and the two soundtracks in the video in the Sindhi language, the video makes itself accessible to the Sindhi community across the globe that does not speak Sindhi anymore, as well as to a non-Sindhi audience well versed in the English language. Thus, the light, which has not been extinguished since it was brought from Sindh, will remain lit on the virtual medium of the Indian Jhulelal temple forever.

The Jal and Darya

Jhulelal's worship consists of two integral elements: the *jyot* and the *jal*. According to oral narratives about Jhulelal, he is an avatar of the River Indus, or of the Vedic God Varuna; according to the Islamic version, he is the protector of the sailors and the boatmen (on the River Indus). Both narratives thus stress a connection to water. This second material element of Jhulelal worship, the element of water or *jal*, therefore contributes significantly to the remembrance process. It is believed that a symbolic gift of water, as a sign symbol of fertility and prosperity, was given by Jhulelal to Pugar, his cousin, to whom he also gave spiritual leadership of the community. Since worship centred on water, it can be presumed that there was no compulsion to build a physical space: it is commonly said that the Daryapanthis could perform their rituals on the banks of the Indus river itself. Hence, it can be presumed that early on there was no need to construct bodies of water as a part of Jhulelal worship, due to the availability and accessibility of the River Sindh. This is how the tradition is described in the narrative from 1926.

However, with changes in geographical location and in the course of the Indus river, this element of water worship acquired new forms. In the present day, in many places including Udero Lal, the final rituals involving water worship as part of Jhulelal traditions are performed near a canal or a well (*khooh*). The procession that starts with the *darshan* of the *jyot* usually ends with the *jal*, at the well or a canal. This symbolises the journey or pilgrimage of the devotee from one manifestation of Jhulelal to another. The ritual of the immersion in water of the elements used during Jhulelal worship marks the successful completion of its rituals by a devotee. Since Jhulelal is believed to be an incarnation of water, realising all the stages of Jhulelal's worship through the final step of immersion in water could be argued to represent a devotee's merging with the divine. At Udero Lal, the *khooh* is the very symbol of Jhulelal and according to a version of the narrative tradition, it is said that Jhulelal disappeared forever after entering this well. In the present day, however, the *mata* (or mother figure) performs the most important rituals (as we shall see with the case of the *bahraano*s, described below) near the well; these always end with the immersion of the offerings in that well. The *mata* also uses the water from the well to perform the ritual of *chhando*, the sprinkling of holy water on the devotees as a sign of blessing.

The tradition claims that this well in Udero Lal *darbar* was built by Pugar. It is said to be very deep and to connect with the Indus. From some of the inscriptions on the well, written in Khudavadi script, one of the oldest Sindhi scripts, one can deduce that the well was renovated in the late nineteenth century. The well is about 6 metres in circumference, with a marble edge. Due to the lack of historical sources available, and the many divergent opinions expressed in narratives about the tradition, not much more is known about its history. Nonetheless, above the well, there is a free-standing marble sculpture in the round of Jhulelal on a horse along with two other horsemen. Another interesting element is that the well has a name: Balanbo Sahib. There is no consensus about its meaning or etymology in Sindhi. Nonetheless, Balanbo Sahib is considered as a kind of manifestation of Jhulelal, more than a simple symbol. It is a part of him, since it hosts holy water associated with Jhulelal, the god of water. Consequently, the remembrance process is strongest when a devotee performs a ritual, or prays beside the Balanbo Sahib. In doing this, he or she comes as close as possible to Jhulelal, and thus can benefit from his blessings and powers. Due to its importance in Jhulelal's tradition in Sindh, the name of Balanbo Sahib can be found in other sacred places, even when these are not devoted to Jhulelal.

On the other hand, the Chaliha temple site in India includes an inland pool for the performance of Jhulelal worship rituals. This static body of water, called the *sarovar* (tank) by the temple authorities, is comparatively recent in its current form and dates from rebuilding and construction of the temple complex. Before these changes, however, this indoor body of water was still an integral part of the Jhulelal *mandir*. It took the form of a small pond which served as the 'military *talaav*'.[12] From the Partition years onwards till the 1990s, the military *talaav* was used for making the religious offerings (*akho*) and *matki* (earthen pot) immersions that formed part of the Jhulelal rituals in this temple.

The size of the present *sarovar* is approximately 12×24 m^2. It is further divided into two sections: the frontal two-thirds of the water body is not used for any immersions; that is to say it is kept clean and looks aesthetically like a river. The remaining one-third, which has a Jhulelal statue in a *mandir* on the top of the *sarovar*, is the section that is used for the immersions. This section is called the *darya* or 'river' and is used for *akho* and for *matki* immersions, alongside the other offerings. These offerings are collected by the temple authorities and then immersed in the Ulhas river on a regular basis. Regular cleaning of both sections of the *sarovar* is an integral element of the upkeep of the *sarovar*'s hygiene regime (Fig. 3.2).

The *sarovar* serves as the medium; it is seen as being connected to the River Sindh, despite its being man-made. The idea of water, and more specifically the idea of the River Sindh, was a core ritual for the worship of Jhulelal and his festivals in undivided India. Now, with Partition, the Sindhi Hindus' Chaliha temple of Ulhasnagar continues with Jhulelal worship and his rituals through the use of a body of water that is not the River Sindh. However, by continuing the rituals in the *sarovar*, the devotees imagine themselves to be a part of the larger Sindhi community worshipping Jhulelal on the other side of the border, which still has access to the River Sindh. Through this imagined worship at the River Sindh, the temple authorities recover the lost access to the river by creating a local, static form of access instead. This identification with the Sindhis worshipping Jhulelal and the River Sindh on the other side of the

---

[12] This military *talaav* was part of the British army barracks that constituted the five camps, which were collectively termed Ulhasnagar.

Top left -- photo of the *khooh* (water-well) in the *darbar* in Uderolal, Pakistan, picture taken during the fieldwork trip in 1997; bottom left -- close up photo of the *khooh* enclosed in a metal structure at the darbar in Uderolal, picture taken during the fieldwork trip in 2016. Top right -- photo of the *sarovar* (water-pool) in the Chaliha Sahib mandir in Ulhasnagar, India; photo courtesy of the Chaliha Sahib mandir website.

Fig. 3.2 Photo of Khoo (copyright Boivin and Rajpal) and screenshot of the *sarovar* from www.chalinhasahib.com. Accessed 15 June 2017

border helps the Sindhis in India to continue to negotiate their cultural heritage by recreating and reappropriating some aspects of its imagined identity.

REMEMBRANCE PROCESS THROUGH A VERNACULAR RITUAL OBJECT: THE BAHRAANO

While the above sections outlined the significance of the *jyot* and the *jal* in the remembrance process of Jhulelal, this section examines the ritual of the *bahraano sahib* (an offering made of food, fruits, ground rice and sugar) amongst the Hindu Sindhis. The *bahraano* ritual can be said to form the core of the Sindhi cultural religious practice. It forms the integral part of the remembrance process for and the embodiment of Jhulelal, both in Pakistan and in India: while one can not dispute the role played by light (*jyot*) and water (*jal*), the *bahraano* is at the centre of the main ritual. It also brings together the two elements of the *jyot* and the *jal*. The *bahraano* ritual comprises three successive steps: the first is the making of the *bahraano* and lighting of the *jyot*; the second is the procession; and the third is the immersion of the *bahraano* in the *jal*. According to a private document provided by Kumar Lal Thakur (d. 2015) from Thane, near Mumbai, 48 elements are necessary to make a 'proper' *bahraano*.[13] The guidelines for making the *bahraano* are not the same everywhere, though the basic items required, sugar, rice, oil and fruits, remain constant in both countries and across the globe. In many cases, simplified guidelines are used.

The origin of the word *bahraano* is not well known, but the ritual can be seen as a system of gift and counter-gift. Before Partition, *bahraano*s were offered to the Indus River in hope of future prosperity (such as a good harvest, good health, the birth of healthy children and prosperity in business). According to Upendra Thakur, the *bahraano* in pre-partitioned Sindh was performed when the Indus river was about to flood 'as a welcome to the river-god'.[14] The *bahraano* was made to obtain the generosity of the Indus. Upon further examination, the composition of the *bahraano*, mostly vegetables, grains and fruits, seems to express a wish to feed the river, so that in return, it will feed the devotees. Later on the *bahraano* came to symbolise happiness, so that it was made for every joyful event, or that event's commemoration.

Today, in Pakistan as well as in India, the *bahraano* is performed in a number of circumstances, beyond the main festivals devoted to Jhulelal, such as Chetichand or Asu. *Bahraano*s are also performed when a certain wish made by the devotee is fulfilled. According to Nitin Thakur from Mumbai, the *bahraano* is made at home, so that it can bring happiness to a new home, a new-born child or of course a marriage.[15] Furthermore, the *bahraano* is made when a family is going through a hard time, since it has the power, empowered by Jhulelal himself, to solve all difficulties. Before Partition, *bahraano*s were made by the priest caste of the Daryapanth, the Thakurs. Today, they have all left for India, where they are in competition with the new sacerdotal classes. The Thakurs still make *bahraano*s for families and visit them in those families' homes; in the temples, they are made and sacralised by the new priests, usually known as *maharaj*s.[16]

---

[13] Personal interview, Thane (Mumbai), April 2012.

[14] U.T. Thakur, *Sindhi Culture* (Bombay: University of Bombay, 1959), 123.

[15] Personal interview, Mumbai, February 2012.

[16] Most *maharaj*s belong to the Lohana caste, whose members are primarily involved in trade and business.

Bahraanos also constitute an important role in the 40-day Chaliha festival celebrated by the Sindhis. For instance, in the Chaliha Sahib temple in Ulhasnagar, on the fortieth day of the Chaliha festival, devotees from all backgrounds arrive in the Chaliha Sahib *mandir* to immerse their *bahraano*s in the *sarovar* at the Chaliha *mandir*. In an interview with the temple authorities, we were informed that the last day of the festival is termed the *matki mela* day at the Chaliha Sahib *mandir*, and priests offer prayers all day long for the safe immersion of the *matki*s and the *bahraano*s. While people offer *bahraano*s and immerse them throughout the festival of Chaliha, the dedicated *matki mela* day witnesses the immersion of over 1000 *matki*s in the *sarovar*. This collective celebration of the *bahraano* at the Chaliha *mandir* becomes another step in the remembrance process, whereby Sindhis in Ulhasnagar experience a collective community experience in their rituals for the worship of Jhulelal.

CONCLUSION

Even before Partition, Jhulelal's tradition never went through a process of standardisation or centralisation: there was no effort to create a single and homogenised community. The different sites as well as the first printed sources give evidence that Jhulelal's followers belonged to local communities who may have gathered in the *darbar* of Udero Lal to perform the main festival. In present-day Pakistan, the *dargah*-like structures are usually the oldest sites, but after Partition, the built structures became more diverse in terms of their spacial organisation and style. Nonetheless, the sacred symbol of Jhulelal worship continues to be the *jyot*, which plays a major role in the main ritual itself and is also a part of the *bahraano*.

In the year 1947, Hindu Sindhis migrated to India in large numbers. Ulhasnagar became known popularly as Sindhunagar, in honour of its Sindhi residents.[17] In this new environment, they had to reconstruct a past which created a new relationship with their lost motherland. The *jyot* played a pivotal role in the process of reimagining the tradition's past

---

[17] Since Ulhasnagar's allocation to the Hindu Sindhi refugees at the time of Partition, this community has wished to rename Ulhasnagar as 'Sindhunagar'. Despite a range of different political parties making promises to the Sindhi community about the renaming of the city, and extensive media coverage of such promises, this has not yet occurred.

on the other side of the border, as described above. The remembrance process was framed through a narrative locating the *jyot* in the sacred land of Sindh. Finally, through the *jyot*, we argue, the Sindhis of India have built a new Sindh, their own Sindh in the nation state of India.

Jhulelal's tradition has recently been invigorated on both sides of the border. This reflects both a form of continuity between the traditions in Pakistan and India and the increased circulation of people and objects related to Sindhi and Jhulelal worship. For example, the statue of Jhulelal which was installed in the recently renovated temple of Darya Lal in Karachi was made in the city of Ajmer in India. In addition, in present-day India, the Jhulelal Tirathdham, the largest ever Jhulelal *mandir* in the world, is under construction in the state of Gujarat.[18] This continued exchange through objects, people and memories, we argue, is a sign of the fact that the memories of pre-Partition days continue to stay fresh in the minds of Sindhis across the border, albeit through the lens of Jhulelal worship. As this paper is part of an ongoing project, and the project is inspired by the recognition of the ongoing remembrance process that is framing the memories of the Partition and Indo-Pak border, there cannot be a definitive conclusion yet. Placing the Sindhi experience within a larger exploration of Partition Studies, however, is crucial if we are to understand the many dimensions and full range of Partition's legacy.

WORKS CITED

Asodumal, Talhiram. *Janam sakhi Shri Udero Lal Sahab ji*. Hyderabad: Sindhu, 1926.

Bhavnani, Nandita. *The Making of Exile: Sindhi Hindus and the Partition of India*. London: Westland and Tranquebar Press, 2014.

Kothari, Rita. *The Burden of Refugee. The Sindhi Hindus of Gujarat*. Hyderabad: India Orient Longman, 2007.

Kumar, Priya, and Rita Kothari. "Sindh, 1947 and Beyond." *South Asia: Journal of South Asian Studies* 39, no. 4 (2016): 773–789.

Parwani, Lata. "Myths of Jhuley Lal: Deconstructing a Sindhi Cultural Icon." In *Interpreting the Sindhi World. Essays on Society and Culture*, edited by Michel Boivin and Matthew Cook, 1–27. Karachi: Oxford University Press, 2010.

---

[18] Please check its website http://www.jhulelaltirathdham.com/ for further details.

Ramey, Steven. *Hindu, Sufi, or Sikh: Contested Practices and Identifications of Sindhi Hindus in India and Beyond.* New York: Palgrave Macmillan, 2008.

Ray, Anita C. "Varuna, Jhūlelāl and the Hindu Sindhis." *South Asia: Journal of South Asian Studies* 35, no. 2 (2012): 219–238.

Thakur, U. T. *Sindhi Culture.* Bombay: University of Bombay, 1959.

Zamindar, Vazira Fazila-Yacoobali. *The Long Partition and the Making of Modern South Asia.* Karachi: Oxford University Press, 2008.

CHAPTER 4

Between Mini-India and Sonar Bangla: The Memorialisation and Place-Making Practices of East Bengal Hindu Refugees in the Andaman Islands

Philipp Zehmisch

INTRODUCTION

Recounting an official tour to the Andaman Islands[1] in the 1960s, the renowned Bengali politician, activist and social worker for refugees and female empowerment, Dr. Phulrenu Guha, commented in an interview

---

[1] The Indian Union Territory of the Andaman and Nicobar Islands is located about 1000 km south–east of the Indian subcontinent in the Bay Bengal. The tropical archipelago is comprised of 572 islands, reefs and rocks. See Pankaj Sekhsaria, "When Chanos Chanos Became Tsunami Macchi: The Post-December 2004 Scenario in the Andaman and Nicobar Islands," *Journal of the Bombay Natural History Society* 106 (2009): 256. The main geological body of the Andamans, Great Andaman, is surrounded by many small islands, and stretches as a long narrow piece of land measuring around 250 km from north to south, with an average breadth of 32 km from east to west. Bengali Hindu refugees were settled exclusively in the Andamans.

P. Zehmisch (✉)
LMU Munich, Munich, Germany
e-mail: Philipp.Zehmisch@ethnologie.lmu.de

© The Author(s) 2018   63
C. Mahn and A. Murphy (eds.), *Partition and the Practice of Memory*,
https://doi.org/10.1007/978-3-319-64516-2_4

on how she had perceived the situation as East Bengal Hindu refugees settled across the islands:

> We saw the various settlements set up by the refugees from East Bengal, saw how they had adapted marvellously to the new set-up. The natural beauty of the Andamans is no less than that of Bangladesh, in fact many regions are even more beautiful than East Bengal. The children of the settlers studied in schools opened specially to cater their needs. On the whole, East Bengalis led a happy and productive life. They informed us in one voice that their decision to migrate to the Andamans, rather than stay back in the refugee colonies in West Bengal, had enabled them to look forward to a better future.[2]

This passage demonstrates several hegemonic but contested tropes of refugee settlement in the Andaman Islands that I seek to critically examine in this chapter: the refugees' good adaptation to the Andaman environment; the role of the state as a caring, paternalist custodian; and the social mobility resulting from the rehabilitation of refugees as landowning farmers. Such narratives have until the present day continued to dominate the official narrative. The overall positive character of this representation stands, however, in stark contrast to most accounts of East Bengal Hindu refugee rehabilitation in mainland India, especially outside West Bengal. Narratives in other locations describe a several-decades-long process characterised by hardship: this involved a great deal of inadequate planning and the application of force by state actors, as well as difficulties experienced by refugees in adapting to camps and rehabilitation settlements, where they experienced hunger, disease and violence.[3]

Describing the state-directed settlement of 3652 East Bengal Hindu refugee families in the Andamans as an overall successful project, Dr. Guha—herself from East Bengal and familiar with refugees' hardships on the mainland—tends to reproduce the dominant narrative of

---

[2] Phulrenu Guha, "Rehabilitation, East & West," in *No Woman's Land: Women from Pakistan, India & Bangladesh Write on the Partition of India*, ed. Ritu Menon (New Delhi: Women Unlimited, 2004), 195–196.

[3] Abhijit Dasgupta, *Displacement and Exile: The State-Refugee Relations in India* (New Delhi: Oxford University Press, 2016); Jhuma Sen, "Reconstructing Marichjhapi: From Margins and Memories of Migrant Lives," in *Partition: The Long Shadow*, ed. Urvashi Butalia (New Delhi: Zubaan, 2015), 102–127.

the multi-ethnic Andaman migrant and settler society as a whole. Her account fits neatly into hegemonic representations of the post-Partition colonisation of the islands: the state's settlement policies were instrumental in settling various communities of subaltern refugees, repatriates, landless people and labour migrants on the islands in order to fortify the national claim on this potentially vulnerable strategic location with a visible 'Indian' population. As a result of territorial expansion and state-sponsored development, with the government providing land and employment to the rapidly growing population, society on the islands can be broadly described as upwardly mobile, but, at the same time, as strongly structured by class and new forms of inequality. Seeking to avoid social turmoil, and to declare post-Partition settlement policies as a success, state actors have literally embedded the islands' society within mainstream nationalist discourse by calling it a 'Mini-India'. The term signifies the peaceful and cosmopolitan cohabitation of 400,000–500,000 residents hailing from most of the regions, languages, religions, ethnicities and castes of South Asia, and presents the Andamans as a showcase example of Indian secularism and communal 'harmony'.[4]

Accounts of refugee rehabilitation in the Andamans such as Dr. Guha's must therefore be interpreted within the discourse of nation-building. Positive narratives of refugee rehabilitation have, however, not only been endorsed by the central government and officials of the local administration, but have, due to the hegemonic character of nationalist propaganda, become omnipresent in collective modes of self-definition among Bengali refugees and their descendants. Declarations that rehabilitation has been a complete success, however, as I will show in the course of this chapter, have also turned into a problem for the refugees and their descendants in their current political struggle to gain better access to the avenues of social mobility being provided by the state via affirmative action.

Keeping in mind the impact of the dominant state ideology and its particular demands in representing refugee rehabilitation, I will explore ethnographic data in order to throw light on the cultural and political

---

[4]Philipp Zehmisch, *Mini-India: The Politics of Migration and Subalternity in the Andaman Islands* (New Delhi: Oxford University Press, 2017).

dimensions of memorialising the refugee experience in the Andaman Islands.[5] In so doing, I seek to answer several questions, as follows:

1. What were the official reasons for the settlement of East Bengal refugees in the Andamans and what effects did resettlement have on the refugees and their descendants when they started a new life in the islands?
2. In what ways are the psychological, ecological, socio-economic and cultural challenges implied in the rehabilitation process remembered 70 years after Partition and what meaning do they have for the community in the here and now?

I will proceed by first providing a condensed overview of the historical context of Bengali refugee settlement in the Andamans along with an analysis of the key motivations, ideologies and discourses in which these processes were embedded. I will then identify some of the multiple and hybrid layers of belonging contained within the figure of the Bengali Hindu refugee in the Andamans. Concentrating on the memories and representations of processes of place-making,[6] as narrated by Bengali refugees and their descendants, my analysis focusses on two entangled and overlapping aspects. First, I will highlight how the diasporic memory of East Bengal has contributed to the formation of a distinctly 'local' reconstruction of 'Bengali-ness' in the Andamans: this implies, on the one hand, a dynamic process involving an 'ethnic' transformation of

---

[5] The data presented in this chapter stems largely from 20 months of qualitative fieldwork conducted between 2006 and 2012. My PhD research in social and cultural anthropology focussed on questions of migration and subalternity in the diasporic settler society of the Andaman Islands and, thus, on the interaction of various communities that have unequal access to means of production as a result of settlement policies. Consequently, I did not primarily concentrate on the Bengali Hindu refugees, but collected data among them when investigating the history of colonisation and refugee rehabilitation, as well as their status, directly attributable to that history, as a landowning community with political influence in the larger Andaman society.

[6] Akhil Gupta and James Ferguson, "Culture, Power, Place: Ethnography at the End of an Era," in *Culture, Power, Place: Explorations in Critical Anthropology*, ed. Akhil Gupta and James Ferguson (Durham: Duke University Press, 1997), 1–32; John Gray, "Community as Place-Making: Ram Auctions in the Scottish Borderland," in *Realizing Community: Concepts, Social Relationships and Sentiments*, ed. Vered Amit (London: Routledge, 2002), 38–59.

the cultivated landscape, environment and sociocultural infrastructure according to ideas transmitted from their lost homeland, and on the other, an adaptation of the local norms, values and practices in the cosmopolitan Andaman society. Second, I am going to discuss the intersection of memories and politics in the Andaman context by concentrating on the context in which political identifications—as 'Indians', Bengalis or refugees—are appropriated to articulate belonging and political voice.

A Short History of Colonisation

As a colony of the British Empire and the ensuing Indian nation state, the Andaman Islands in the Bay of Bengal have been the destination of various migrations from different parts of South and South East Asia. After the mutiny of 1857, a British penal colony was installed on the lands of the indigenous hunter-gatherer population of the Andamans. The function of the rapidly expanding colony was to remove potentially 'dangerous' convicts from their surroundings on the subcontinent, and to rehabilitate them as a sedentary settler population.[7] The colonisation of the islands with convict settlers, and, from the 1920s onwards, with several other forest-dwelling, labouring and farming communities, must be regarded as form of 'ecological warfare' against the 'jungle', that is the tropical rainforest covering the entire islands, and its indigenous inhabitants.[8] These policies resulted, on the one hand, in a gradual ethnocide of the indigenous 'Andaman Islanders',[9] and on the other, in the formation of a distinctly 'local' settler population. Among the various 'pre-42' groups, that is, people who lived there before the Japanese occupation of 1942–1945, the so-called 'local-born' community is worth mentioning. The local-born may be described as a hybrid and cosmopolitan amalgam of communities representing a large variety of the caste,

---

[7] Clare Anderson, *Legible Bodies: Race, Criminality and Colonialism in South Asia* (Oxford/New York: Berg, 2004); Satadru Sen, *Disciplining Punishment: Colonialism and Convict Society in the Andaman Islands* (New Delhi: Oxford University Press, 2000); and Aparna Vaidik, *Imperial Andamans: Colonial Encounter and Island History* (Hampshire/New York: Palgrave Macmillan, 2010).

[8] Satadru Sen, *Savagery and Colonialism in the Indian Ocean: Power, Pleasure and the Andaman Islanders* (Routledge: New York, 2010), 65.

[9] Alfred R. Radcliffe-Brown, *The Andaman Islanders* (London: Weidenfeld & Nicholson, 1922).

class, linguistic, ethnic and religious backgrounds of the Indian sub-continent; this community came into being as a result of matchmaking between convict settlers and, later on, their offspring, which had regularly crossed rigid rules of caste, religious and ethnic endogamy.[10]

Before Partition, the status of the Andaman and Nicobar Islands had remained undecided due to the rival claims of India, Pakistan, Burma and Britain. In spite of having a sizeable pre-42 Muslim population, the islands were finally given to the Indian Union—the reasons for this still await further academic investigation. Independence did not, however, bring about a marked change in the priorities of governance. Following the intellectual design of British policies in the islands, the post-Partition administration conceptualised the largely forested islands, in which the indigenous population had been severely reduced to a couple of hundred individuals, as a *terra nullius*, a space which should be rendered productive through the commercial exploitation of forest resources and agricultural expansion.[11] This agenda may have been influenced by the objective of achieving agricultural self-sustainability in the islands, an aim which had a colonial genealogy: in earlier decades, the British had not achieved their goal of reducing local dependency on food imports through increased agricultural production.[12]

Postcolonial settlement policies in the Andamans were ideologically dominated by the objectives of governance in the new nation state. These can be tentatively summarised by identifying two broad paradigmatic motivations. First, the establishment of rehabilitated refugees as pioneering farmers at the frontier served the objective of colonising the Andamans, both from within and in the name of the new nation. As on the mainland, such as in the dreaded Dandakaranya project in central India,[13] 'poor' Bengali refugees, who had lost everything and were in need of state assistance, could be settled on cleared tracts of forest that

---

[10] Zehmisch, *Mini-India*, 61.

[11] Uditi Sen, "Dissident Memories: Exploring Bengali Refugee Narratives in the Andaman Islands," in *Refugees and the End of Empire: Imperial Collapse and Forced Migration in the Twentieth Century*, ed. Panikos Panayi and Pippa Virdee (Basingstoke, Hampshire: Palgrave Macmillan, 2011), 222.

[12] Kiran Dhingra, *The Andaman and Nicobar Islands in the 20th Century: A Gazetteer* (New Delhi: Oxford University Press, 2005), 187; Sita Venkateswar, *Development and Ethnocide: Colonial Practices in the Andaman Islands* (Copenhagen: Iwgia, 2004), 126.

[13] Dasgupta, *Displacement and Exile*, 53–58.

had been inhabited by Adivasis.[14] Typical of a settler-colonial attitude, the process implied that the 'weaker' indigenous communities had to give way to 'the right of conquest'.[15] Creating an ordered agricultural landscape in the supposedly 'unproductive' forests and 'filling' these with a permanent settler population, constituted the transformation of 'nature' into 'culture', too. Further, the act of removing downtrodden Bengali refugees to the Andamans, and transforming them into sedentary peasant settlers and loyal, governable subjects, served to place a visible 'Indian' and 'Hindu' settler population on the islands in order to prevent possible claims by other nation states, especially Pakistan, Burma and China, on the lowly populated islands.

Second, the colonial 'garbage dump ideology',[16] that is, the deportation of 'problem' populations to the islands in order to increase the governability of the mainland, was continued after Partition. The transportation of Bengali refugees to the Andamans was influenced by the ideological framework of government policies towards East Bengal Hindu refugees in West Bengal, which crucially distinguished refugees on the basis of class and caste.[17] The integration and assimilation of the urban upper-caste *bhadralok* from East Bengal, who had largely arrived soon after Partition (1947–1949) and settled in Kolkata and other cities, had been depicted as comparatively smooth; as these classes were well connected and financially sound, many of their unauthorised colonies were quickly regularised and most of them soon found means of making a livelihood.[18] In contrast, the *chotolok*—peasants, sharecroppers and agricultural labourers belonging to the lower and lowest castes, most of them Namasudras—who had come to West Bengal after being targeted in communal violence from late 1949 onwards, were perceived as a law-and-order problem by the state; consequently, a discriminatory policy of rehabilitation was applied which 'sanitised' Kolkata and its vicinity of lower-class refugees, placed them in transit camps and scattered

[14] Nandini Sundar, *Subalterns and Sovereigns: An Anthropological History of Bastar (1854–2006)*, 2nd ed. (New Delhi: Oxford University Press, 2007), 196–197.

[15] Venkateswar, *Development and Ethnocide*, 130.

[16] S. Sen, *Disciplining Punishment*, 238.

[17] Dasgupta, *Displacement and Exile*, 21–22; J. Sen, "Reconstructing Marichjhapi," 103.

[18] J. Sen, "Reconstructing Marichjhapi," 104.

them in different parts of India.[19] The majority of Bengali refugees who were settled in the Andamans belonged to the second category, the *chotolok* whom the state sought to distribute.[20] According to a survey conducted in 1953, 66 per cent of Andaman refugee settlers were from the Namasudra caste; a present survey identified Namasudra, Paundra Kshatriya, Mahswa, Jale Das and Kaibarta as the numerically dominating castes.[21] Most of the refugees hailed from the districts of Barisal, Jessore and Khulna.[22]

With terminology reminiscent of colonial times, Bengali Hindu refugees were settled in the Andamans under so-called 'colonisation and rehabilitation' schemes that spanned over several decades from 1949 until 1980.[23] Each rehabilitated family was provided with five acres of hilly and five acres of paddy land as well as one acre to build a homestead—families settled after 1967 received only five acres of land and less than an acre for house construction.[24] With some variation according to year and place, settlers were provided with licences to extract firewood, leaves, bamboo and cane, and were also supplied with food, timber for construction, pesticides, a buffalo, a milk cow, some cash allotments and loans. Fishermen received motorised boats and nets, too.[25]

The first 'colonisation scheme' was organised by the West Bengal government in 1949. It aimed to settle East Bengali Hindu refugees in South Andaman, both in previously existing villages, on vacant plots that had been left by colonial settlers after the Japanese occupation, and on cleared patches of forest.[26] Soon after, the Andaman administration

---

[19] Ibid., 104. Madhumita Mazumdar, "Dwelling in Fluid Spaces: The Matuas of the Andaman Islands," in *New Histories of the Andaman Islands: Landscape, Place and Identity in the Bay of Bengal, 1790–2012*, ed. Clare Anderson, Madhumita Mazumdar, and Vishvajit Pandya (Cambridge: Cambridge University Press, 2015), 177–178.

[20] Swapan K. Biswas, *Colonization and Rehabilitation in Andaman and Nicobars* (Delhi: Abheejit Publications, 2009), 141.

[21] Ibid.

[22] U. Sen, "Dissident Memories," 223.

[23] Biswas, *Colonization and Rehabilitation in Andaman and Nicobars*, 76–91.

[24] Ibid., 100.

[25] Laxman P. Mathur, *Kala Pani: History of Andaman & Nicobar Islands with a Study of India's Freedom Struggle* (New Delhi: Eastern Book Corporation, 1985), 266; Cecil J. Saldhana, *Andaman, Nicobar and Lakshadweep: An Environmental Impact Assessment* (New Delhi: Oxford & IBH, 1989), 14.

[26] Biswas, *Colonization and Rehabilitation in Andaman and Nicobars*, 75–79.

took over this scheme and continued it until 1961 in cooperation with the West Bengal Ministry of Rehabilitation; under the scheme, settlers were placed on new clearings of rainforest in South Andaman, Havelock, Baratang, Middle Andaman and North Andaman Island.[27] In 1967, the Ministry of Relief and Rehabilitation at New Delhi set up a new, so-called 'rehabilitation scheme'; functional until 1980, it served to colonise some of the remaining 'empty' forest spaces of Middle Andaman, Neil Island and Little Andaman as well as Great Nicobar and Katchal Islands.[28]

These schemes led to the settlement of 3652 refugee families,[29] approximately 18,260 persons, if estimated by an average of five persons per family. However, in order to get a more appropriate idea of these families' demographic composition in the present, one must add the refugees' descendants in the second, third and fourth generations, who are also, identity-wise and administratively, counted as 'settlers'. Moreover, if one speaks broadly of those who identify themselves broadly with the larger group of East Bengal Hindu refugees, one may take into account numerous relatives, friends or neighbours of Bengali settlers, who moved to the islands on their own volition in later decades, sometimes from other camps in India or even crossing the border from East Pakistan or Bangladesh. While the latter received no land themselves because they had not been formally rehabilitated by the state, they often settled near their rehabilitated relatives by encroaching on, leasing or purchasing land.

These settlement policies as well as subsequent migrations from Bengal contributed to the shaping of several regions in the Andamans, in which one can find villages or clusters of villages with distinct characteristics of a Bengali diaspora. Some prominent 'Bengali' locations are:

---

[27] Ibid., 89.

[28] Ibid., 90.

[29] The state settled 4531 families altogether, out of which roughly 80 per cent were Bengali refugees; see Dhingra, *The Andaman and Nicobar Islands in the Twentieth Century*, 167. The decision to include other groups such as Burmese and Tamil repatriates and Chotanagpuri Adivasi department labourers from Ranchi, as well as landless people from other regions in the rehabilitation and colonisation schemes, was possibly influenced by a memorandum submitted by the Andaman Indian Association. This political interest group, which arose from the local-born community, had demanded that no more East Bengal refugees be settled. The association had argued that increasing numbers of Bengali Hindu settlers would disrupt the "homogeneous community" of the previous residents of Mini-India. See Biswas, *Colonization and Rehabilitation in Andaman and Nicobars*, 90.

along the western coast of South Andaman; in Havelock Island, nowadays the most sought-after tourist destination; in Neil Island, which is locally called the 'vegetable bowl' due to its agricultural productivity; in North Andaman, the so-called 'rice bowl', where paddy production dominates the livelihood of large numbers of settlers; and, in Little Andaman, where many settlers have earned large profits due to the rising market prices of *supari* (betel nut), which they grow on their plantations.

RECREATING BENGALI HOMELANDS IN MINI-INDIA

Due to popular narratives and media reports about the devastating effects of convict transportation to the penal colony, the Andaman Islands were dreaded all over the subcontinent as *kala pani* (black waters), a place of banishment where one loses ties to one's homelands and thus one's caste and social identity. Bengali refugees were aware of this discourse when they agreed to be settled in the islands.[30] Nonetheless, most of them willingly chose to come to the Andamans after being persuaded by government officials in refugee camps on the mainland.[31] Being uprooted from their homelands and properties, they were attracted by the prospect of receiving 10 acres of free land and other facilities.[32] One interlocutor, who had fled communal violence with his family as a young boy from Khulna District in 1949, told me they had crossed the border with a train to Bangav in the Nadia district of West Bengal. He recollected how they had met officials of the West Bengal Ministry of Rehabilitation, who offered to send them to the Andamans with the first batch of refugee settlers: "They invited us, saying 'Follow us! We'll take you to the camp. You will become settlers. The government of India will give you everything. Your food, clothing, and we will even take you to the places where we'll give you land to settle. And we'll construct houses for you and give you all facilities.'" However, while some families were directly sent to the Andamans in this way after crossing the border, many others spent years in refugee camps across the

---

[30] Clare Anderson, Madhumita Mazumdar, and Vishvajit Pandya, "Introduction," in *New Histories of the Andaman Islands: Landscape, Place and Identity in the Bay of Bengal, 1790–2012,* ed. Clare Anderson, Madhumita Mazumdar, and Vishvajit Pandya (Cambridge: Cambridge University Press, 2015), 7.

[31] Mazumdar, "Dwelling in Fluid Spaces," 184; U. Sen, "Dissident Memories," 227.

[32] Ibid., 228.

country before being settled on the islands. Apart from the difficulties implied in starting a new life in the Andamans, Bengali refugees also had to deal with their individual and collective traumas of turmoil, displacement and camp life; this was a process in which recourse to religiosity and spirituality played a big role.[33]

When arriving in the islands from 1949 onwards, refugees faced public protest from the colonial 'pre-42' settlers, who were afraid of being overpowered[34] and who resented the favourable conditions under which the refugees were rehabilitated.[35] The refugees, thus, came to be rapidly confronted with the political factuality of Mini-India, where communities compete with each other to gain an influence on the bureaucracy and funds associated with administrative power. They did, consequently, not only cross physical, geographical borders into Indian state territories to become citizens of a democratic nation state, but, in a more metaphorical way, also cross the borders of Mini-India by renegotiating the Self in the light of localised discourses of nation, ethnicity, religion, gender, class and caste. Practices of border-crossing may be usefully understood as a form of ethics that is dependent on situating oneself as different from the Other through 'incommensuration', i.e., 'the creative production and elaboration of incommensurable difference'[36] while, at the same time, searching for a common ground with those demarcated as Others by identifying affinities on the basis of shared characteristics evolving from similar social, cultural, ecological and political conditions structuring everyday life.

Being settled as agricultural pioneers on forest lands, Bengali refugees crafted a diasporic identification by combining reconstructed cultural traditions, rituals and traits from their lost homelands in East Bengal with appropriated values, norms and practices from the cosmopolitan Andaman society. Refugee settlers thus display a hybrid diasporic belonging encompassing both localised 'Indian-ness' and trans-local 'Bengali-ness'. In order to disentangle some of the dominant strands of this hybrid form of diasporic identification, and to analyse this process with regards to

---

[33] Mazumdar, "Dwelling in Fluid Spaces," 188–189.

[34] Biswas, *Colonization and Rehabilitation in Andaman and Nicobars*, 90.

[35] Anderson, Mazumdar, and Pandya, "Introduction," 8.

[36] Jonathan Mair and Nicholas H.A. Evans, "Ethics Across Borders: Incommensurability and Affinity," *HAU: Journal of Ethnographic Theory* 5 (2015): 201.

spatial relationships, I employ the concept of place-making. Place-making may be defined as the social, cultural, religious, economic and political transformation of spaces into places through naming practices, rituals and institutions.[37] By establishing social and economic relations, transforming the physical infrastructure of landscapes and settlements and forging political and religious or spiritual alliances, people inscribe their collective self-definition in a particular locality and environment.[38]

The place-making processes of Bengali refugees in the Andamans were influenced by their emplacement as agricultural pioneers who colonised newly cleared plots of "jungle" at the frontier.[39] Over the course of several decades, their mode of production as farming settlers influenced the emergence of a new nomenclature, which is based on a local administrative category that came to redefine their group identity in the multiethnic local society: the now common term 'Bengali settlers' indicates the symbolic transformation of previous downtrodden, marginalised and 'poor' refugees from East Bengal into landed Andaman residents and citizens of India, implying both changes in class composition and national belonging. This transformation process can be understood when we consider several effects of adaptation and social change resulting from place-making practices.

The first step in becoming settlers, as it was commonly narrated by settlers and their descendants I spoke to in the course of my fieldwork, was that of ecological adaptation. Making a place for oneself and earning a livelihood in the tropical island environment was surely a difficult task, especially during colonial times and in the decades after Independence. Settling at the edge of the forest, people had to find creative ways to make a living at the perceived frontier between 'civilisation' and 'wilderness': not only are many settlements of refugees in South and Middle Andaman located near the reserve of the indigenous Jarawa, which has contributed to various violent and non-violent conflicts,[40] but the environment around settlements is also replete with potentially dangerous animals like venomous snakes and saltwater crocodiles. Resulting from

---

[37] Edward S. Casey, *The Fate of Place—A Philosophical History* (Berkeley/Los Angeles: University of California Press, 1996); Gupta and Ferguson, "Culture, Power, Place," 1–32; and Gray, "Community as Place-Making."

[38] Gupta and Ferguson, "Culture, Power, Place," 6–13.

[39] U. Sen, "Dissident Memories," 222.

[40] Venkateswar, *Development and Ethnocide*, 126–127.

the very moist climate—until two decades ago, there were torrential rains for 6–9 months of the year—infections and diseases have continued to be major health issues. In remote areas, communication, transport, health care and welfare have not been effectively provided by the state.

Several older settlers confirmed in personal conversations with me that, in the years after their arrival, they had been afraid of both the 'jungle' and the sea, and that they had felt more than awkward about being placed in a new, and potentially threatening environment in a remote forest area without proper communication and infrastructure.[41] Nonetheless, my interlocutors emphasised that they mastered the task of constructing their own houses and of clearing most of the rapidly growing 'jungle' from their allotted lands for cultivation. Not being used to the island conditions, including the heavy monsoon rains and the high humidity throughout many months of the year, some of their fellow refugee settlers left during the initial years of colonisation. However, the majority who remained in the islands subscribe to the narrative of having 'domesticated' the forest and transformed it into a rural landscape dominated by agricultural activities. After having made their homes, settlers have had a life of comparable material plenty—with safe drinking water, agricultural and horticultural crops, livestock as well as forests and creeks in which to hunt, fish and gather. Reminiscent of a settler-colonial mindset, several informants revealed that they continued to regard the 'untamed', dense forest vegetation as 'wilderness' that must be cleared with the objective of creating a 'proper' and 'clean' agricultural landscape suitable to their farming mode of production.

Here, place-making led to the active shaping and reshaping of the environment according to collectively shared ideas, values and practices that decisively influenced the ways in which a new homeland in a diasporic context was created. One may tentatively assume that the emergence of a particular sense of place among Bengali refugee settlers in the Andamans, among other components, built a symbolic inscription

---

[41] In such situations, it is safe to assume that most Bengali refugees relied on each other's support and solidarity, such as those who settled on Havelock Island from 1956 onwards, for whom 'isolation and an altogether new habitat and environment gave rise to a feeling of insecuredness […] which in turn resulted into [*sic*] a strong sense of unity and interdependence'. See Kakali Chakrabarty, Chhanda Mukhopadhyay, and Kanchan Mukhopadhyay, "A New Trend in Marriage Practice: Case Studies from a South Andaman Village," in *Anthropology of Small Populations*, ed. Anthropological Survey of India (Calcutta: Anthropological Survey of India, 1998), 226.

of reconstructed 'Bengali-ness' into the landscape of the islands: refugee settlers have to a certain extent 'imported' their imaginations of an
ordered agricultural landscape to the islands from Bengal. This is especially visible in the aesthetic transformation of the landscape through the
construction of ponds (*diggis*), gardens and plantations resembling, on
a superficial level, the landscape of their homelands. Apart from utilising locally available species, Bengali settlers also raised certain imported
plants—medicinal and ornamental as well as crops—with which they
had been familiar on the mainland, in their gardens and plantations.
This transformed, 'ethnicised' landscape may therefore be understood to
function as carrier and signifier of a reconstructed diasporic memory of
East Bengal.

I found other examples of a firmly emplaced Bengali diaspora in
existence all over the rural areas of the islands: place names such as
Nabagram, Subhashgram, Kalighat, Durgapur, Swarajgram, Kadamtala,
Bakultala or Netajinagar indicate diasporic belonging. In public
space, statues of iconic national 'heroes' from Bengal like the poet
Rabindranath Tagore or the anti-colonial freedom fighter Subhash
Chandra Bose reinforce the impression that the Andamans are a place
with a visible Bengali presence and character. In the bazaar areas of villages with Bengali majorities, one can buy Bengali products and food,
while inscriptions on stores are often written in Bangla. Most settlers and
their descendants speak a colloquial Bangla, which is perceived as having
a rural origin, and which marks a contrast to the more formalised, met-
ropolitan Bangla spoken by the urban *bhadralok*. If one is invited into a
home, the hosts often proudly proclaim that they serve 'original' Bengali
food, consisting of rice, fish, pulses and vegetable curries. Bengalis are
stereotyped as having an affinity for politics, and a love for arts, music
and literature.[42] These ascriptions broadly corresponded with my experience of reconstructed 'traditions': the political angle can be observed at
chai shops where people regularly meet and discuss political as well as
village matters and where interlocutors often emphasised that this was a
proof that the Bengali 'tradition' of debate was alive in the Andamans. I
also attended several private concerts in households where Bengali folk
songs and epics were performed; including, among others, *nama sangir-
tan* (songs praising Lord Krishna).

---

[42] B.R. Tamta, *Andaman and Nicobar Islands* (Delhi: National Book Trust, 1991), 127.

Beyond that, religious festivals like Durga Pooja, Lakshmi Pooja, Kali Pooja, Krishna Janmastami, Shiva Ratri and Makarsankranti are regularly celebrated in Bengali villages. They lend a sense of identification to the settlers, not only as Bengali 'Hindus' in a Hindu-majority India, but also as Bengalis who are residents of Mini-India. For example, I went to a Krishna *pooja* (worship, religious ceremony) at a temple in Sundarpur on Little Andaman during the full moon. Without coming across the notion that this was a Matua festival,[43] many elements correspond to Mazumdar's descriptions of such an event[44]: musicians playing harmonium, flutes and drums (*dhol*) performed ecstatically for the audience in the temple. Occasionally the musicians hugged people in the audience, leading some older women to burst into tears. The music as well as the reciting of mantras for Lord Krishna went on non-stop for 24 hours, while the performers would change every one-and-a-half hours. At this event, one Bengali interlocutor told me proudly that the 'culture' of the settlers' ancestral homelands in East Bengal was alive and that only Bengalis would attend this festival. He opined that in many parts of the islands 'traditions' from Bengal were more adulterated than in Little Andaman because in these places, Bengalis had lived together with other communities for many decades and thus they had also participated in each other's religious festivals.

Hinting at the tendency towards cultural creolisation and religious syncretisation that I have observed across the islands, especially among communities who had lost links with their ancestral homelands, this statement may be interpreted by embedding these cultural developments into a temporal framework of settlement: as Little Andaman was settled with refugees as late as the mid-1970s, the reconstructed Bengali 'culture', which my interlocutor was so proud of, seems to be more oriented towards the maintenance of a diasporic 'tradition' and more exclusively ethnically defined than in other places, where Bengali refugees were settled earlier and where they have intermarried and mingled in everyday affairs with neighbouring communities to a larger extent. In the Andamans, it can be generally observed that, over the course of several generations of settlement, most communities tend to neglect the

---

[43] Local people have estimated that more than 80 per cent of East Bengal refugees in the Andamans belong to the Matuas, an anti-caste and egalitarian religious sect that is very popular among Namasudras. See Mazumdar, "Dwelling in Fluid Spaces," 198.

[44] Mazumdar, "Dwelling in Fluid Spaces," 172.

strict maintenance of ethnic and religious boundaries; they gradually merge towards being islanders, who are not only incommensurate with the original settlers in terms of ethnic, religious or caste affiliations, but who also share an affinity, with other communities, of feeling at 'home' in Mini-India. This implies interethnic solidarity, friendship and marriage as well as a preference on the part of islanders towards speaking the local lingua franca, Andaman Hindustani, instead of their respective mother tongues in everyday life.[45]

As a result of leaving behind their homelands and making new homes in the islands, the settlers' social hierarchies were renegotiated, too. For example, a Bengali settler from Kadamtala in Middle Andaman attributed land ownership and similar living conditions in a new environment to a certain form of equality among settlers. As landowners, settlers were not economically dependent on each other and occupied a similar class status to each other. In addition to that, Bengali settlers—like other communities in the islands—do not strictly adhere to the principles of caste interdependence, separation and hierarchy as described by Dumont.[46] Instead, most of them are members of the anti-caste and egalitarian Matua sect.[47] I was told by second-generation Bengali settlers that—due to the decreasing relevance of this practice for them—they have given up arranging marriages according to the matching of *gotras* (patrilineal, exogamous lineage groups). The weakening of practices of caste endogamy, in terms of connubial and commensal restriction, among settlers has also been confirmed by other researchers.[48] A pronounced effect of overseas migration on the softening of caste hierarchies is a phenomenon that can be broadly observed among other migrant groups in the Andamans, too.[49]

---

[45] Zehmisch, *Mini-India*, 98–99.

[46] Luis Dumont, *Homo Hierarchicus: The Caste System and its Implications* (Chicago/London: University of Chicago Press, 1980), 42–46.

[47] Mazumdar, "Dwelling in Fluid Spaces."

[48] See Chakrabarty, Mukhopadhyay, and Mukhopadhyay, "A New Trend in Marriage Practice," 225–230. This does not mean that caste has not continued to function as a means of separation and hierarchy, but that it has been given new meanings according to the diasporic context with class becoming a more significant means of differentiation than caste. There are, of course, cases, in which both concepts overlap: for example, I came across several indications that Bengali settlers, who largely belong to the Namasudra caste, look down upon later-migrated Dalits from West Bengal, who are mostly landless agricultural labourers.

[49] Zehmisch, *Mini-India*, 100–101.

When I asked Bengali settlers and their descendants to evaluate how they now, many decades later, viewed their decision to migrate to the Andamans, the large majority expressed satisfaction about having been provided with land and assistance after their arrival in India without any resources. Congruent with the larger Nehruvian ideological premise of social uplift,[50] most refugee families were proud to state that, as citizens of India, they had indeed experienced considerable class mobility over several generations. Cultivation was the main source of livelihood for the first generation of settlers and it still is, especially for those in Middle and North Andaman, who live far away from the administrative and economic hub on South Andaman. The district of South Andaman, especially the only town and seat of the administration, Port Blair, and its periphery as well as small islands like Havelock and Neil Island, have seen an explosion of real estate prices due to tourist development; in these locations, many Bengali settlers have sold their allotted lands to tourist entrepreneurs or opened guest houses, restaurants, cafes and shops catering to tourists. The booming hospitality industry has, however, also provided jobs to descendants and/or relatives of settlers—especially, to those latecomers who are referred to as 'without', because they migrated to the islands after the rehabilitation and colonisation schemes had been formally closed in various locations and, therefore, were without land, government assistance and approval.[51] Moreover, the success of tourism has also produced envy of those entrepreneurs, most of them mainlanders, who are able to gain the most profit from the lucrative tourist business. Government service is—besides trade, contracting and politics—the most common and desired source of social mobility among refugees and their descendants in the second and third generation. These alternative sources of income have reduced settlers' dependency on agriculture—especially in South Andaman. As a result of settlers leasing out their fields or plantations to sharecroppers or agricultural labourers who have more recently migrated from the subcontinent, mostly from West Bengal and Bangladesh, new class relations have been established between settlers and non-settlers. Over a few generations, the formerly

---

[50] P.A. Mohanrajan, *The Legacy of Nehru: A Centennial Tribute 1889–1989* (Madras: University of Madras, 1991).

[51] Kanchan Mukhopadhyay and Chhanda Mukhopadhyay, "The Transplanted Migrant Villagers in the Andaman Islands," *Journal of Social Anthropology* 3 (2006): 163.

destitute have transformed into landed gentry. Metaphorically speaking, the black waters of *kala pani*, associated with loss and social death, have, over several generations, proven to be *amrit*, the water of life, providing downtrodden, traumatised refugees with a culturally, socially, economically and ecologically 'fertile' existence as landowning settlers on new homelands.

CONTESTED POLITICS OF MEMORISATION

Practices of memorisation among Bengali settlers may be understood as dynamic sociocultural and ecological reconstructions involving a creative fusion of old and new elements in response to diasporic circumstances. As a result of their settlement, they adopted several major threads of identification, based on practices of memorisation. First, there is a certain, albeit weakening nostalgia, for the idea of a 'lost' homeland in East Bengal. Seeking to gain an understanding of how contemporary notions of local belonging among Bengali settlers are linked to diasporic reconstructions of loss, I encountered, of course, the famous trope of *Sonar Bangla* (the golden Bengal) which Hindu refugees from East Bengal left behind when coming to Andaman.[52] When I talked to Ram Das, an elderly Bengali refugee settler in Little Andaman, about his personal connection to the lost homeland, he told me that *Sonar Bangla* was now here at his new home because, as he reasoned, everything he had brought here and planted grew well. His statement indicates that he was able to imagine that his 'home' travelled along with him and that literally as well as figuratively, his life had taken root in his new environment. In contrast to Ram Das, who had migrated to Little Andaman from Bengal after the 1971 war, and who had been 'given land by Indira Gandhi'—as the common expression goes in this island, which was settled from 1974 onwards, fairly late, as compared to other locations—many of the contemporary witnesses of Partition in other places had already passed away by the time of my fieldwork. Narratives of their refugee experience and of their homelands did not play a prominent role among their offspring.

When I asked settler descendants what they knew of their ancestral homelands, they usually replied that they did not have not much of an idea because their parents had either not talked to them about it or

---

[52] See also Tamta, *Andaman and Nicobar Islands*, 127.

they had expressed their longing for *Sonar Bangla* largely among their peers, with whom they had jointly arrived in the Andamans. While one may deduce from these statements that the problem of coping with the trauma of displacement might have remained somewhat confined to the directly affected generation, it may also be assumed that the overall focus on narrating a life-history that is dominated by the positive outcome of successful place-making processes is itself a mechanism for coping with trauma and its associated negative memories. This lack of intergenerational exchange of memories of a distant ancestral homeland may also be linked to an explicitly stated disinterest in that homeland among Bengali settler descendants, which most of them justified with the established fact that they had been born in the Andamans, felt at home there and had no links to their now-almost-mythical places of origin. What mattered in their accounts much more was how their local belonging was contingent upon their parents' struggle to make a place for themselves in the islands, and on their achievements as pioneering settlers who contributed to the colonisation process.

This privileging of a narrative of settlement and place-making over memories of a lost homeland, displacement and violence is also visible within the research of Uditi Sen, a historian who interviewed first-generation refugees in the Andaman Islands about a decade ago. Sen concluded from her data that the refugees' practices of memorialising the personal choices they had made, as well as their triumphs over ecological adversities when settling as agricultural pioneers in the islands, took a much more prominent role in the formation of their collective identity than the experience of being a 'refugee' suffering under state coercion, loss and victimhood.[53] As these narratives place emphasis on agency and successful socio-economic and cultural adaptation, they open up a contrasting representation to the recurring trope of Partition literature depicting the 'low-class' Bengali refugee as a 'passive' victim of various forms of physical and bureaucratic violence and external force. Hence, I argue that one must consider the entanglement of these personalised oral histories with the hegemonic state narrative of Mini-India; presumably, Bengali settlers collectively acknowledged and embodied the omnipresent Mini-India discourse of peaceful cohabitation and social uplift, and integrated it into their own narrations of local belonging.

---

[53] U. Sen, "Dissident Memories."

Apart from the fact that self-projections as industrious, 'roll-your-sleeves-up' pioneering settlers contradict the common stereotyping of Bengalis as lazy, they also appear to be more psychologically appealing components of a diasporic ethno-history than languishing in memories of loss and deprivation. However, one must also take into account the particular sociopolitical context of the Andamans in which these articulations of belonging are voiced: in this former settler colony, public recognition is to a certain extent based on the ascription of collective contributions to the colonisation process. Different communities claim to have been instrumental in the foundation and institutionalisation of the colony and thus, the Indian nation state, in the islands: the pre-42 communities, especially the local-born, tend to present themselves as the 'original colonisers' of the islands, because their convict ancestors laid the foundations of the colony under a strict penal regime, against an inclement and often deadly environment and against the violent resistance of the indigenous hunter-gatherers.[54] Similarly, the Ranchi community, who succeeded the convicts in clearing forests for the timber industry and refugee settlements as well as in erecting the major infrastructure, claims a status as the 'builders of modern Andaman'.[55] Analogous to these claims, it appears reasonable to understand the self-projections of Bengali settlers as 'agricultural pioneers'[56] as being influenced by the local context of political competition for recognition and access to state sinecures.[57]

---

[54] Philipp Zehmisch, "Manufacturing India beyond India: Migration, Social-Engineering, and Politics in the Andaman Islands," *ISA e-Symposium for Sociology* 6, no. 1 (2016), http://www.sagepub.net/isa/admin/viewEBPDF.aspx?&art=EBul-Zehmisch-Mar2016.pdf&type. Accessed May 7, 2017.

[55] Philipp Zehmisch, "The Invisible Architects of Andaman: Manifestations of Aboriginal Migration from Ranchi," in *Manifestations of History: Time, Space and Community in the Andaman Islands*, ed. Frank Heidemann and Philipp Zehmisch (New Delhi: Primus, 2016), 122–138.

[56] See also U. Sen, "Dissident Memories."

[57] As a result of distributions of welfare as well as a politics of recognition along lines of community, Andaman politics may be understood as a field in which coexisting, separate 'containers' of community compete for access to state benefits and influence. These politics have become enmeshed with ethnic and racial stereotyping and have thus impacted the social relations between different communities. See Zehmisch, *Mini-India*, 102–115.

When it comes to formulating ethnic belonging in the political arena of Mini-India, Bengali settlers tend to identify with Greater Bengal as a cultural 'container' differentiating them from other communities. In the Andaman diaspora, the term 'Bengalis' refers to East Bengal refugees and later-coming migrants from Bangladesh and West Bengal, and Bangla speakers from other states. Thus, in spite of the separate positionality of settlers hailing from as East Bengal, they contextually merge with other migrants with whom they share more sociocultural norms, values, practices and particular political interests than with other groups. An institution that lends an overall feeling of belonging to Bengalis in Port Blair is Atul Smriti Samiti, the so-called 'Bengali Club' where, apart from hosting cultural programmes and festivals for the Bengali community, committed social workers and patrons conduct various forms of advocacy and counselling for their clients.

One of the collective means of reified cultural identification with Bengal is based on the hegemonic memory of the anti-colonial struggle. All over India, the Andamans are remembered as a destination to which political prisoners, the majority of them Bengalis, were deported by the British in order for them to be incarcerated and violently disciplined in the Cellular Jail.[58] Consequently, many Bengali interlocutors displayed an ethno-historical consciousness as a community by glorifying political prisoners from Bengal for their sacrifices in the service of national liberation. Further, they also took pride in the link between the Andamans and the famous Bengali nationalist 'Netaji' Subhash Chandra Bose, who installed an INA (Indian National Army) 'puppet' government on the islands during the times of the Japanese occupation in World War II. Regardless how little local Bengalis may be personally related to actual freedom fighters, such identification with national heroes appears to enhance the prestige of this ethnic group, in a considerably nationalist overseas setting that encourages the mainstream groups to compete in displaying their patriotism by highlighting their collective contributions and efforts they have invested in nation-building.

---

[58] The Cellular Jail gained notoriety all over India through prison narratives and literature produced by 'bourgeois-nationalist' ex-inmates. Due to the discursive nationalisation of local history, the islands have come to embody a site of nationalist 'pilgrimage', in which VIPs as well as tourists from the mainland come to hail freedom fighters at several locations in Port Blair. See Zehmisch, *Mini-India*, 118–123.

Another site of ethnic reification is the field of politics. The approximately 130,000 Bengalis are the numerically strongest linguistic group in the Andaman society, and thus the politically most influential group. Among them, refugee settlers and their descendants are vested with the economic and political powers of patronage because they act as employers or landlords for more recently migrated Bengalis. Due to their numerical supremacy and the tendency to form vote banks on linguistic lines, Bengali politicians dominate the *panchayats* (institutions of communal governance) in those regions and villages with a Bengali majority. What's more, in the last few decades, every elected Member of Parliament from the Andamans has been a Bengali. Islanders of all sorts regularly blame the former office bearer, who was in power for several decades, for having facilitated and willingly supported the migration of Bengali migrants to the islands in order to increase his ethnic vote bank. Broadly generalising, the electoral dominance of Bengalis enables certain political players both to channel state sinecures and influence more efficiently when working for the benefit of their voting clients. One visible outcome of the strength of the vote bank of the Andaman Namasudras is that politicians have repeatedly demanded to introduce Scheduled Caste (SC) reservation in the islands in line with their SC entitlements on the Indian mainland.

Another effect of political dominance could be observed about a decade ago, when affirmative action on the basis of the Other Backward Classes (OBC) scheme was implemented in the Andamans. In comparison with the four pre-42 communities, the OBC commission had identified Bengali settlers as 'educationally and historically backward'.[59] By giving reservation to the, on average, landed and comparatively economically sound communities, the outcome of this decision did not take present socio-economic disparities between various islanders into account, but was clearly influenced by an articulation of the political voice of influential community leaders. When I interviewed spokespersons for the Bengali settlers, they repeatedly reiterated the notion of 'backwardness', which was, accordingly, conditioned both by the historical injustice of their displacement from East Bengal and by their isolated settlement in remote forest areas, replete with 'dangerous animals' and 'hostile savages' but lacking in communication and infrastructure. Further, because

---

[59] Biswas, *Colonization and Rehabilitation in Andaman and Nicobars*, 133.

Bengali settlers had been brought to the Andamans by the state, it would have to take responsibility for their welfare, too. Justifying demands *from* the state by highlighting collective efforts *for* it, as well, such claims of backwardness were consecutively linked up to the larger argument that Bengali settlers had contributed to the colonisation of the islands by bringing 'development' and 'civilisation' to the 'jungle'. One can observe that the notion of historical backwardness put forward in this kind of argument does not clearly correspond with the master narrative of successful refugee rehabilitation; this incongruence and disjuncture between the two discourses demonstrates that representations of the past must, in most cases, be regarded as contextually determined by collective desires to articulate and display certain components of identity in the present, especially when such identifications are linked to political demands.

This assumption may also be confirmed by another observation: while East Bengal refugee settlers tend to adopt a collective, reified community identity as 'Bengalis' when it comes to making certain cultural, historical or political claims which benefit them, there are paradoxically other moments in which they deny this connection for the very same reason—political expediency. For example, I encountered strong anti-migrant rhetoric among representatives of the Settlers' Offspring Welfare Association in Diglipur, who were arguing against the influx of migrants from West Bengal and Bangladesh. Putting forward arguments relating to overpopulation and environmental damage, they especially blamed illegalised Bangladeshi migrants, stating that they had no right to come to the islands because they were foreigners. When I pointed out that most Bangladeshis were from the same region as their own ancestors—the majority were Hindus, too, and had also suffered from socio-economic deprivation and, possibly, communal tensions— I was told that these migrants had homes to which they could return, while the refugee settlers and their offspring could go nowhere else; their homes were now here, in the Andamans. Moreover, as Bengali refugees, they were Indians because their homelands had been in undivided India before Partition when they became part of Pakistan. These examples demonstrate that representations of memories of the past must always be interpreted by considering their embeddedness into an overarching discursive setting, both local and trans-local, and the various political agendas which inflect how they are narrated and communicated to the public.

CONCLUSION

This chapter has analysed the reasons for and effects of refugee settlement in the Andaman Islands in the light of different cultural, socioeconomic, historical and political strands emerging at the intersection of memory and place. The refugees' overall positive representation of their settlement and their place-making processes embeds the narrative of refugee rehabilitation in the Andamans within the nationalist master narrative of Mini-India, in which a patronising state apparatus had provided for its 'happy children' well. Particular to the Andaman case is—especially when compared to the accounts of refugee rehabilitation on the mainland—the prominence that narratives of successful place-making processes seem to have in composing the specific ethno-history and identification of Bengali refugees, over against the expression of nostalgia for what they had left behind or memories of violence and deprivation.[60] This 'loss of relevance of Partition' in their memories runs counter to the 'received wisdom' on Bengali refugees, which portrays them as 'passive victims of a harsh, ill-conceived and inadequate regime of rehabilitation'.[61]

East Bengal Hindu refugees in the Andamans are better understood by looking beyond the dominant narrative of Partition as primary means of identification. Their place-making practices are closely intertwined with dynamic sociocultural and ecological reconstructions of Bengaliness emerging in response to diasporic circumstances and involving a creative fusion of old and new elements. The reconstructed notion of Bengal emerges here as a flexible trope of memory that becomes manifest in the present at the level of sociocultural practices, notions of belonging and politics. Consequently, refugees and their descendants contextually appropriate, silence or engage different notions of memory in order to underline collective claims of 'Indian-ness' in the national context, 'Bengali-ness' in the diasporic Andaman context and socially less relevant caste identities as well as 'refugee-ness' in the context of reservation policies.

---

[60] See also U. Sen, "Dissident Memories," 220.
[61] Ibid., 220–221.

WORKS CITED

Anderson, Clare. *Legible Bodies: Race, Criminality and Colonialism in South Asia.* Oxford/New York: Berg, 2004.

Anderson, Clare, Madhumita Mazumdar, and Vishvajit Pandya. "Introduction." In *New Histories of the Andaman Islands: Landscape, Place and Identity in the Bay of Bengal, 1790–2012,* edited by Clare Anderson, Madhumita Mazumdar, and Vishvajit Pandya, 1–27. Cambridge: Cambridge University Press, 2015.

Biswas, Swapan K. *Colonization and Rehabilitation in Andaman and Nicobars.* Delhi: Abheejit Publications, 2009.

Casey, Edward S. *The Fate of Place: A Philosophical History.* Berkeley/Los Angeles: University of California Press, 1996.

Chakrabarty, Kakali, Chhanda Mukhopadhyay, and Kanchan Mukhopadhyay. "A New Trend in Marriage Practice: Case Studies from a South Andaman Village." In *Anthropology of Small Populations,* edited by Anthropological Survey of India, 225–230. Calcutta: Anthropological Survey of India, 1998.

Dasgupta, Abhijit. *Displacement and Exile: The State-Refugee Relations in India.* New Delhi: Oxford University Press, 2016.

Dhingra, Kiran. *The Andaman and Nicobar Islands in the 20th Century: A Gazetteer.* New Delhi: Oxford University Press, 2005.

Dumont, Luis. *Homo Hierarchicus: The Caste System and Its Implications.* Chicago/London: University of Chicago Press, 1980.

Gray, John. "Community as Place-Making: Ram Auctions in the Scottish Borderland." In *Realizing Community: Concepts, Social Relationships and Sentiments,* edited by Vered Amit, 38–59. London: Routledge, 2002.

Guha, Phulrenu. "Rehabilitation, East & West." In *No Woman's Land—Women from Pakistan, India & Bangladesh Write on the Partition of India,* edited by Ritu Menon, 195–202. New Delhi: Women Unlimited, 2004.

Gupta, Akhil, and James Ferguson. "Culture, Power, Place: Ethnography at the End of an Era." In *Culture, Power, Place: Explorations in Critical Anthropology,* edited by Akhil Gupta and James Ferguson, 1–32. Durham: Duke University Press, 1997.

Mair, Jonathan, and Nicholas H.A. Evans. "Ethics across Borders: Incommensurability and Affinity." *HAU: Journal of Ethnographic Theory* 5, no. 2 (2015): 201–225.

Mathur, Laxman P. *Kala Pani: History of Andaman & Nicobar Islands with a study of India's Freedom Struggle.* New Delhi: Eastern Book Corporation, 1985.

Mazumdar, Madhumita. "Dwelling in Fluid Spaces: The Matuas of the Andaman Islands." In *New Histories of the Andaman Islands: Landscape, Place and Identity in the Bay of Bengal, 1790–2012,* edited by Clare Anderson, Madhumita Mazumdar, and Vishvajit Pandya, 170–200. Cambridge: Cambridge University Press, 2015.

Mohanrajan, P.A. *The Legacy of Nehru: A Centennial Tribute 1889–1989.* Madras: University of Madras, 1991.

Mukhopadhyay, Kanchan, and Chhanda Mukhopadhyay. "The Transplanted Migrant Villagers in the Andaman Islands." *Journal of Social Anthropology* 3 (2006): 161–173.

Radcliffe-Brown, Alfred R. *The Andaman Islanders.* London: Weidenfeld & Nicholson, 1922.

Saldhana, Cecil J. *Andaman, Nicobar and Lakshadweep: An Environmental Impact Assessment.* New Delhi: Oxford & IBH, 1989.

Sekhsaria, Pankaj. "When Chanos Chanos Became Tsunami Macchi: The Post-December 2004 Scenario in the Andaman and Nicobar Islands." *Journal of the Bombay Natural History Society* 106 (2009): 256–262.

Sen, Jhuma. "Reconstructing Marichjhapi: From Margins and Memories of Migrant Lives." In *Partition: The Long Shadow,* edited by Urvashi Butalia, 102–127. New Delhi: Zubaan, 2015.

Sen, Satadru. *Disciplining Punishment: Colonialism and Convict Society in the Andaman Islands.* New Delhi: Oxford University Press, 2000.

Sen, Satadru. *Savagery and Colonialism in the Indian Ocean: Power, Pleasure and the Andaman Islanders.* New York: Routledge, 2010.

Sen, Uditi. "Dissident Memories: Exploring Bengali Refugee Narratives in the Andaman Islands." In *Refugees and the End of Empire: Imperial Collapse and Forced Migration in the Twentieth Century,* edited by Panikos Panayi and Pippa Virdee, 219–244. Basingstoke, Hampshire: Palgrave Macmillan, 2011.

Sundar, Nandini. *Subalterns and Sovereigns: An Anthropological History of Bastar (1854–2006),* 2nd edn. New Delhi: Oxford University Press, 2007.

Tamta, B.R. *Andaman and Nicobar Islands.* Delhi: National Book Trust, 1991.

Vaidik, Aparna. *Imperial Andamans: Colonial Encounter and Island History.* Hampshire/New York: Palgrave Macmillan, 2010.

Venkateswar, Sita. *Development and Ethnocide: Colonial Practices in the Andaman Islands.* Copenhagen: Iwgia, 2004.

Zehmisch, Philipp. "Manufacturing India beyond India: Migration, Social-Engineering, and Politics in the Andaman Islands." *ISA e-Symposium for Sociology* no. 6, 1 (2016), http://www.sagepub.net/isa/admin/viewEBPDF. aspx?&art=EBul-Zehmisch-Mar2016.pdf&type. Accessed May 7, 2017.

Zehmisch, Philipp. "The Invisible Architects of Andaman: Manifestations of Aboriginal Migration from Ranchi." In *Manifestations of History: Time, Space and Community in the Andaman Islands,* edited by Frank Heidemann and Philipp Zehmisch, 122–138. New Delhi: Primus, 2016.

Zehmisch, Philipp. *Mini-India: The Politics of Migration and Subalternity in the Andaman Islands.* New Delhi: Oxford University Press, 2017.

PART II

The Archive and the Literary

CHAPTER 5

The Story of Partition from the Official and the Alternate Archives

Pallavi Chakravarty

Seventy years after the event itself, the story of the Partition of the Indian subcontinent has come into its own. A vast number of contemporary accounts, scholarly works, cinematic and literary representations and dedicated websites have contributed towards bringing Partition to the centre of the narrative that otherwise describes the emergence of two nations and their citizens. This has been made possible by the use of a diverse array of sources that allow sometimes radically different perspectives, viewpoints and insights into the experience, history and impact of Partition. It is because of these changing sources that our understanding of Partition has changed so much over time, and is likely to continue to do so. This essay looks at the various sources that have been used in Partition studies, to assess some of their strengths and limitations, and to understand their relationship. Our focus is on the interplay of the official and the alternate archives. Stuart Blackburn's research on a mid-nineteenth-century conflict between two tribes in Arunachal Pradesh—the Apatanis and the Nyshis—shows that whereas the official records on this issue brought to light a very partisan view of the conflict, use of the

P. Chakravarty (✉)
Ambedkar University Delhi, New Delhi, India
e-mail: pallavi@aud.ac.in

© The Author(s) 2018
C. Mahn and A. Murphy (eds.), *Partition and the Practice of Memory*,
https://doi.org/10.1007/978-3-319-64516-2_5

alternate archives (oral testimonies, in this case), even nearly a century later, could uncover otherwise unknown and unexpected aspects of the same event.[1] When compared with these oral accounts, in Blackburn's own words, the official record "appears like a badly-cropped photograph, a snapshot that distorts not by what it shows but by what it leaves out."[2] Partition Studies, perhaps by definition, has become a primary location for the insight that history, overall, is no longer a subject that can rely upon research based solely upon the written document as preserved in the official archives, but must also involve—and in ever-changing ways—the identification of new sources, new archives: the alternate archives.

This paper is divided into two sections. The first section briefly discusses the phases in Partition historiography and how each phase has made a distinct contribution in terms of method and process. In the second section I have identified a few examples to demonstrate how the official and alternate archives have been used to explore these themes in the context of the Partition in the east, i.e. on the Bengal border. What can be concluded is that whereas some aspects of Partition history are adequately addressed through the official archives, alternate sources such as literature, cinema and oral evidences prove to be useful for a social history of partition. However, what will also be seen, as has been pointed out by Stuart Blackburn, is that it is only through the use of *both* these sources that the "complete picture" can be brought to light.

THE HISTORIAN'S ARCHIVE AND PARTITION HISTORIOGRAPHY[3]

The earliest works on Partition were the contemporary accounts of the administrators and politicians involved in this messy business of dividing a country and its people. A close reading of these works show that

---

[1] Stuart Blackburn, "Colonial Contact in the 'Hidden Land': Oral History Among the Apatanis of Arunanchal Pradesh," *IESHR* 40, no. 3 (2003): 335–365.

[2] Ibid., 350.

[3] For a more detailed discussion on Partition historiography refer to Pankhuree R. Dube, "Partition Historiography," *The Historian* 77, no. 1 (Spring 2015): 54–79; David Gilmartin, "The Historiography of India's Partition: Between Civilization and Modernity," *The Journal of Asian Studies* 74, no. 1 (February 2015): 23–41; Joya Chatterji, "New Directions in Partition Studies," *History Workshop Journal* 67, no. 1 (2009): 213–220; and Joya Chatterji, "Partition Studies: Prospects and Pitfalls," *The Journal of Asian Studies* 73, no. 2 (May 2014): 309–312.

these accounts are heavily biased in accordance with the nationality of the author. Thus while Indian and Pakistani authors held each other responsible for this event, British authors believed Partition was the only solution to this great Indian conundrum, and that they had solved it with "surgical accuracy".[4] However, apart from these published contemporary memoirs and accounts, the decades following Partition also saw the opening up of unpublished archival documents from the period to the general public and scholars. Administrative reports, correspondences, secret files, legislative assembly debates, institutional and the private papers of various political parties, politicians and administrators and so on, made up the newly available official archives, and could be accessed at various archives/institutes situated in India, Pakistan, Bangladesh and the United Kingdom. Access to these sources allowed scholars to flesh out a more detailed understanding of the political history of this event.

Asim Roy argues that the first scholarly works in Partition historiography engage with what he calls the "high-politics" debate around what led to Partition.[5] These works, using these, then new sources, remained restricted to exploring the theme of what had led to Partition and who was to be "blamed" for it, and here too the focus was on the "big three"—the Indian National Congress, the Muslim League and the British. Often these works also revolved around the individuals concerned—Jawaharlal Nehru, Gandhi, Jinnah and Mountbatten.[6] Thus, while the contribution of such works was immense with regard to bringing out the theme of Partition as an independent area of research, utilising newly available archival sources, they could not explain the true meaning of this event in terms of the immense impact it had

---

[4]C.M. Ali, *The Emergence of Pakistan* (New York: Columbia University Press, 1967); Maulana Abul Kalam Azad, *India Wins Freedom* (New Delhi: Orient Longman, 1988); B.R Ambedkar, *Pakistan or Partition of India* (Bombay: Thacker and Company Ltd, 1946); Rajendra Prasad, *India Divided* (Bombay: Hind Kitab Publishers, 1946); and Francis Tuker, *While Memory Serves* (London: Cassell, 1950).

[5]Asim Roy, "The High Politics of India's Partition: The Revisionist Perspective," in *India's Partition, Process, Strategy and Mobilization*, ed. M. Hasan (New Delhi: OUP, 2001).

[6]David Page, *Prelude to Partition: Indian Muslims and the Imperial System of Control 1920–1932* (Delhi, 1982); R.J. Moore, *Escape from Empire: The Attlee Government and the Indian Problem* (Oxford: Clarendon, 1983); A.I. Singh, *The Origins of the Partition of India: 1936–1947* (New Delhi: Oxford University Press, 1987); and Ayesha Jalal, *The Sole Spokesman: Jinnah, the Muslim League and the Demand for Pakistan* (Cambridge: Cambridge University Press, 1985).

on the people who were actually affected by it. As a result, this work remained limited in its scope.

It was, as noted by Urvashi Butalia and Gyanendra Pandey, the turbulent 1980s in India that resurrected the ghost of Partition once again, and this time from a new perspective. A telling comment made by a Sikh survivor of the 1984 anti-Sikh pogrom in Delhi—"this was just like 1947 for us..."—made Butalia rethink how the event of Partition was taught and researched in India. A new source, oral testimonies, was pursued by scholars as a means to explore Partition from a new perspective; from this emerged ground-breaking works by Butalia, Ritu Menon and Kamla Bhasin.[7] According to Pandey, the social history of Partition had previously been either relegated to the margins, as a short concluding paragraph in the grand narrative of the Indian nationalist movement, or, as noted above, had been disregarded entirely in favour of a study of its causes. Partition was treated as an unwanted anomaly in the narrative of the otherwise successful national movement.[8] It was the "human dimension" of Partition—i.e. a descriptive account of the event and not a debate over the factors that led to it—that was taken up in the next phase of Partition Studies. And in this phase, it is the alternate archives which have been instrumental. So, what are these alternate archives?

As mentioned above, the works of Butalia, Menon and Bhasin have demonstrated how oral testimonies can lead Partition Studies in entirely new directions. It is through the series of interviews conducted by these scholars that we learn about the true meaning of Partition for the people who actually went through this loss and displacement. Such alternate archives, further, allowed for a new kind of return to the official archives. A Dalit woman's interview in Butalia's work, for example, set the ball rolling for many scholars to look at Partition from the point of view of marginalised communities. This encouraged scholars to revisit the official archives to search for the caste dimension in Partition; of course, there are records to construct a history of Partition from this perspective

---

[7] Urvashi Butalia, *The Other Side of Silence* (New Delhi: Viking, 1998); *Borders and Boundaries: Women in India's Partition*, ed. Ritu Menon and Kamla Bhasin (New Delhi: Kali for Women, 2000).

[8] Gyanendra Pandey, *Remembering Partition: Violence, Nationalism and History in India* (Cambridge: Cambridge University Press, 2001).

as well.[9] After all, as noted by Raphael Samuel, oral history compels us to revisit the official archives, not eschew them: "Oral evidence should make the historian hungrier for documents, not less."[10] Thus, oral testimonies today have become a primary source material for every Partition historian, in themselves and in dynamic interaction with official archives of various kinds. The interviews with Partition victims recorded by Andrew Whitehead for the BBC are maintained at the SOAS library in London. Jadavpur University has published a collection of interviews conducted in the Bijoygarh Colony (*Dhongsho O Nirman: Bangiya Udbastu Samajer Swkathit Bibaran*, 2007). Similarly, the second volume of the series *Trauma and Triumph* (2009) edited by Jashodhara Bagchi and Subhoranjan Dasgupta is a collection from varied sources, with interviews forming a very significant part of it. The *Partition Archive* is another venture, created by the survivors themselves, in order to record their stories, lest we forget them. To date they have created a bank of more than 5000 interviews with survivors of Partition across the borders of India, Pakistan, Bangladesh, the UK and even the USA.[11]

While contemporary accounts by administrators and politicians have discussed the trauma of Partition to a degree, the experiences of people have come to be known to us mainly through the collection of interviews years later.[12] However, such trauma did not go unwritten even in those times. Here I am referring to now-classic works of literature such

---

[9] Ramnarayan Rawat, "Partition Politics and Acchut Identity: A Study of the Scheduled Castes Federation and Dalit Politics in UP, 1946–48," in *Partitions of Memory: The Afterlife of the Division of India*, ed. Suvir Kaul (New Delhi: Permanent Black, 2001); Ravinder Kaur, "The Last Journey: Exploring Social Class in 1947 Partition Migration," *Economic and Political Weekly* 41, no. 22 (June 3–9, 2006): 2221–2228; Ravinder Kaur, *Since 1947: Partition Narratives Among Punjabi Migrants of Delhi* (ND: OUP, 2007); Vazira Fazila-Yacoobali Zamindar, *The Long Partition and the Making of Modern South Asia: Refugees, Boundaries, Histories* (New York: Columbia University Press, 2007); and Akanksha Kumar, "Locating Dalits in the Midst of Partition and Violence," JSHC 2, no. 2 (2016) http://jshc.org/locating-dalits-in-the-midst-of-partition-and-violence/. Accessed 15 November 2017.

[10] Raphael Samuel, "Local History and Oral History," *History Workshop Journal*, no. 1 (Spring, 1976): 191–208, 204.

[11] www.1947PartitionArchives.org. Accessed 18 November 2017.

[12] Several interviews have revealed that the second and third generation of these survivors had been regularly fed with what we might call "Partition stories" by their parents and grandparents respectively. They did not need to refer to any textbook to understand Partition and its meaning.

as those by Saadat Hasan Manto. His *Siyah Hashiye* ("Black Borders") is perhaps the most curt yet accurate description of the many experiences of partition—violence, loss, displacement, victimhood and futility. In *Toba Tek Singh*, Manto makes a novel argument about the "insanity" of the whole act of Partition itself, which makes us revisit the whole argument of the British authors at the time of Partition, who saw it as the only option available to solve the problem at hand. At the same time, Manto's work also made a few scholars think about the impact of this tragic event upon the margins of the marginalia—asylum and prison inmates.[13] A short story by Rajinder Singh Bedi, "Lajwanti", and Amrita Pritam's classic *Pinjar* are two influential works from literature which have guided Partition studies towards another lesser-known aspect— abducted women and their plight during Partition. Thus, while the cold facts and numbers, as recounted in the files concerning abducted women, had already presented us with this horrifying aspect of Partition violence, stories like these humanised the experience to give a larger commentary on gender-based violence. Literary works have thus offered nuanced portraits of everyday trauma that move beyond historical fact; in Jasbir Jain's words, literature "goes beyond the empirical reality, beyond treaties and wars and probes the silence of the human mind... literature is "writing" about what cannot be written about."[14] A fine selection of such short stories and novels have been translated from various languages into English by Alok Bhalla for his indispensable four-volume magnum opus, *Stories about the Partition of India*.[15] Works like this, as demonstrated by essays in this volume, have continued to be written. We now have several such compendia on the stories of Partition, each

---

[13] Anirudh Kala, Alok Sarin, and Sanjeev Jain, "The Psychiatrist's Partition," in *Himal Southasian*, http://old.himalmag.com/component/content/article/1426-the-psychiatrists-partition.html. Accessed 24 April 2017; Anupama Roy, "Sifting, Selecting, Relocating Citizenship at the Commencement of the Republic," CWDS Occasional paper no. 54, source: www.cwds.ac.in/OCPaper/occassionalpaper54.pdf. Accessed 16 March 2011.

[14] Jasbir Jain, *Reading Partition/Living Partition* (New Delhi: Rawat Publishers, 2007), 5.

[15] Alok Bhalla, ed., *Stories About the Partition of India*, vols. I–IV (New Delhi: Harper Collins, 1994).

highlighting the "human dimension" through the lens of personal catas-
trophe and trauma that is intertwined with a story of the nation and
national birth.[16]

Yet another component of the alternate archives of Partition history
has been cinema. M. S. Sathyu's classic *Garam Hawa,* (1973) is noted
for its representation of the plight of the Muslim in post-Partition India.
In Bengal, the role of cinema in bringing to light the human dimension of Partition has been perhaps even more significant. Not having
witnessed the kind of horrific violence or the one-time mass migration
seen on the Western border, the experience of Partition in Bengal was
subtle and difficult to grasp from official records. Ritwik Ghatak, and his
famous trilogy on the entire experience of Partition in the east—*Meghe
Dhaka Tara, Subarnarekha, and Komal Gandhar* (1960, 1965 and 1961
respectively) provided new insight into the experience of Partition. Nita
(in *Meghe Dhaka Tara*) epitomised the category of the "refugee woman"
and her struggle in post-Partition Bengal, while Sita (in *Subarnarekha*)
depicted the subtle forms of violence experienced by women in Bengal.
Cinema, like literature, has also opened up new areas of research in
Partition studies. We now find many edited volumes on Partition which
compile diverse alternate sources that have the common aim of showing us the "human dimension" of the event, and not the "high-politics"
debate.[17]

Thus, we see that the second phase in Partition historiography went
far beyond earlier works in describing to us the meaning of that event,
rather than what led to it. But there are limitations here as well; the most
important being that in restricting the meaning of Partition to violence
alone, such research limited its own time frame so that it only extended
a little later than 1947, since what were known as the "Partition riots"
culminated in the early months of 1948. Also, a preoccupation with the
experience of catastrophic violence entailed a Punjab-centric perspective, marginalising the different kinds of violence in regions other than

---

[16]Bashabi Fraser, *Bengal Partition Stories: An Unclosed Chapter* (London: Anthem
Press, 2008); Debjani Sengupta, *Mapmaking: Partition Stories from 2 Bengals* (New Delhi:
Stree, 2003); and Tarun K. Saint, *Witnessing Partition: Memory, History, Fiction* (Delhi:
Routledge, 2010).

[17]Mushirul Hasan, ed., *India Partitioned: The Other Face of Freedom*, 2 vols. (Delhi: Roli
Books, 1998); S. Settar, and Indira Beptista Gupta, eds., *Pangs of Partition: The Human
Dimension* (New Delhi: Manohar, 2002).

Punjab—Bengal, Sind, Assam and so on. More recent work in Partition historiography therefore looks towards filling up the gaps still left behind, adopting and expanding research themes from its predecessors and exploring new alternate archives. We also find a return to the theme of high politics, but now looking at politics in post-independent India, Pakistan and Bangladesh.[18] The time frame has been extended well into the 1970s and many new approaches—such as comparative analysis, cross-boundary research and so on—have been utilised to present a revised history of partition. As a result, new themes in Partition studies have been unearthed—on citizenship, on refugees and their rehabilitation, border studies, cities and urbanisation and gender roles, for example.[19] The result is that now we have before us a very detailed account of the event, its causes and its consequences.

We can see, therefore, that official and alternative archives offer substantively different kinds of representations. These representations enable radically different narratives of Partition to emerge. This will be demonstrated here through examination of three themes that emerge in the literature on Partition: the "high politics" debate; the description of the event; and the aftermath of Partition.

THE STORY AT THE INTERSECTION OF THE OFFICIAL AND ALTERNATE ARCHIVES

For the survivors in Bengal, not only is Partition seen as the handiwork of distant actors and as something forced upon the people by fiat, but also, the year 1947 is viewed not as the year of independence, but rather as the year of Partition—*deshbhag*. This grave disruption in their

---

[18] Yasmin Khan, *The Great Partition: Making of India and Pakistan* (New Haven: Yale University Press, 2007); Neeti Nair, *Changing Homelands: Hindu Politics and Partition of India* (Cambridge, Massachusetts: Harvard University Press, 2011).

[19] Joya Chatterji, *The Spoils of Partition: Bengal and India, 1947–67* (Cambridge: Cambridge University Press, 2007); Sarah Ansari, *Life After Partition: Migration, Community and Strife in Sindh, 1947–62* (Karachi: OUP, 2005); Ravinder Kaur, *Since 1947: Partition Narratives Among Punjabi Migrants of Delhi* (New Delhi: Oxford University Press, 2007); Ian Talbot, *Divided Cities: Lahore, Amritsar and the Partition of India* (Karachi: Oxford University Press, 2006); Willem van Schendel, *The Bengal Borderland: Bengal State of Nation in South Asia* (London: Anthem Press, 2005); and Vazira Zamindar, *The Long Partition and the Making of Modern South Asia: Refugees, Boundaries, Histories* (New York: Columbia University Press, 2007).

everyday life had a greater meaning than independence itself. Ganesh Halui, a Bengali refugee, voices such feelings explicitly, "Swadhinata noye, Deshbhager Panchash Bachar" (Not independence, it is the 50 years of Partition).[20] After all, for these refugees independence brought permanent displacement from their homelands and dependence upon the state for their existence in a distant land. Therefore, their sorrow at being uprooted upon Partition was greater than any joy of freedom.

Examining Partition though alternate sources alone, three perspectives emerge: one, communal violence was a result of the "outsiders"; second, Partition of the subcontinent and the resulting large-scale displacement of the people was enforced from above and not desired by the people themselves; and, finally, for the victims of this displacement, the memory of Partition which holds greater importance than independence itself. Hence, the answer to the question about what led to Partition is emotionally charged in the oral sources, and cannot be found using these statements alone. As far as literature and cinema are concerned, neither medium explicitly conveys any message in this regard. Rather, only implicit meanings can be deciphered. The picture that emerges from such sources is also one of an amicable Hindu-Muslim society, and disruption is brought herein through British policies and senior government leaders. But, in general, the picture is of an idyllic society where Hindus and Muslims enjoyed a peaceful coexistence. These sources point out a sudden change in the attitudes of erstwhile neighbours.

This type of characterisation of the causes of Partition, however, requires qualification. This is where the official archives prove to be more useful. Those records, for instance, show that communalism was not a spontaneous development. Gyanendra Pandey observes that communalism did not emerge against the trend of nationalism; rather "nationalism was nothing but communalism driven into secular channels—and that too not sufficiently driven... the age of communalism was concurrent with the age of nationalism; they were part of the same discourse."[21] A fine example of how useful archival records have been in helping us

---

[20] Ganesh Halui interview in Tridib Chakrabarti, Nirupama Roy Mandal, and Paulami Ghoshal, eds., *Dhwangsho O Nirmanr: Bangiyo Udbastu Samajer Swokathito Bibaran* (Kolkata: Seriban, 2007).

[21] Gyanendra Pandey, *The Construction of Communalism in Colonial North India* (NY: Oxford University Press, 1990), 236.

trace the development of communalism in Bengal is Suranjan Das' work on communal riots there.[22] Das observes that while the earliest instance of communal riots in Bengal had a class character, and religion was not important, from the Dacca riots onwards in 1924 he notes a decline in this class character and the emergence of a communal character. The communalisation process of riots was complete, according to Das, by the time of the notorious Calcutta and Noakhali riots in 1946, which led to what are called "Partition riots" across India. Using the official archives, Das is able to show that communalism had a longer history than had been thought and was not as spontaneous as had been suggested in the alternate archives, i.e. personal testimonies.

While it is not surprising that the official archives play an important role in the explication of the causes of Partition, they also prove to be indispensable in balancing, and in some cases, correcting the description of that event available in the alternate archive. As mentioned before, Gyanendra Pandey notes that 1947 was not only about independence, but also about Partition, and Partition was primarily an experience of violence. The view of this violence within the official archives has three main limitations: only a particular form of violence is recorded in these archives, i.e. direct violence which involved mass killings; such violence is represented in terms of numbers; and finally, violence is reported selectively, and is thus highly politicised.

To take the first theme first, the state defined violence in a different way to the people themselves. Mass killings in Punjab from the months of March 1947 onwards was accepted as "real" violence by the state. The more subtle forms of violence which led to a systematic squeezing out of the minorities from East Pakistan was dismissed as "psychological" fear and went unrecorded in the official archives. As pointed out by Nehru,

Honourable Members have said that people in East Bengal have not been led to come away because of newspaper articles or by public speeches, that there are other causes. Of course there are other causes. Who says any newspaper speech or an article can make a million people come away? … *but when there is this huge upset in people's minds and people are frightened and are full of fear, then every little thing counts…* we are dealing with not

---

[22] Suranjan Das, *Communal Riots in Bengal 1905–1947* (Oxford: OUP, 1991).

only an economic upset or social upset but a *psychological problem of the greatest magnitude.*[23]

That there was a policy in Pakistan of systematically squeezing out the minorities from East Pakistan was largely ignored by the government of India, and hence the existence of this violence in the East is de-emphasised if one relies solely upon the official archives. A description of such violence comes across more clearly in the oral or literary narratives on partition.

The second theme covered in the official archives is a statistical analysis of Partition violence. The fortnightly reports of the Home Political department or CID records simply enumerate the number of people killed in "mob violence". At the same time it is regretted by most scholars that we still do not know how many people actually lost their lives in this tragedy. The official records may have either a conservative estimate of the numbers or a rather exaggerated account of the same. It is, thus, difficult to study Partition violence in terms of numbers alone. Finally, the political motives behind such exaggerated or conservative estimates of violence cannot be ignored. Both states were at pains to show the other as the more aggressive agent with respect to violence against minorities and women. While incidents of violence against Muslims in Bengal are very hard to find in the archives in India, there is ample evidence of the atrocities faced by the Hindus in East Pakistan.[24] The rhetoric of the state was that the Indian side had upheld its secular principles, based upon which the minorities were treated better in India than in Pakistan. There are hardly any records in India which show the migration of Muslims from West Bengal to East Pakistan, but those showing the continuing migration of Hindus from East Pakistan to the Indian side are far more numerous. Likewise, one of the reasons for Rameshwari Nehru's opposition to the Abducted Persons Recovery and Restoration Act (1948) was what she called the "political angle"; i.e., far fewer women were

---

[23] Reply to the debate in Parliament on the situation in Bengal, 9 August 1950. *SWJN*, Vol. 15 part I, 279.

[24] Although it should be remembered that even these evidences were toned down to show that these figures were not alarming enough because the primary aim of the Union Government in India was to reduce the influx of refugees from East Pakistan.

recovered from Pakistan than from India, and if this were to continue it would seem to show that India was the more aggressive country.[25]

Thus, the picture that emerges from the official archives on Partition violence is at best only a partial image. This lacuna is filled in by the alternate sources. That the violence was not from the "Other" only emerged from the oral testimonies recorded by Butalia, Menon and Bhasin. Further, that violence could be far more subtle than the recorded forms is evident from the oral testimonies of refugees from Bengal. Hiranmoy Bandopadhyay[26] mentions the reasons cited by the refugees for their migration from East Pakistan: no security of life and property, threat to the honour of their women and finally, quite a few of them migrated due to their political ideologies—they had fought for a united India under the party and leaders of their choice, and Pakistan was neither what they had desired, nor could they ever support it.

Bandopadhyay cites a Bengali refugee—"Shotti toh emon kichu mard-har-khoonjakham hoy nee. Tobe bujhle ki na sokoler shojjo shakti saman noye" (That there was no mass-scale violence and rioting is true, but not everybody has the same tolerance level).[27] Talking about the ever-looming threat to women, one of them narrates an incident where, when a few women went to take a bath in the pond, some of the Muslim men remarked teasingly, "Pak Pakistan, Hindur Bhatar Mussolman" (This is Pakistan, the husband of a Hindu will be a Muslim). In yet another incident narrated by the refugees, one of the Muslim men called out to the ladies in the pond "E bibi, bela je bede cholo. Aar deri keno? Ebar ghore cholo" (Oh Bibi, its evening now, why delay any further, let's go home).[28]

That the women in East Pakistan, too, were abducted, raped and forcibly married, is not well recorded in official documents. Such incidents

---

[25] Rameshwari Nehru, "Memorandum on Recovery of Women: Review of the Position since October 1948" [dated 1950 (?)] *Rameshwari Nehru Report No. 1*, Rameshwari Nehru Papers, NMML.

[26] The District Magistrate of 24-Parganas and later Rehabilitation Commissioner in the government of West Bengal, who was also a migrant from East Bengal, recollected his experience of helping in the rehabilitation of refugees from East Pakistan in a memoir titled *Udvastu* (Kolkata: Bangiya Sahitya Samsad, 1970).

[27] Hiranmoy Bandopadhyay, *Udvastu* (Kolkata: Sahitya Samsad, 1970), 13. The translation from the original Bangla is mine.

[28] Ibid., 16. The translation from the original Bangla is mine.

were ignored or hushed up because the state was at pains to show that there was no real violence in the East. However, Jyotirmoyee Devi's classic novel *Epar Ganga Opar Ganga* (*The River Churning By*) presents a useful case study for gender-based violence and its precipitation of exclusion from the family.[29] Sutara, the protagonist in the novel, witnesses the murder of her father, and the rape and suicide of her mother and sister. She is rescued by her Muslim neighbours who keep her at their home with the intention that as soon as the violence subsides they can send Sutara back to her brother's home in Calcutta. And true to their word, they do send her as conditions improve. But by then a long time has passed and her brother's wife, and also her family (except the father), do not accept Sutara because she has lived in the house of a Muslim. Although the text is fictional, it offers a powerful account of how intimate lives and relations were distorted and destroyed by Partition. Another example is the poignant story of "Hoina", where Arati is rejected by Saroj when he comes to know of her harrowing tale of abduction and rape.[30] When Saroj returns to take Arati back, having realised that the information he had got about her was wrong, she refuses to go with him because she realises that Saroj would not have come had the information been correct.

At this point it is important to note the silences in the alternative archives as well. Whereas it is easy to find real testimonies from people about incidents which they have seen or heard, it is very difficult to find the voices of women, and even more difficult to find the voices of such women who were abducted or raped and yet survived. One observes this silence in the oral testimonies, alongside a simple enumeration of some cases of violence against women recorded in official account.[31] Yet another drawback in the oral testimonies lies in the fact that these, too, depict the violence as only being one-sided. Thus in all narratives of the Hindu migrant, it is the Muslim who is shown as the aggressor. That the victim too could be a perpetrator of violence does not come through from these accounts. One such rare account can be found in Nonica

---

[29] Jyotirmoyee Devi, *Epar Ganga Opar Ganga* (English translation by Enakshi Chatterjee, *The River Churning*) (New Delhi: Kali for Women, 1995).

[30] "Hoina," short story by Santosh Kumar Ghose, *Seminar*, 510 (February 2002).

[31] So while we have countless numbers of stories of women who "sacrificed" their life for the "honour" of the family, community and nation, there are hardly any stories which speak of the women who survived, who were abducted and then returned to their families.

Datta's *A Daughter's Testimony*.[32] Subhashini, the narrator sees the mass killings of Muslims in her village in 1947 as a worthy revenge for the killing of her father by Muslims in 1942. For her, therefore, 1947 was a moment of celebration and redemption. Yet another such rare account is to be found, rather implicitly, in one of the interviews recorded by Urvashi Butalia wherein her Sikh narrator to this day seeks penance for his silent culpability in the abduction of a Muslim woman by a group of Hindu men, as he made no attempt to save her.[33] On the whole, there are very few such reminiscences but the few that exist give us a different perspective with which to view Partition violence.[34]

The value of the interplay of sources is also visible in the attempt to address issues related to refugees and their rehabilitation. What is most striking is the conflicting definitions of the refugee we find, when we compare the definition obtained from the official archives with that used by the refugees themselves in the alternate archives. With India not being a signatory to either the United Nations Convention on Refugees (1951) or to the Protocol (1964), the universally applied definition of the refugee is not applicable in India. India therefore referred to this group as "displaced persons" in all official correspondence at the time. The "displaced person" was defined as follows:

> … any person who, on account of the setting up of the Dominion of India and Pakistan, or on account of civil disturbances, or the fear of such disturbances in any area now forming part of Pakistan, has after the first day of March, 1947, left or been displaced from, his place of residence in such area and who has been subsequently residing in India, and includes any person who is resident in India and who for that reason is unable or has been made unable to manage, supervise or control any immovable property belonging to him in Pakistan.[35]

---

[32] Nonica Datta, *Violence, Martyrdom and Partition: A Daughter's Testimony* (New Delhi: OUP, 2009).

[33] Urvashi Butalia, *The Other Side of Silence* (New Delhi: Viking, 1998).

[34] A rare example would be Ajay Bhardwaj's *Rabba Hun Kee Kariye* (2007) which is a documentary work on a village in Indian Punjab in which the survivors talk of the violence they inflicted upon Muslims, and how this act of theirs made them suffer so many years later, either with ill health, misery in general or simply out of a sense of guilt.

[35] "An Act to provide for the registration and verification of claims of displaced persons in respect of immovable property in Pakistan," *Acts of Parliament* (Delhi: Ministry of Law, 1950).

In practice, this definition only applied to the refugees coming from West Pakistan. Those from East Pakistan were defined differently based upon the intention of the government to include or exclude them from the prospective rehabilitation schemes. The definitions for displaced persons coming from East Pakistan depended upon their time of arrival,[36] the type of violence they had suffered[37] and the degree of rehabilitation required.[38] This is the picture that emerges from a close reading of the official documents.[39] Also implicit in the official records is an understanding of the refugee as an "economic liability". All the government-sponsored publications appear to be self-congratulatory about the Herculean task being diligently performed by the people in power, with little or no appreciation of the role played by the refugees themselves.[40]

The "refugees", on the other hand, are dismissive of that term and feel betrayed by the state's failure to adequately acknowledge/reward them for their supreme sacrifice to the cause of independence. In my fieldwork in Kolkata, for example, I observed a strong objection to the use of the term "refugee" by the "refugees" themselves. They found it derogatory and not truly representative of their plight. They believed that government aid was their right. They should be seen as "political

---

[36] Old migrants: (those who came during the period from 1947 to 31 March 1958); illegal migrants: (those who came between 1 April 1958 and 31 December 1963); new migrants (those who came between 1 January 1964 and 1971).

[37] Partition violence started early in 1946 in the districts of Noakhali and Comilla, hence, the definition of displaced persons from East Pakistan made room for including them as well.

[38] Thus, there was the RG group (rehabilitable group, which included the "able-bodied male" refugee) and the PL group (permanent liability group, which included "unattached women" and old or disabled refugees); then there were the BLC (borderline cases). Refugees were also grouped according to their place of rehabilitation—camp (government refugee camps) and colony (colonies made by refuges on lands they had forcibly acquired, by their own initiative). Those who fled from the ill-equipped camps were termed "deserter" refugees; and finally those who stayed on at the camps even after the government stopped all aid and assistance to these sites were called "ex-campsite" refugees. The terms themselves show the irregular and inadequate assistance given to the refugees coming from East Pakistan.

[39] The documents mentioned here are the Ministry of Rehabilitation files, legislative assembly debates and letters of correspondence between officials or ministers.

[40] U. Bhaskar Rao, *The Story of Rehabilitation* (Delhi: Department of Rehabilitation, 1967); Mohanlal Saxena, *Some Reflections on the Problem of Rehabilitation* (Delhi: n.p., 1950).

sufferers" or "martyrs", because they were the ones who had sacrificed everything for the country's independence. They felt betrayed by the state and the political leadership of the time because none of the promises made by those actors were fulfilled. Their entry from East Pakistan was regulated, and at times prevented as well. This was not the welcome they had looked forward to. They prefer to use the term *udvastu* (uprooted) or *bastuhara* (who has lost their homeland) for themselves. Becoming *udvastu* meant leaving behind the land of their ancestors— "*saat-purusher bhite-maati*". In all, what comes out of these narratives and oral testimonies is that the refugees saw themselves as those who had made the greatest sacrifice for the country, they had been betrayed by its leadership and they had eventually emerged as survivors without the help of the state or the host population.[41] Such feelings have been penned most eloquently by Jyotirmoyee Devi in the following lines:

> So you no longer seem to recognise us...
> Still we came.
> You have given us a new name 'refugees' and
> stamped it on us as our hallmark,
> Driven out from our land, despised and disgraced
> in our new habitat
> We are the valueless price
> paid for you(r) acquisition of dominion, Delhi and Dacca ...[42]

The other refutation of the state narrative by the refugees is that they contest the idea that they were a burden on the state; rather, they could have been used as a valuable asset for the country. This brings us to a discussion of how the theme of rehabilitation is dealt with in these two different sources.

The official archives are absolutely indispensable for a thorough study of government policies regarding the rehabilitation of refugees. Copious amounts of information can be found in the annual reports of the

---

[41] Indubaran Ganguly's *Colonysmriti* (Calcutta: n.p, 1997); Anil Sinha's *Paschim Bongo Udvastu Upanibesh* (Calcutta: Book Club, 1995); and Debobrata Dutta, *Bijoygarh: Ekti Udvastu Upanibesh* (Calcutta: n.p., 2001).

[42] Jyotirmoyee Devi, "We are the Valueless Price" (poem) in *Asoka Gupta Papers*, Asoka Gupta Archives, School of Women's Studies, Jadavpur University, Kolkata. Translated from Bangla by Saibal Gupta.

Ministry of Rehabilitation, the files of correspondence between the concerned ministries, the heads of state and ministers of rehabilitation, and of course the government-sponsored official publications. A close look at these sources shows that rehabilitation of the refugees coming from West Pakistan followed a certain pattern: evacuation → relief → rehabilitation → compensation. But this could not be followed for the refugees from East Pakistan. The justification given was that the conditions in the east were very different from those in the west, hence different policies were developed for these groups of refugees.[43] According to the government, despite all the odds, the matter of rehabilitation was solved with only "residuary problems" remaining. But this was not so for the refugees. A strong critique of this justification from the refugees and their organisations is found in the alternate archives. According to the refugees, the whole rehabilitation programme in the east was a sham or, as one of them put it, a "mockery".[44] What emerges from the alternate archives is that the refugees refused to be the "*mukhopekhi*"[45] of the state, and rehabilitation in the east was largely the work of the refugees themselves. What is found, by contrast, in the official archives, is a record of the stiff resistance of the refugees to the rehabilitation policies of the state. For example, the post-1964 refugees from East Pakistan were packed off to Dandakaranya[46] by the state. Facing a hostile environment and host society here, many of them returned to West Bengal within a few years. This was reported in the official documents as the inability of the refugees to work towards their rehabilitation. These refugees were branded as "deserter refugees" and overall, the impression of the Bengali refugees in the documentation, in contrast to that of the Punjabi refugees, was that of their being "lazy", "immobile", lacking self-initiative and forever pining for the homeland.[47]

---

[43] This distinction in treatment meted out to the refugees coming from West Pakistan and those coming from East Pakistan is the subject of my PhD research, and the forthcoming publication, *Rehabilitating the Refugee: An East–West Story* (New Delhi: Primus Publications, forthcoming).

[44] Interview with Haripada Das, 10 January 2010, Shodepur, West Bengal.

[45] Dependent.

[46] A barren land in the hostile geographical area around present-day Chattisgarh and Odisha in central India.

[47] U.B. Rao, *The Story of Rehabilitation* (New Delhi: Government of India, 1964).

What is not reported in the official archives are the reasons for the mass desertion of the refugees from Dandakaranya. This comes through memoirs from the refugees themselves, as well as scholarly articles by Saibal Gupta, Chairman of the Dandakaranya Development Authority. Refugee narratives present a totally different picture of Dandakaranya and the rehabilitation efforts outside West Bengal to the state accounts. The barely human level of existence in these camps is described vividly in the personal memoirs of not only refugees but also of some sympathetic administrators, who have described how truly impossible it was for refugees to stay on.[48] At the same time, the refugees talk of their self-initiative in the setting-up of the squatter colonies—*jabardakhal* colonies—in West Bengal, in order to contest the "lazy", "lacking self-initiative" image constructed by the state for refugees from East Pakistan.[49] A detailed description is found in these texts of the founding of such colonies, and the role of women in the process of setting them up and defending them. These narratives show that though it is the image of the "law-breaking" refugee which predominates official archives, it must not be forgotten that these refugees also played a constructive role in the development of their colonies.[50] The constructive role of the refugee gets

---

[48] Saibal Kumar Gupta, *Eder Kotha Bhulbe Na* [Do not forget them (meaning those who were sent to Dandakaranya)], *Compass* 21 November 1964, 14–15, SWS, JU, Kolkata. Most of the articles and reports regarding this project authored by him and his wife, Smt Asoka Gupta (renowed Gandhian and social worker) have been preserved in the Asoka Gupta archives in the School of Women Studies library at Jadavpur University, Kolkata. There are numerous examples from literary works as well which highlight the poor conditions in Dandakaranya: Narayan Sanyal's *Aranya Dandak* ("The Forest Dandak," 1961) and Shaktipada Rajguru's *Dandak Theke Marichjhapi* ("From Dandak to Marichjhapi," written 1980–1981) among others.

[49] There are several pamphlets/souvenirs and full-fledged books written and published by the refugees which describe the formation of these squatter colonies. Indubaran Ganguly's *Colonysmriti* (Calcutta: n.p., 1997); Anil Sinha's *Paschim Bongo Udvastu Upanibesh* (Calcutta: Book Club, 1995); and Debobrata Dutta's *Bijoygarh: Ekti Udvastu Upanibesh* (Calcutta: n.p., 2001).

[50] Especially because, after much struggle and resistance, the refugees did manage to compel the government to regularise the squatter colonies. But the government made it clear that this was as much as they could do. The development would be solely the responsibility of the refugees themselves. Eventually, the state did help in the development projects; yet the initial thrust was from the refugees only—the founding of schools, clubs, libraries, the construction of roads and drainage work, for example, was largely done by the refuges themselves.

washed away under the more aggressive and rebellious image projected by accounts of the resistance movements, which have been documented in the official archives.

The long-dominant image of the women in Partition history has been one of the "chief-sufferer":[51] she was abducted and raped. But since Bengal did not see this kind of violence, literary and cinematic works have brought out yet another image of the "refugee-woman" from the east—that of the breadwinner in the refugee family.[52] First the novel and later the film of the same name, *Meghe Dhaka Tara*, epitomised in the character of Nita the typical refugee-woman in the east. Even oral testimonies from the east point towards the courageous character and indispensable financial role of the woman in the family. Now we also have studies which look at the economic role of refugee women from West Pakistan.[53] Thus, while the official archives are indispensable for the study of rehabilitation policies—to mark the east–west contrast, to understand the principle behind the rehabilitation programmes on both fronts, to point out the implications of the rehabilitation programmes (or lack of them) in the lives of these displaced persons—a qualitative analysis must also take place within the alternative archives to unearth the contradictions and limitations of state policies, and their impacts. At the same time, the voices in the alternate archives do not themselves offer a full picture.

Conclusion

This paper has examined how the official and alternate archives work best in tandem, to enable the exploration of various themes around the Partition of India, particularly at the eastern border. It can be seen that while the official archives are indispensable for looking at what led to this tragic event, alternative archives are crucial for understanding what the

[51] Andrew J. Major, "'The Chief Sufferers': Abduction of Women During the Partition of the Punjab," *South Asia: Journal of South Asian Studies* 18 (1995): 57–72.

[52] Term used by Gargi Chakravartty, *Coming Out of Partition: Refugee Women of Bengal* (New Delhi: Bluejay Books, 2005). This shows the alternative image of women during Partition.

[53] Karuna Chanana, "Partition and Family Strategies: Gender-Education Linkages Among Punjabi Families in Delhi," *EPW* 28, no. 17 (24 April 1993); Anjali Bhardwaj Datta, "Gendering Oral History of Partition," *EPW* 41, no. 22 (3 June 2006).

event actually meant to the people who experienced it. As has been discussed, the official archives do offer valuable information and perspectives. They work best, however, when offset by alternate archival sources, such as oral testimony and creative works. The emphasis on the human experience in Partition is now even more important than ever before. With an increase in the use of alternate sources and newer approaches, Partition studies have moved beyond the view from above; the focus is now on the implications of the event for the people actually affected. To understand the event fully, however, a view from all vantage points—above, below and across—is necessary.

WORKS CITED

"An Act to provide for the registration and verification of claims of displaced persons in respect of immovable property in Pakistan," *Acts of Parliament*. Delhi: Ministry of Law, 1950.

Ali, C.M. *The Emergence of Pakistan*. New York: Columbia University Press, 1967.

Ambedkar, B.R. *Pakistan or Partition of India*. Bombay: Thacker and Company Ltd, 1946.

Ansari, Sarah. *Life After Partition: Migration, Community and Strife in Sindh, 1947–1962*. Karachi: Oxford University Press, 2005.

Azad, Maulana Abul Kalam. *India Wins Freedom*. New Delhi: Orient Longman, 1988.

Bandopadhyay, Hiranmoy. *Udvastu*. Kolkata: Sahitya Samsad, 1970.

Bhalla, Alok, ed. *Stories About The Partition of India*, Vols. I–IV. New Delhi: Harper Collins, 1994.

Bhardwaj, Ajay (dir.). *Rabba Hun Kee Kariye*, 2007.

Blackburn, Stuart. "Colonial Contact in the 'Hidden Land': Oral History Among the Apatanis of Arunanchal Pradesh." *IESHR*, 40, no. 3 (2003): 335–365.

Butalia, Urvashi. *The Other Side of Silence*. New Delhi: Viking, 1998.

Chakrabarti, Tridib, Nirupama Roy Mandal, Paulami Ghoshal, eds. *Dhwangsho O Nirmanr: Bangiyo Udbastu Samajer Swokathito Bibaran*. Kolkata: Seriban, 2007.

Chakrabarty, Dipesh. "Remembered Villages Representations of Hindu-Bengali Memories in the Aftermath of the Partition." *South Asia* 18 (1995): 109–129.

Chakrabarty, Pallavi. *Rehabilitating the Refugee: An East-West Story*. New Delhi: Primus Publications, forthcoming.

Chakravartty, Gargi. *Coming Out of Partition: Refugee Women of Bengal*. New Delhi: Bluejay Books, 2005.

Chanana, Karuna. "Partition and Family Strategies: Gender-Education Linkages among Punjabi Families in Delhi." *EPW* 28, no. 17 (24 April 1993).

Chatterji, Joya. "New Directions in Partition Studies." *History Workshop Journal* 67, no. 1 (2009): 213–220.

Chatterji, Joya. *The Spoils of Partition: Bengal and India, 1947–67*. Cambridge: Cambridge University Press, 2007.

Das, Suranjan. *Communal Riots in Bengal 1905–1947*. Oxford: Oxford University Press, 1991.

Datta, Anjali Bhardwaj. "Gendering Oral History of Partition," *EPW* 41, no. 22 (3 June 2006).

Datta, Nonica. *Violence, Martyrdom and Partition: A Daughter's Testimony*. New Delhi: Oxford University Press, 2009.

Devi, Jyotirmoyee. "We are the Valueless Price." In *Asoka Gupta Papers*, Asoka Gupta Archives, School of Women's Studies, Jadavpur University, Kolkata. Translated from Bangla by Saibal Gupta.

Devi, Jyotirmoyee. *Epar Ganga Opar Ganga* (English translation by Enakshi Chatterjee, *The River Churning*). New Delhi: Kali for Women, 1995.

Dhongsho O Nirman: Bangiya Udbastu Samajer Swkathit Bibaran, 2007

Dube, Pankhuree R. "Partition Historiography." *The Historian* 77, no. 1 (Spring 2015): 54–79.

Dutta, Debobrata. *Bijoygarh: Ekti Udvastu Upanibesh*. Calcutta: n.p., 2001.

Fraser, Bashabi. *Bengal Partition Stories: An Unclosed Chapter*. London: Anthem Press, 2008.

Ganguly, Indubaran. *Colony Smriti*. Calcutta: n.p., 1997.

Ghose, Santosh Kumar. "Hoina." *Seminar*, 510 (February 2002) http://www.india-seminar.com/2002/510.htm. Accessed 15 May 2017.

Gilmartin, David. "The Historiography of India's Partition: Between Civilization and Modernity." *The Journal of Asian Studies* 74, no. 1 (February 2015): 23–41.

Gupta, Saibal Kumar, Eder Kotha Bhulbe Na. Compass, *SWS*, JU, Kolkata, 21 November 1964, 14–15.

Hasan, Mushirul, ed. *India Partitioned: The Other Face of Freedom*, 2 vols. Delhi: Roli Books, 1998.

Hashmi, Taj ul-Islam. *Pakistan as a Peasant Utopia: The Communalization of Class Politics in East Bengal, 1920–1947*. Boulder, CO: Westview Press, 1992.

Jain, Jasbir. *Reading Partition/Living Partition*. New Delhi: Rawat Publishers, 2007.

Jalal, Ayesha. *The Sole Spokesman: Jinnah, the Muslim League and the Demand for Pakistan*. Cambridge: Cambridge University Press, 1985.

Joya, Chatterji. "Partition Studies: Prospects and Pitfalls." *The Journal of Asian Studies* 73, no. 2 (May 2014): 309–312.

Kala, Anirudh, Alok Sarin, and Sanjeev Jain. "The Psychiatrist's Partition." In *Himal Southasian*, http://old.himalmag.com/component/content/article/1426-the-psychiatrists-partition.html. Accessed 24 April 2017.

Kaur, Ravinder. "Exploring Social Class in 1947 Migration." *Economic and Political Weekly*, 3 June 2006.

Kaur, Ravinder. *Since 1947: Partition Narratives among Punjabi Migrants of Delhi*. New Delhi: OUP, 2007.

Khan, Yasmin. *The Great Partition: Making of India and Pakistan*. New Haven: Yale University Press, 2007.

Kumar, Akanksha. "Locating Dalits in the Midst of Partition and Violence." *JSHC* 2, no. 2 (2016).

Mansergh, Nicholas, and Penderel Moon, eds. *The Transfer of Power*, Vols. XI–XII. London: HMSO.

Menon Ritu, and Kamla Bhasin, eds. *Borders and Boundaries: Women in India's Partition*. New Delhi: Kali for Women, 2000.

Moore, R.J. *Escape from Empire: The Attlee Government and the Indian Problem*. Oxford: Clarendon, 1983.

Nair, Neeti. *Changing Homelands: Hindu Politics and Partition of India*. Cambridge, Massachusetts: Harvard University Press, 2011.

Narain, Iqbal, ed. *A Centenary History of the Indian National Congress, 1947–64*, Vols. I–V. New Delhi: Academic Foundation.

Nehru, Rameshwari. "Memorandum on Recovery of Women: Review of the Position since October 1948." *Rameshwari Nehru Report No. 1*, Rameshwari Nehru Papers, NMML, 1950.

Page, David. *Prelude to Partition: Indian Muslims and the Imperial System of Control 1920–1932*. New Delhi: Oxford University Press, 1982.

Pandey, Gyanendra. *The Construction of Communalism in Colonial North India*. Oxford University Press, 1990.

Pandey, Gyanendra. *Remembering Partition: Violence, Nationalism and History in India*. Cambridge: Cambridge University Press, 2001.

Pirzada, S.S. *Foundation of Pakistan: All India Muslim League Documents 1906–47*, 2 vols.

Prasad, Rajendra. *India Divided*. Bombay: Hind Kitab Publishers, 1946.

Rao, U. Bhaskar. *The Story of Rehabilitation*. Delhi: Department of Rehabilitation, 1967.

Rawat, Ramnarayan. "Partition Politics and Acchut Identity: A Study of the Scheduled Castes Federation and Dalit Politics in UP, 1946–48." In *Partitions of Memory: The Afterlife of the Division of India*, edited by Suvir Kaul. New Delhi: Permanent Black, 2001.

"Reply to the Debate in Parliament on the Situation in Bengal." 9 August 1950. *SWJN*, vol. 15 part I, 279.

Roy, Anupama. "Sifting, Selecting, Relocating Citizenship at the Commencement of the Republic" *I. CWDS* Occasional Paper no. 54 www.cwds.ac.in/OCPaper/occassionalpaper54.pdf. Accessed 16 March 2011.

Roy, Asim. "The High Politics of India's Partition: The Revisionist Perspective." In *India's Partition, Process, Strategy and Mobilization*, edited by M. Hasan. New Delhi: OUP, 2001.

Saint, Tarun K. *Witnessing Partition: Memory, History, Fiction*. Delhi: Routledge, 2010.

Samuel, Raphael. "Local History and Oral History." *History Workshop Journal*, no. 1 (Spring, 1976): 191–208.

Saxena, Mohanlal. *Some Reflections on the Problem of Rehabilitation*. Delhi, 1950.

Schendel, Willem van. *The Bengal Borderland: Bengal State of Nation in South Asia*. London: Anthem Press, 2005.

Sengupta, Debjani. *Mapmaking: Partition Stories from 2 Bengals*. New Delhi: Street, 2003.

Settar, S., and Indira Beptista Gupta, eds. *Pangs of Partition: The Human Dimension*. New Delhi: Manohar, 2002.

Singh, A.I. *The Origins of the Partition of India: 1936–1947*. New Delhi: Oxford University Press, 1987.

Sinha, Anil. *Paschim Bongo Udvastu Upanibesh*. Calcutta: Book Club, 1995.

Talbot, Ian. *Divided Cities: Lahore, Amritsar and the Partition of India*. Karachi: Oxford University Press, 2006.

The Displaced Persons (Claims) Act (1950), Acts of Parliament, 1950, Ministry of Law, India.

The Partition Archive. www.1947PartitionArchives.org. Accessed 18 November 2017.

Tuker, Francis. *While Memory Serves*. London: Cassell, 1950.

Zaidi, A.M, S.G. Zaidi, and S. Zaidi, eds. *The Encyclopaedia of the Indian National Congress*, Vols. I–XXVII. New Delhi: S. Chand.

Zamindar, Vazira. *The Long Partition and the Making of Modern South Asia: Refugees, Boundaries, Histories*. New York: Columbia University Press, 2007.

CHAPTER 6

Narrating Trauma, Constructing Binaries, Affirming Agency: Partition in Muslim Women's Autobiographical Writing

Siobhan Lambert-Hurley

Nearly twenty years on from Urvashi Butalia's game-changing *The Other Side of Silence* (1998), Partition historiography—by which I mean the body of historical writing addressing the Partition and Independence of the Indian subcontinent in 1947—looks very different than it did before. The statistics inevitably used to open these accounts have changed little: around twelve million refugees, 1 million dead from slaughter, malnutrition and disease, 75,000 women abducted and raped, thousands of families divided by new borders drawn on a map to represent the newly independent nations of India and Pakistan.[1] But, whereas earlier generations of historians sought to understand Partition primarily in terms of the "high politics" that facilitated the transfer of power, now we can

---

[1] Urvashi Butalia, *The Other Side of Silence: Voices from the Partition of India* (New Delhi: Penguin, 1998), 3.

S. Lambert-Hurley (✉)
University of Sheffield, Sheffield, UK
e-mail: s.t.lambert-hurley@sheffield.ac.uk

© The Author(s) 2018
C. Mahn and A. Murphy (eds.), *Partition and the Practice of Memory*,
https://doi.org/10.1007/978-3-319-64516-2_6

appreciate the impact of that event—or perhaps better, process—on the lives of "ordinary people".[2] Historiographical trends that hit Indian history-writing more generally in the early 1980s, leading to the creation of Subaltern studies, permeated this discourse a few years later to create a "new" history of Partition "from below". The catalysts were many: renewed communal violence in India associated with the assassination of Indira Gandhi in 1984, the destruction of the Babri Masjid in 1992 and the Gujarat riots in 2002 alongside the golden and diamond jubilees of Independence in 1997 and 2007 primarily.[3] Debates on ethnic cleansing and sectarian conflict elsewhere in the world—from Bosnia to Iraq—also figured in this story.[4] Butalia's insistence that we think of Partition as "one of the great *human* convulsions of history" has given rise to a Partition historiography with a *human* face.[5]

The feminist commitment that infused not just Butalia's effort, but also Ritu Menon and Kamla Bhasin's *Borders and Boundaries*, published in the same year, has placed women, gender and sexuality at the heart of this "new" history of Partition.[6] Women, it became clear, had experienced Partition in a unique way, not least because their bodies had been "singled out" as "privileged sites of violence": for rape, abduction, mutilation, murder and suicide.[7] The "honour" of the family/community/nation became invested in women such that they bore the brunt of Partition's

---

[2] For a concise overview of these shifts in Partition historiography, see Pippa Virdee, "Remembering Partition: Women, Oral Histories and the Partition of 1947," *Oral History* 41, no. 2 (Autumn 2013): 49–53.

[3] Butalia identifies the events of 1984 especially, but also 1992, as inspiring her own study (*The Other Side of Silence*, 4–7), as does Gyanendra Pandey in *Remembering Partition* (Cambridge: Cambridge University 2001), x. As examples of the historiographical clustering around an independence jubilee, see Yasmin Khan, *The Great Partition: The Making of India and Pakistan* (New Haven: Yale University Press, 2007); Ian Talbot, *Divided Cities: Partition and Its Aftermath in Lahore and Amritsar 1947–1957* (Karachi: Oxford University Press, 2007).

[4] For these parallels, see Ritu Menon and Kamla Bhasin, *Borders & Boundaries: Women in India's Partition* (New Delhi: Kali for Women, 1998), 63; Karan Mahajan, "A People's History of Partition," *New York Sun* (10 October 2007). http://www.nysun.com/arts/peoples-history-of-partition/64254/. Accessed on 10 October 2007.

[5] Butalia, *The Other Side of Silence*, 3. Italics added.

[6] Bhasin and Menon, *Borders and Boundaries*.

[7] Jill Didur, *Unsettling Partition: Literature, Gender, Memory* (Toronto: University of Toronto Press, 2006), 7.

"most horrific crimes", even as they may have colluded in them too: in its most extreme form, a type of "femicide" was given validation as "honour killings".[8] In the aftermath, patriarchal families joined interests with a patriarchal state to reclaim "its" women, restoring abducted women's sanctity by passing judgement on their sexual "purity"—a process of rehabilitation in which many female relief workers played a key role. Women thus came to represent "something more than ordinary individuals"; they were "sacred to the people".[9] The function of women, gender and sexuality in these analyses, then, was not simply to "supplement more orthodox historiography", to quote Suvir Kaul, but rather to demonstrate its "constitutive centrality": how it "interrogates and rewrites the narratives".[10] To understand the "story of 1947" as a "gendered narrative" was to overturn binary constructions of "public" and "private", "victims" and "heroes", that had infused nationalist and communitarian discourses.[11]

At the same time, what these accounts often neglected were the particular experiences of Muslim women. Butalia, for instance, makes extensive use of Anis Kidwai's well-known Partition memoir, *Azadi ki Chhaon Main*, on working with refugees and abducted women in the uncertain and often violent environs of Delhi between September 1947 and June 1948.[12] But she otherwise recognises that her study has a "major lacuna" in that it is "one-sided": relating only to the Partition of Punjab through the use of Indian documents and interviews.[13] Her own critique of her

---

[8] Pippa Virdee, "Negotiating the Past: Journey through Muslim Women's Experience of Partition and Resettlement in Pakistan," *Cultural and Social History* 6, no. 4 (2009), 469.

[9] Virdee, "Negotiating the Past," 471–472.

[10] Suvir Kaul, ed., *The Partitions of Memory: The Afterlife of the Division of India* (New Delhi: Permanent Black, 2001), 10.

[11] Bhasin and Menon, *Borders and Boundaries*, 9; Urvashi Butalia, "Community, State, and Gender: Some Reflections on the Partition of India," in *Inventing Boundaries: Gender, Politics and the Partition of India*, ed. Mushirul Hasan (New Delhi: Oxford University Press, 2000), 203–204.

[12] Anis Kidwai's *Azadi ki Chhaon Main* was originally published in Urdu in 1974 (New Delhi: National Book Trust, 1974), transliterated into Hindi (the version Butalia uses) by Noor Nabi Abbasi in 1978 (Delhi: National Book Trust, 1978) and, most recently, translated into English by Ayesha Kidwai as *In Freedom's Shade* (Delhi: Penguin, 2011). For examples of how it is employed, see Butalia, *The Other Side of Silence*, 146–147, 259–261, 302–303. It is also key evidence in her "Community, State, and Gender."

[13] Butalia, *The Other Side of Silence*, 22.

own work is one applicable to Partition's "new history" more generally. As Pippa Virdee notes, it is "predominantly Indian-centric" and focused on the "plight of Punjabis". While the latter may be appropriate if gauging the "worst of the atrocities", it results in a historiography that is, in her own words, "geographically limited".[14] Increasingly, these limitations are being overcome. A starting point perhaps was Gyanendra Pandey's recognition in *Remembering Partition* (2001) of the "third" Partition by which, soon after the "official" Partition, refugees began flooding into Delhi and the United Provinces especially.[15] The Partition stories of refugees and families divided in Delhi and Karachi have since attracted growing attention.[16] Bengal, overlooked for some time on the assumption that Partition's impact was somehow less significant there, has also come into the frame, particularly through Joya Chatterji's study of the specific political negotiations, migration patterns and economic ruptures of 1947 and after.[17]

Partition is thus coming to be explored as a historical happening pertinent not just to Punjab, or even Punjab and Bengal—but, still, the Indian-centricity persists, even among feminist scholars. The effect is that less than a handful of authors have focused on 1947's memories and meanings from the perspective of Pakistani women or, more broadly, Muslim women in India, Pakistan and Bangladesh. Several explanations are offered for Muslim women's "virtual anonymity" in Partition historiography.[18] For the Indian researchers who pioneered the field, the matter

---

[14] Virdee, "Remembering Partition," 52. On Punjab's Partition, see Ian Talbot and D.S. Tatla, *Epicentre of Violence: Partition Voices and Memories from Amritsar* (Delhi: Permanent Black, 2006); Ishtiaq Ahmed, *The Punjab Bloodied, Partitioned and Cleansed* (Karachi: Oxford University Press, 2012).

[15] Pandey, *Remembering Partition*, 35–39.

[16] Ravinder Kaur, *Since 1947: Partition Narratives among Punjabi Migrants of Delhi* (New Delhi: Oxford University Press, 2007); Vazira Fazila-Yacoobali Zamindar, *The Long Partition and the Making of Modern South Asia: Refugees, Boundaries, Histories* (Delhi: Penguin, 2007).

[17] Joya Chatterji, *The Spoils of Partition: Bengal and India, 1947–1967* (Cambridge: Cambridge University Press, 2007). On Partition from the perspective of Bengali Muslims, see Neilesh Bose, *Recasting the Region: Language, Culture and Islam in Colonial Bengal* (Delhi: Oxford University Press, 2014). On the Partition experiences of women in Bengal, see Jasodhara Bagchi and Subhoranjan Dasgupta, eds., *The Trauma and the Triumph: Gender and Partition in Eastern India* (Calcutta: Bhatkal and Sen, 2003).

[18] I borrow this observation from Rabia Umar Ali, "Muslim Women and the Partition of India: A Historiographical Silence," *Islamic Studies* 48, no. 3 (Autumn 2009): 428.

is largely practical: relevant historical subjects and sources are understood to be located primarily on the "other side" of the border. Butalia, for instance, explains that, as an Indian citizen, she had "no access to information, interviews or anything else from Pakistan"; only researchers from a "third country" could get permission to consult Partition documents and memories across South Asia.[19] The importance of contact is underscored by Uma Chakravarti: only after teaching a women's studies course in Lahore was she inspired to think about Partition from the "standpoint" of Pakistani women on the "other side".[20] Others highlight cultural limitations connected to *izzat* and *sharam*, honour and shame, considered more prevalent in Muslim South Asia. In an article lamenting the "historiographical silence" on Muslim women and Partition, Rabia Umar Ali points to "patriarchal constraints and societal norms" that have made it "taboo" for Muslim women especially to divulge stories that may include rape, abduction and forced conversion.[21]

How, then, to recover the Muslim women's voices that have remained marginalised even after the turn in Partition historiography to "ordinary lives"? Following Butalia's lead, many scholars favour oral testimony for its "ability to empower those unexpressed utterances"—in this case, the "silent history" of Muslim women's Partition—that would "otherwise remain undocumented."[22] Notable here is Pippa Virdee's work, based on targeted interviews in Pakistan's west Punjab. A "locality-based approach"—by which she pursued "multiple interviews in a geographically tight space" in and around Ludhiana and Lyallpur—provided a "glimpse" into the "lived experiences" of Muslim women, including the illiterate, the less privileged and the rural. At the same time, it flagged up ethical and methodological concerns: the responsibility of the interviewer for "constructing and creating an account" based on traumatic, often buried or forgotten memories.[23] The difficulty of actually interviewing women who have been "conditioned to feel they have little value to contribute to society" is also highlighted. Particularly in male company,

[19] Butalia, *The Other Side of Silence*, 22.

[20] Uma Chakravarti, "Betrayal, Anger, and Loss: Women Write the Partition in Pakistan," in *Speaking of the Self: Gender, Performance and Autobiography in South Asia*, ed. Anshu Malhotra and Siobhan Lambert-Hurley (Durham, NC: Duke University Press, 2015), 123.

[21] Ali, "Muslim Women and the Partition of India," 428.

[22] Virdee, "Remembering Partition," 53; Virdee, "Negotiating the Past," 467.

[23] Virdee, "Remembering Partition," 53–54.

women proved reluctant to talk, partly because the memories were still too raw to be expressed and partly because they could not conceive of their experiences or memories as having worth.[24] Her observations remind us of Gayatri Spivak's probing of whether the subaltern woman can actually "speak" in any meaningful sense when proscribed by a patriarchal discourse that defines what she may say, do and even think.[25]

Recognising these constraints, other scholars have employed fiction, primarily in the form of novels, poetry and film, to examine Muslim women's experiences of Partition. An early effort was Mushirul Hasan's reading of Attia Hosain's well-known Partition novel, *Sunlight on a Broken Column* (1961), as "one of the most compelling *archives* of Muslim experience before, during, and after partition."[26] His treatment of novels as "historical texts" justifies Jill Didur's observation that early commentators tended to overlook how Partition literature was a "re-presenting", rather than a "documenting", of violence in particular. Her corrective when reading *Sunlight* is to follow Kaul in encouraging a more "vigilant or critical reading" in which the "discursive construction of subjectivity, agency, nationalism and history" are understood as part of the "narrativization".[27] For Antoinette Burton, who also tackles Hosain's novel, Partition literature can thus be "reimagined" as a "dwelling place" of "legitimate historical practice" by scrutinising it for its "forms and fictions": the ways in which memories are structured, articulated and materialised.[28] Accordingly, the aforementioned Chakravarti analyses three Partition novels composed by female authors in Pakistan: Mumtaz Shah Nawaz's *The Heart Divided* (1948), Khadija Mastur's *Aangan* (1952) and Zaheda Hina's *Na Junoon Raha Na Pari Rahi*

---

[24] Virdee, "Remembering Partition," 55–56.

[25] Gayatri Chakravorty Spivak, "Can the Subaltern Speak?," in *Colonial Discourse and Postcolonial Theory: A Reader*, ed. Patrick Williams and Laura Chrisman (New York: Harvester Wheatsheaf, 1993), 66–111, especially 90.

[26] Mushirul Hasan, *Legacy of a Divided Nation: India's Muslims Since Independence* (Boulder, CO: Westview Press, 1997), 62. This description is applied to Hasan's work by Antoinette Burton in her *Dwelling in the Archive: Women Writing House, Home, and History in Late Colonial India* (Delhi: Oxford University Press, 2003), 106. Italics added.

[27] Didur, "Introduction: Unsettling Partition," 5–6. Also see her chap. 4: "A Heart Divided: Education, Romance and the Domestic Sphere in Attia Hosain's *Sunlight on a Broken Column*," 94–124. For the original quote from Kaul, see *The Partitions of Memory*, 13.

[28] Burton, *Dwelling in the Archive*, 102.

(1996). Her starting point is to recognise that, though these novels are not autobiographical in a "strict sense", they enable women to "speak for a larger feminine self beyond personal experience". Through the protagonists, the writings "speak back" to her of a Partition defined for Muslim women as a group by anger, loss and nostalgia.[29]

Another form of Partition literature,—identified, but rarely explored for the purpose of recovering *individual*, as well as *collective*, Muslim women's voices—is autobiography. As an example, Ali lists a handful of male and female authors whose autobiographical "outpourings of their experience have lent expression to many silent voices"—but fails to tell us more.[30] Similarly, five of the twelve authors or interviewees extracted in Ritu Menon's edited collection, *No Woman's Land* (2004), are Muslim women from India, Pakistan and Bangladesh, but there is only cursory analysis of their contributions in the short introduction.[31] In fact, there is a plethora of autobiographical writings by South Asian Muslim women, including memoirs, travelogues and short journal articles, both published and unpublished, in which to explore the theme of Partition from their unique perspective. In particular, this body of material published from 1947 onwards enables analysis of how Partition memories are constructed in relation to gender, class and community at different historical moments and locations. Of particular interest, as suggested by my title, is autobiography's cathartic function for narrating trauma, but also the selective deployment of silences as a means of dealing with pain and complicity. Other major themes include the creation of binaries between self and Other, assertions of victimhood and agency and the role of rumour in remembrance.

The assumed requirement for literacy to produce autobiography means most Muslim female authors of autobiography are, in general terms, "elites" within South Asia's complex social hierarchy: upper or middle class, *sharif* of the old sort or new. Most of the authors were not just educated, but educated to the degree level and beyond—an accreditation that meant they often pursued an occupation when few

[29] Chakravarti, "Betrayal, Anger and Loss," 123.

[30] Ali, "Muslim Women and the Partition of India," 433.

[31] The authors and interviewees include Sara Suleri, Ismat Chughtai, Shehla Shibli, Anees Kidwai and Hasna Saha. On their contributions in the introduction, see Ritu Menon, ed., *No Woman's Land: Women from Pakistan, India and Bangladesh Write on the Partition of India* (Delhi: Women Unlimited, 2004), 4, 8–10.

women and even fewer elite Muslim women did. Their jobs varied, but by far the majority were educationalists, writers, politicians and performers.[32] When compared to oral testimony as a source, it means less social variation, admittedly: female authors of South Asian autobiography rarely go beyond what Virdee calls "more accessible, educated and urban voices".[33] Saying that, the cast of characters that they depict, including servants, students, clients, audiences and voters, often do. Autobiographies also offer insight into Partition experiences beyond one locality or region. Authors from both Punjab and Bengal can be considered alongside those from other Muslim centres in South Asia, including Aligarh, Rampur, Bhopal and Hyderabad, thus enabling some discussion of the regional specificities of Partition experiences and memories.[34] Moreover, autobiographies can disclose the construction of memories unmediated by a researcher or fictional lens.[35] To get a sense of the complexity of themes within this rich body of Partition literature by Muslim women, let us turn in the remainder of this chapter to a case study.

Chosen for close analysis is an autobiographical account of Partition by a Bengali Muslim woman named Jobeda Khanam (1920–1990). Her autobiography, *Jiban Khatar Pataguli* ("Pages from My Life"), was published only in Bengali by a press in Dhaka in 1991.[36] Its circulation appears to have been fairly limited outside Bangladesh despite the author's earlier fiction, including short stories and children's books, garnering some attention.[37] Nonetheless, it represents a wider proliferation

---

[32] This summary is based on chap. 2: "The Sociology of Authorship" in my forthcoming monograph on *Gender, Autobiography and the Self in Muslim South Asia* (Redwood City: Stanford University Press, forthcoming).

[33] Virdee, "Remembering Partition," 56.

[34] On where Muslim women writing autobiography have been located in geographical terms, see chap. 3: "The Autobiographical Map" in my forthcoming monograph.

[35] That is not to deny the role of an editor or ghost writer. On the part played by these external figures in constructing autobiography, see chap. 4: "Staging the Self" in my forthcoming monograph.

[36] Jobeda Khanam, *Jiban Khatar Pataguli* (Dhaka: Kathamala Prakashani, 1991). I am extremely grateful to Sarmistha Gupta, with whom I worked in Delhi to prepare translations from the text.

[37] An example of her short-story collections widely available in North American university libraries is: Jobeda Khanam, *Ekati Surera Mrtyu* (Dhaka: Adila Bradarsa, 1974). Her writing for children is addressed in: Peter Hunt, ed., *International Companion Encyclopedia of Children's Literature*, vol. I, 2nd ed. (London: Routledge, 2004), 1087. Other writings include: *Ananta Pipasa* (Dhaka: Naoroja Kitabistana, 1967); *Chotadera Ekankika* (Dhaka: Bangla Ekadami, 1963); and *Mahasamudra* (Dhaka: Bangladesh Shishu Academy, 1977).

of autobiographical writing by Bangladeshi women from the 1980s—
with more than 40 authors producing life stories of various types over
a thirty-year period.[38] Like many of these women, Jobeda wrote at the
end of her life to capture the many political and social changes that she
had experienced. As one near-contemporary, Khatenamara Begam (born
c. 1923–1924), summarised:

> We—I mean, people of my age group—have seen all three ages (past, pre-
> sent and future). The first 23/24 years of our lives were under the mighty
> British colonizers; our youth was spent in a lot of confusion and strug-
> gle under Pakistan; and our mature years passed in difficulty as independ-
> ent citizens of Bangladesh. Today, at the end of my life when I see the
> past, I see we have crossed many strong waves over many years. We have
> seen epoch-making political changes. We have gathered many different and
> strange experiences. With great excitement, I have seen the great changes
> that have taken place in the field of women's education and her social
> environment.[39]

For Jobeda, too, living through these "three ages" motivated autobiographical reflection.

The author's social and educational background also made her representative of Muslim women writing autobiography in the twentieth
century. Born in 1920 in the small town of Kushtia—then in colonial
Bengal's Nadia district, but now in south-west Bangladesh—her childhood experiences were framed by a fairly affluent extended family that
practised strict seclusion (*purdah*). Though her grandfather was a
respected local *pir* (or spiritual guide), her father, as a younger son, had
been sent to school and then college to receive a "modern" education
that would facilitate access to the colonial bureaucracy. Duly, he landed
a "very big" job as sub-inspector in the Education Department that
meant his immediate family often moved to different postings within
colonial Bengal. While in Basirhat (now in West Bengal), Jobeda's father

---

[38] I discuss this proliferation in chaps. 2 and 3 of my forthcoming monograph.

[39] Khatemanara Begam, "Nari Shiksha: Ami Ja Dekhechhi," in *Kaler Samukh Bhela*, ed.
Nurunnahar Faizunnessa (Dhaka: Muktodhara, 1988), 70.

was pressured by Muslim friends to send his daughter to a local purdah school, but, as she was nearly eleven, he demurred on the basis that she was of marriageable age. Still, he recognised her desire to learn by teaching her the rudiments of Bengali and mathematics at home. Only after her marriage at the age of thirteen to a Westernised "gentleman" from Calcutta over twenty years her senior did she begin to study in earnest, passing her matriculation examination five years later. Ultimately, she pursued education to the Master's level and beyond, even going abroad in the 1950s to study at the University of London and the University of Kentucky.[40]

Midway through her published autobiography, Jobeda paused to reflect consciously on the process of writing her life at the age of seventy years old when her memories were no longer "sharp". As she explained of her narrative: "It is from my memory and thus not a continuous history. The memories that come to my mind are just jotted down. That is why sometimes I write things that have happened later and sometimes things that have happened earlier. Many things I do not remember in sequence. Many things I remember very clearly, but I do not remember their dates and years."[41] Her frank observation calls to mind academic analyses under the rubric of "memory studies" by which individual recollections, as contained in oral histories or autobiographies, are characterised as "unstable", "shifting", even "whimsical".[42] At the same time, it evokes a fragmentary quality so often identified with women's writing by which their autobiographies in particular are seen to resist chronology and construction.[43] The process of writing—by which memories were just "jotted" down—becomes inscribed on a text free of chapter breaks or a proper conclusion. The abrupt end to the text may, in fact, be a result of the author's death mid-composition. Certainly, the book was published posthumously.

---

[40] This biographical summary is based on the first half of Jobeda Khanam's *Jiban Khatar Pataguli*, especially, 1–28, 43, 88–89.

[41] Ibid., 87.

[42] I draw here on the analysis of "Gender, Performance, and Memory" by Anshu Malhotra and myself in our Introduction to *Speaking of the Self*, especially 18.

[43] For a summary of the "difference" theory of women's autobiography, see Sidonie Smith and Julia Watson, "Introduction: Situating Subjectivity in Women's Autobiographical Practices," in *Women, Autobiography, Theory: A Reader*, ed. Sidonie Smith and Julia Watson (Madison: The University of Wisconsin Press, 1998), 18.

Nevertheless, *Jiban Khatar Pataguli* is roughly chronological, with the main section on Partition appearing as part of a wider discussion of the author's struggle to attain educational qualifications after 1939. That watershed moment is defined, not by the outbreak of World War II, but by her husband's premature death from typhoid that left her a widow with two young children at the age of just eighteen. Unwilling to return to her natal home where she would be a "burden" on others, she sought employment as a teacher, which would allow her to provide for her children while pursuing higher education.[44] Her narration thus moves from the process of completing her IA and BA in the early 1940s against a backdrop of war and famine, to her return to Calcutta in 1946—aged around 26 years—to pursue formal teaching training (BT). That Jobeda retained her links to her native district of Nadia in central Bengal—soon to be partitioned in 1947—underlines the autobiography's status as "memories from the border" in line with this volume's wider intention.[45] Subsequent to this core passage, Partition reappears frequently as a marker of time "before" or "after" which politics or culture or government operated according to one strict imperative or another. The author's telling of later episodes of violence as East Pakistan transmuted into Bangladesh—including during the Language Movement that reached its peak in 1952, and the 1971 war resulting in independence—encourages reflection on how her Partition memories may have been inflected through that lens.

Of particular note is that Jobeda Khanam begins the passage on Partition proper with a nationalist trope: that, "before the troubles", there had been communal harmony in Bengal, with Hindus and Muslims united in their opposition to the British and their Indian collaborators in the police force. The "binary formulation" that she creates here between "idyllic cohabitation" on one hand and "antagonism and violence" on the other, to borrow Mahua Sarkar's descriptors, is somewhat belied by the author's own telling of intercommunal relations in her childhood.[46] We may consider here, as example, a passage early in the text in which

[44] Jobeda Khanam, *Jiban Khatar Pataguli*, 44.

[45] On Nadia's "demographic contours" as a "border district," see Subhasri Ghosh, "Population Movement in West Bengal: A Case Study of Nadia District, 1947–1951," *South Asia Research* 34, no. 2 (2014): 113–132.

[46] Mahua Sarkar, "Changing Together, Changing Apart: Urban Muslim and Hindu Women in Pre-Partition Bengal," *History & Memory* 27, no. 1 (Spring/Summer 2015): 9.

Jobeda describes making a "special friend" of a neighbour girl, Lolita, while living in the Hindu-majority Krishnanagar district. The poor girl ended up "beaten black and blue" for letting a "Muchalman"—a derogatory term for Muslim—spoil a room of foodstuffs with her touch when she came to play. As Jobeda introduces the anecdote: "We"—read, Muslims—"were always worried that we would create ritual pollution by touching them"—read, Hindus—"or their things." Because Jobeda's father was the inspector and Lolita's father the headmaster of the local school, no one from Lolita's family dared to "scold" Jobeda—but "at home I was slapped for going to their house".[47] The apparent "conviviality" of pre-Partition Bengal is thus brought into tension, even in a context of complex status hierarchies.[48]

To evoke a past peace before intercommunal violence engulfed Bengali society thus offers a moment for nostalgia in the text, but not one that is readily sustained. Indeed, in narrating Partition, the author moves immediately back to a position of creating strict binaries between "self" and "other"—with "self" as Muslim and "other" as Hindu. As she writes: "Congress was the united force of Hindus and Muslims. In unity, everybody fought against the British. But when the Muslims saw that Hindus were only working for their own welfare, then the Muslims established the Muslim League …".[49] Once set, the subsuming of individuals into groups defined by religious community (in the case of Indians) or nation (in the case of Britons) is sustained throughout. Hence, she writes that, after the horror in Calcutta that signified Direct Action Day in August 1946, "the Hindus, the Muslims and the British had almost agreed to the fact of Partition".[50] A more accurate telling of the delicate political negotiations that signified this shift may have referenced, as above, the Indian National Congress or the All-India Muslim League or even the British *rulers* or *government*. But, in Jobeda's retrospective telling, political groupings were synonymous with community.

What she suggests, however, is that the discord between these groups was not necessarily innate in a way focal to more antagonistic versions of the "two nations theory". On the contrary, it was created by Hindu

[47] Jobeda Khanam, *Jiban Khatar Pataguli*, 20–21.

[48] I draw here again on Sarkar, "Changing Together," 17.

[49] Jobeda Khanam, *Jiban Khatar Pataguli*, 51.

[50] Ibid., 62.

majoritarianism and exclusion both at an individual and a more general level. So, still narrating the events of 1946, Jobeda records that she had some difficulty gaining entrance to David Hare Training College for her teacher training because the principal, a Mr. K.D. Ghosh, did not want to give her entry and the "three Muslim professors" did not stand up for her. Only by calling on "Suhrawardy Sahib", no less—the Muslim League politician, then Premier of Bengal with whom she had cultivated a connection since 1940—was she able to gain access. Even then, as the only "Muslim woman" among just four or five "Muslim students" in the whole school, she lived in an otherwise "Hindu" hostel in a Hindu-dominated area of the city (on Hungerford Street in Ballygunge). Significant are the taunts she reports having received from a "Hindu girl": "why did you hurry to get admitted here? When Pakistan is created you could go there and get admitted easily." According to Jobeda's own telling, her response was the following: "I could not help but answer her ridicule. I told her—the day Pakistan is created, I will go there. Now, Pakistan is mixed with India, so we have our own rights here."[51]

Later in this same section, the author reports in a similar vein: "Our movement for another country was very irritating to Hindu society. They behaved as if India was theirs. They would not let India be divided. One day a quarrel broke out between me and two of my Hindu class mates during which one commented that Suhrawardy and Jinnah were traitors. I got extremely angry. I said very forcefully that your whole Hindu society is a traitor. You all want to keep the Muslims as your servants. That is why Jinnah and Suhrawardy fight against this."[52] This anecdote, read alongside the previous one, offers a clear sense of how, from the sympathetic location of late-twentieth-century Bangladesh at the least, Jobeda conceived of "Muslims" as an underclass in pre-Partition India being pushed out by "Hindus". At the same time, these passages are highly revealing of her own agency: Muslims may be victims, but she is willing to talk and to act. Even when "scared for our lives", she would do "daring things": put a vermillion dot on her forehead and a *shankha*, or conch-shell bangle, on her wrist so that, disguised as a married Hindu woman, she could buy books on College Street or visit her relatives.[53] She also

---

[51] Ibid., 52.

[52] Ibid., 53.

[53] Ibid., 62.

writes at length about her eager participation in various meetings and processions, as well as her work in the relief camps after the riots.[54]

Of course, it is significant that she did the latter work, not just as a matter of political conviction or philanthropy, but also to gain the wages necessary to pay for schooling, accommodation and food for her and her children. Some of the most inspirational passages in *Jiban Khatar Pataguli* are those in which Jobeda narrates how, throughout 1946 and early 1947, she would teach in the morning and then go to college in the afternoon before working in the relief camps in the evening, all the while making arrangements for her children's schooling and care.[55] Included in this section is a revealing quotation attributed to an associate, Anwara Begam, who was then a Muslim League parliamentarian. She supported Jobeda, when she was trying to acquire another teaching job at a Muslim girls' high school in Park Circus in central Calcutta, by lambasting the reluctant principal: "A Muslim girl is fighting to stand on her own two feet and you will not help her."[56] Ultimately, Jobeda was granted employment, indicating how Partition could offer opportunities to those women seeking to take them. And yet it would be problematic to read women's agency here as an unequivocal good. As Jobeda puts it: "I got the job. I got the job, but I did not have any rest from morning to night."[57]

Furthermore, women's agency can also be located in their collusion in violence. A number of incidents narrated by the author—about others, if not herself—point to how women were responsible for providing their menfolk with weapons with which to fight, primarily in the form of domestic objects like kitchen knives. As Jobeda writes about Direct Action Day: "The riot started. But how would Muslims fight?... If I had not seen it with my own eyes I would not have believed it. I saw women giving their men anything they could find for the men to fight with."[58] She also depicts Muslim women of differing classes as responsible for spurring on their sons to fight and die. Consider the following passage as an illustrative example: "I remember one lady very clearly. She was the

---

[54] Ibid., 53, 60–62.

[55] Ibid., 60.

[56] Ibid., 60.

[57] Ibid., 60.

[58] Ibid., 56.

mother of a rickshaw puller. She touched her heart and said—"This is our jihad. Nobody can destroy the Muslims. To defend the honour of the Muslims, my son will give his life." The fire I saw in that thin woman's eyes on that day, I still remember clearly to this day."[59] These anecdotes confound one of the oft-perpetuated "myths" of Partition violence that it was "largely male", with women as the "victims of violence, not its perpetrators, not its agents".[60] According to Butalia, these narratives "contained and circumscribed" women's "potential for violence" to keep them within an "ordained boundary" that defined them as "non-violent".[61] As a Muslim, a Bangladeshi and an independent woman, Jobeda had no such compunction.

Nevertheless, there is still a strong undercurrent of victimhood and trauma in *Jiban Khatar Pataguli*. The author, for instance, reports the intense fear that she experienced in the days following Direct Action Day, during which she ended up hiding, separated from her children, in the offices of the *Millat* newspaper with a number of other single Muslim women. Though they had no bedding, food or bathing facilities, their greatest distress came from the night sounds: "In the dead of night, we could hear different kinds of noises. Jai Hind, Jai Hind, Allah Ho Akbar, Allah Ho Akbar. Every noise stopped our heart beating. Even the water that trickled down the tap sounds like Jai Hind, Jai Hind ... How would we be safe?"[62] They begged for poison only to be reassured by male Muslim leaders: "We will not let our daughters fall into their hands."[63] We may conjecture that her experience of living through the equally traumatic circumstances of the 1971 independence struggle— during which so many Bengali women and girls were, in her own telling, "butchered" and "humiliated" by "cruel Pakistani soldiers"—may have reinvigorated and framed these earlier memories.[64] The young woman that she was in 1946 could only have imagined what may have happened to her if the offices were attacked; after 1971, she knew through personal

---

[59] Ibid., 55.

[60] Butalia, *The Other Side of Silence*, 169.

[61] Jobeda Khanam, *Jiban Khatar Pataguli*, 170–171.

[62] Ibid., 57–58.

[63] Ibid., 58.

[64] Ibid., 124, 125, 129.

observation, the experiences of friends and family, and, notably, rumour how women could be raped, murdered and dismembered.

The author also recounts in very explicit terms the specific horrors that she observed during the era of Partition, particularly when travelling through Calcutta in a government car under police protection to her exams in July and August of 1947: one foot stuck out of a bag on the side of the road, a headless body hanging from a tree. On the latter occasion, she reports being so disturbed that she vomited in the car before breaking into a howl in the examination hall.[65] Other tragedies were not observed, but "heard" as rumours or news stories: how people were tied, like cattle, then thrown over bridges, how others were torn in half by their legs or burnt to "coal", how naked women with their breasts sliced off were left abandoned on the road. Faced with photographs taken by a reporter friend, she again began to "howl".[66] These passages point to how autobiography may take on a therapeutic function: as a means of coming to terms with past trauma by articulating and thus containing it.[67] Jobeda herself notes that, after Partition, she tried to "forget everything" and "feel at peace": "But that did not happen".[68] Unable to suppress the memories—especially in a political context where ongoing violence meant they were constantly being invoked—she appears to have turned instead to writing the pain as a form of catharsis. Yet it is noteworthy that she is neither perpetrator, nor victim in these accounts—and she remains silent as to the identities of both.

Elsewhere, there are just a few occasions on which the reader may glimpse at fractures in the strict binaries created by the author between "Hindu" and "Muslim". A representative passage is that in which she describes how, after the riots following Direct Action Day, she returned to her hostel to be warmly received by her relieved friend Aruna and the other "Hindu" girls.[69] There are also several ruptures in the author's portrayal of "Muslims" as a group. For instance, she chooses to include anecdotes about how certain Muslims—from the rickshawallahs in Dhaka

---

[65] Ibid., 63–64.

[66] Ibid., 79–80.

[67] The best analysis of trauma's place in contemporary memoir is Leigh Gilmore's *The Limits of Autobiography: Trauma and Testimony* (Ithaca, NY: Cornell University Press, 2001).

[68] Jobeda Khanam, *Jiban Khatar Pataguli*, 80.

[69] Ibid., 59.

to a later minister in the Pakistan government—sought to take advantage of Partition's chaos for their own economic gain.[70] Her inclusion of these incidents problematises her earlier claim that, during Partition, "all Muslims wanted to help each other."[71] Jobeda also points to how Muslim rioters were "those we considered as goons"—in other words, just thugs, whether they were Muslim or not.[72] Even more revealing are the differences that she highlights between "fellow Muslims" once they found themselves in the new Pakistan. There, refugees from West Bengal and others, like herself, who had spent time in cosmopolitan Calcutta pursuing education, were ostracised by locals. As she writes: "We had the air of being foreigners in our ways and the way we talked."[73]

Notable is the significance of women to these discourses of difference, whether between Hindus and Muslims or Calcutta Muslims and Dhaka Muslims. The author notes, for instance, how the "goons" referred to above participated in the violence on the pretext of taking "revenge" on those who have "disrespected our mothers and sisters".[74] There are other references to women's "honour" too: how girls sought to escape the riots "with their honour intact", how rioters promised to protect "their daughters", how girls could not escape the "lustful looks" as they waited at Sealdah railway station to go to Dhaka.[75] But honour, or *izzat*, as a concept is actually evoked far less than one may expect from existing Partition literature.[76] On the contrary, Jobeda appears to make only passing reference to honour, seemingly as a token explanation drawing on a wider discourse—but without its being a matter of real significance to her own remembrance of Partition in Calcutta.

Indeed, where the issue of women's honour appears with much greater clarity in the text is on the author's arrival in Dhaka shortly after Partition proper—at which point differences between migrants and locals became epitomised by their attitudes to veiling practices in particular.

---

[70] Ibid., 61–62.

[71] Ibid., 60.

[72] Ibid., 55.

[73] Ibid., 69.

[74] Ibid., 55.

[75] Ibid., 55, 58, 65.

[76] Butalia, for instance, dedicates an entire chapter to "Honour" in *The Other Side of Silence*, 137–194.

Consider, as example, the following anecdote: "One day a funny incident occurred. A lady and I were walking towards the radio office. All of a sudden two men came and stood in front of us. One of them looked at us angrily and said, 'Look, this is Pakistan—a country of the Muslims. Walking shamelessly like this will not be tolerated here.' My friend stood firm and said, 'In which law of Pakistan is this written? Just show me that. If we do not listen to you, what will you do? Beat us? Will you be able to beat women? I will go to the radio station now, and then I will go to the market. Let me see what you all can do.'"[77] As the passage suggests, by this point in the narrative Jobeda and her "lady" friend had found new employment in Dhaka working for the local radio station. They, like many other women who had come from Calcutta, were unveiled, highly educated and economically independent. For the men on the street, the honour of Pakistan as a new nation was invested in "its" women—but Jobeda makes clear that their vision was contested: that she and other women would not be reduced to symbols that divested them of agency.

These observations may lead us, in conclusion, to ask how Partition was defined for this particular Bengali Muslim woman. Certainly, it was by a whole range of emotions. The first was a sense of loss: the loss of Calcutta, the loss of a united Bengal, the loss of family and friends left behind. Particularly poignant is a passage in which the author reflects on how, to go to the new Pakistan, she will have to leave her husband's grave behind in Calcutta where it will remain untended: "the pain that we will not have any claim on Calcutta kept hurting us".[78] The second emotion was uncertainty. Throughout her section on Partition is a refrain in which she asks about other people, though also herself: "what will happen to us now?"[79] And yet even stronger than these negative feelings was a sense of Partition as a positive new beginning. A third emotion, then, was relief. Jobeda notes, for instance, how, after the dangerous and uncertain journey from Calcutta, she arrived in Pakistan full of happiness, excitement and hope. As she writes: "On the border we could see a signboard. On it, in big letters, was written: 'Pakistan'. There was so much jumping and merrymaking inside the carriage. Everybody

[77] Jobeda Khanam, *Jiban Khatar Pataguli*, 71.
[78] Ibid., 64–65.
[79] Ibid., 74.

was laughing. Everybody was shouting, 'Pakistan, Pakistan. We have reached Pakistan. Now there is no more fear.' I also smiled. I heaved a sigh of relief. There is no more fear in life. To save one's life one will not have to walk with worry. Now we are free, independent."[80]

This mantra of "no more fear" is repeated several times in *Jiban Khatar Pataguli* as the author recounts the immediate aftermath of Partition, and also the empowerment of "going to an independent country as an independent citizen".[81] This meaning seems to define Jobeda's memories of Partition more than any other: that of the opportunities that it provided her as an independent Muslim woman. Hence, she reports how, immediately after Partition, she was offered a teaching job at the reputable Eden Girls' School in Dhaka alongside working on the radio. She also joined the All Pakistan Women's Association (APWA) through which she became involved with rehabilitation work with refugees.[82] Partition is thus portrayed as acting as a springboard for the author's later very successful career: as a teacher, as a radio artiste, as a writer, as a school inspectress, as an aid worker and as a government employee. Ultimately, she was appointed deputy director of East Pakistan's Bureau of National Reconstruction and, in 1976, the founding director of the Bangladesh Shishu Academy—an autonomous body under the Ministry of Women and Children's Affairs, dedicated to children's welfare. Today, her work is memorialised in the names of the Academy's library and a girls' college in Khulna.[83]

What Jobeda Khanam offers in *Jiban Khatar Pataguli*, then, is a multifaceted and often ambivalent representation of Partition that reflects her specific identities and locations—at the time and at the time of writing. As an educated, middle-class Bengali Muslim woman freed of her husband by widowhood and her father by economic independence, she lived through Partition without the encumbrances that enforced silence and accentuated honour. There is some trauma for sure, but there are no clear heroes and no clear victims either. There is a sense of loss and

---

[80] Ibid., 66–67.

[81] Ibid., 66.

[82] Ibid., 67, 73.

[83] See, in *Banglapedia*, the entries for "Bangladesh Shishu Academy" http://en.banglapedia.org/index.php?title=Bangladesh_Shishu_Academy and "Koyra Upazila" http://en.banglapedia.org/index.php?title=Koyra_Upazila.

betrayal, but also a sense of possibility—a sense of opportunity for women with real agency. Her relentless categorising of "Hindus" and "Muslims", "refugees" and "locals", synchronises with strained memories of communal harmony in pre-Partition Bengal to highlight the complexities of "living together": how coexistence need not eradicate boundaries, nor strong claims on identity require open discord.[84] Like other sources used to create Partition's "new" history, this narrative enables a more personalised telling that underscores women's centrality to 1947 as a gendered story. But it also points to how widening the corpus to include autobiographical writings by Muslim women—not just from Bangladesh, but India and Pakistan too—can establish new parameters and possibilities for our understanding of Partition.[85]

WORKS CITED

Ahmed, Ishtiaq. *The Punjab Bloodied, Partitioned and Cleansed.* Karachi: Oxford University Press, 2012.

Ali, Rabia Umar. "Muslim Women and the Partition of India: A Historiographical Silence." *Islamic Studies* 48, no. 3 (Autumn 2009): 425–436.

Bagchi, Jasodhara, and Subhoranjan Dasgupta, eds. *The Trauma and the Triumph: Gender and Partition in Eastern India.* Calcutta: Bhatkal and Sen, 2003.

Begam, Khatemanara. "Nari Shiksha: Ami Ja Dekhechhi." In *Kaler Samukh Bhela*, edited by Nurunnahar Faizunnessa. Dhaka: Muktodhara, 1988.

Bose, Neilesh. *Recasting the Region: Language, Culture and Islam in Colonial Bengal.* Delhi: Oxford University Press, 2014.

Burton, Antoinette. *Dwelling in the Archive: Women Writing House, Home, and History in Late Colonial India.* Delhi: Oxford University Press, 2003.

Butalia, Urvashi. "Community, State, and Gender: Some Reflections on the Partition of India." In *Inventing Boundaries: Gender, Politics and the Partition of India*, edited by Mushirul Hasan, 178–207. New Delhi: Oxford University Press, 2000.

---

[84] I reference here a body of scholarship exemplified by Mushirul Hasan and Ashim Roy's edited volume, *Living Together Separately: Cultural India in History and Politics* (Delhi: Oxford University Press, 2005).

[85] It is my intention to further explore these "parameters and possibilities" in a fuller study of intercommunal interactions and Partition in Muslim women's autobiographical writings in due course.

Butalia, Urvashi. *The Other Side of Silence: Voices from the Partition of India*. New Delhi: Penguin, 1998.

Chakravarti, Uma. "Betrayal, Anger, and Loss: Women Write the Partition in Pakistan." In *Speaking of the Self: Gender, Performance and Autobiography in South Asia*, edited by Anshu Malhotra and Siobhan Lambert-Hurley, 121–140. Durham, NC: Duke University Press, 2015.

Chatterji, Joya. *The Spoils of Partition: Bengal and India, 1947–1967*. Cambridge: Cambridge University Press, 2007.

Didur, Jill. *Unsettling Partition: Literature, Gender, Memory*. Toronto: University of Toronto Press, 2006.

Ghosh, Subhasri. "Population Movement in West Bengal: A Case Study of Nadia District, 1947–1951." *South Asia Research* 34, no. 2 (2014): 113–132.

Gilmore, Leigh. *The Limits of Autobiography: Trauma and Testimony*. Ithaca, NY: Cornell University Press, 2001.

Hasan, Mushirul. *Legacy of a Divided Nation: India's Muslims Since Independence*. Boulder, CO: Westview Press, 1997.

Hasan, Mushirul, and Ashim Roy, eds. *Living Together Separately: Cultural India in History and Politics*. Delhi: Oxford University Press, 2005.

Hunt, Peter, ed. *International Companion Encyclopedia of Children's Literature*, Vol. I, 2nd ed. London: Routledge, 2004.

Kaul, Suvir, ed. *The Partitions of Memory: The Afterlife of the Division of India*. New Delhi: Permanent Black, 2001.

Kaur, Ravinder. *Since 1947: Partition Narratives among Punjabi Migrants of Delhi*. New Delhi: Oxford University Press, 2007.

Khan, Yasmin. *The Great Partition: The Making of India and Pakistan*. New Haven: Yale University Press, 2007.

Khanam, Jobeda. *Ananta Pipasa*. Dhaka: Naoroja Kitabistana, 1967.

Khanam, Jobeda. *Chotadera Ekankika*. Dhaka: Bangla Ekadami, 1963.

Khanam, Jobeda. *Ekati Surera Mrtyu*. Dhaka: Adila Bradarsa, 1974.

Khanam, Jobeda. *Jiban Khatar Pataguli*. Dhaka: Kathamala Prakashani, 1991.

Khanam, Jobeda. *Mahasamudra*. Dhaka: Bangladesh Shishu Academy, 1977.

Kidwai, Anis. *Azadi ki Chhaon Main*. New Delhi: National Book Trust, 1974.

Kidwai, Anis. *Azadi ki Chhaon Main*, transliterated into Hindi by Noor Nabi Abbas. Delhi: National Book Trust, 1978.

Kidwai, Anis. *In Freedom's Shade*, trans. Ayesha Kidwai. Delhi: Penguin, 2011.

Lambert-Hurley, Siobhan. *Gender, Autobiography and the Self in Muslim South Asia*. Redwood City: Stanford University Press, forthcoming.

Mahajan, Karan. "A People's History of Partition." *New York Sun*. Accessed on 10 October 2007, http://www.nysun.com/arts/peoples-history-of-partition/64254/.

Malhotra, Anshu, and Siobhan Lambert-Hurley, eds. *Speaking of the Self: Gender, Performance and Autobiography in South Asia*. Durham, NC: Duke University Press, 2015.

Menon, Ritu, ed. *No Woman's Land: Women from Pakistan, India and Bangladesh Write on the Partition of India.* Delhi: Women Unlimited, 2004.

Menon, Ritu, and Kamla Bhasin. *Borders & Boundaries: Women in India's Partition.* New Delhi: Kali for Women, 1998.

Pandey, Gyanendra. *Remembering Partition.* Cambridge: Cambridge University, 2001.

Sarkar, Mahua. "Changing Together, Changing Apart: Urban Muslim and Hindu Women in Pre-Partition Bengal." *History and Memory* 27, no. 1 (Spring/Summer 2015): 5–42.

Smith, Sidonie, and Julia Watson. "Introduction: Situating Subjectivity in Women's Autobiographical Practices." In *Women, Autobiography, Theory: A Reader*, edited by Sidonie Smith and Julia Watson, 3–56. Madison: The University of Wisconsin Press, 1998.

Spivak, Gayatri Chakravorty. "Can the Subaltern Speak?" In *Colonial Discourse and Postcolonial Theory: A Reader*, edited by Patrick Williams and Laura Chrisman, 66–111. New York: Harvester Wheatsheaf, 1993.

Talbot, Ian. *Divided Cities: Partition and Its Aftermath in Lahore and Amritsar 1947–1957.* Karachi: Oxford University Press, 2007.

Talbot, Ian, and D.S. Tatla. *Epicentre of Violence: Partition Voices and Memories from Amritsar.* Delhi: Permanent Black, 2006.

Virdee, Pippa. "Remembering Partition: Women, Oral Histories and the Partition of 1947." *Oral History* 41, no. 2 (Autumn 2013): 49–53.

Zamindar, Vaizra Fazila-Yacoobali. *The Long Partition and the Making of Modern South Asia: Refugees, Boundaries, Histories.* Delhi: Penguin, 2007.

CHAPTER 7

Relocating the Memory
of the Partition in Bapsi Sidhwa's
Defend Yourself Against Me

Daniela Vitolo

This essay asks what happens to the personal and collective memory of the Partition of India and Pakistan when it is recalled by a group of people living far from the subcontinent. It approaches this question through a reading of Bapsi Sidhwa's short story "Defend Yourself Against Me" (2008), to discuss how through her story the author shows that the Partition of the Indian subcontinent, a defining event for the South Asians living in Pakistan, India and Bangladesh, is equally relevant for the South Asian diaspora. Looking at what happens in the story when the remembrance of the facts related to the creation of the borders between India and Pakistan is moved across another border, which is that separating the Asian subcontinent from the USA, it is possible to discuss how the characters confront the memory of that event. Indeed, for the members of the diasporic community pictured in the story, recognising

D. Vitolo (✉)
University of Naples 'L'Orientale', Naples, Italy
e-mail: daniela.vitolo@hotmail.it

© The Author(s) 2018
C. Mahn and A. Murphy (eds.), *Partition and the Practice of Memory*,
https://doi.org/10.1007/978-3-319-64516-2_7

137

it as part of their history appears to be something both unavoidable and useful for the definition of their identity. While the characters relate to that memory in different ways according to their personal experience of the event, they also process it together. In this way, remembering becomes something that unites a group comprised of various ethnic and religious communities whose members recognise that their roots can be traced back to a distant place and to a common past.

The following discussion pays close attention to the connection between memory and narration that appears fundamental for the development of a shared narrative of 1947. While Sidhwa uses fiction as a means to remember and to promote a public conversation, she also introduces in this short story a metanarrative that promotes literary fiction as a means to deal with the memories of the Partition. In "Defend Yourself Against Me" the narrator, who is also one of the protagonists, is a Pakistani Christian who teaches English in an American university and who is also a writer who has begun to work on a novel about Partition. The use of a narrator that is both one of the characters involved in the process of remembering and the only person conscious of the mechanisms of fiction writing, allows the author to stress how individual and collective acts of remembering and of narrating are intertwined. At the same time, however, fiction is only one of the many ways in which memory can be transmitted. Indeed, in the story the characters recall and share memories through a dialogue which allows them to develop a collective narrative of past trauma. This takes place both among people who feel an urge to remember and others who face the difficulty of bearing testimony.

Following the logic of the "two nations theory", nationalist discourses tend to recall Partition in a selective way, focusing on the violence perpetrated by one group against another and highlighting the idea that each of them is naturally distinct and distant from the other. However, in the case here analysed, the approach chosen by the author does not consider identity construction as determined by the nation. Instead, it focuses on the way in which people can develop their sense of belonging to a group, as well as to a culture and a place, although they have differing ethnic or religious backgrounds. For the community depicted by Bapsi Sidhwa, recalling Partition is useful for the development of a narrative that, in the process of trying to heal a wound that is still open, allows its members to think about themselves as part of a group that is hybrid and which can conceive of itself as united.

THE WORK OF BAPSI SIDHWA

Joy, the narrator in the story, belongs to a minority group in Pakistan and is an immigrant in the United States; in this she shares some auto-biographical traits with the author. Bapsi Sidhwa was born in Karachi in 1938 in a Parsee family that stayed in Pakistan after 1947, while she later moved to the USA in the 1980s and lives in Houston. She has been both a witness of Partition and one of its narrators with her well-known novel *Cracking India*, which is regarded as having inaugurated a new level of discussion about the Partition and its legacy in Partition Studies.[1] Among the main themes of this novel are the memory of trauma, the impact of communal violence on women, and the possibility of forgiveness. These themes recur in the more recent "Defend Yourself Against Me", which has several traits in common with the more famous novel. In *Cracking India*, the story is narrated from a peripheral perspective because Lenny, the narrator, belongs to the Parsee community established in Lahore, which had a marginal role during Partition. For this reason, she seems outside the interests of the dominant groups of the time.[2] At the same time, she relates the story as it is seen through the eyes of a child, giving the impression that the story has been rendered in an objective way because the girl is too young to misrepresent the events for political reasons.[3] The relevance of the novel lies in the fact that it produces a feminist account of Partition, developing a story where all the main characters are women that experience and deal with it in different ways. The novel focuses on the plight of women, who are regarded as symbolic representatives of their communities and, consequently, how their bodies became tokens to be conquered, spoiled and defaced.

The perspective on women at Partition offered through the eyes of a young Parsee girl Lenny, is thus positioned at the margins in several ways. For this reason, *Cracking India* has been defined a "border work" because it "situates itself upon various borders (generic, discursive,

---

[1] C. Cilano, *Contemporary Pakistani Fiction in English: Idea, Nation, State* (London: Routledge, 2013), 34.

[2] A. Kanwal, *Rethinking Identities in Contemporary Pakistani Fiction: Beyond 9/11* (London: Palgrave Macmillan, 2015), 22.

[3] H. S. Mann, "Cracking India: Minority Women Writers and the Contentious Margins of Indian Nationalist Discourse," *The Journal of Commonwealth Literature* 24, no. 2 (1994): 72–73.

ethnic, political) while it also examines and celebrates [...] the inhabitation of such borders".[4] Inhabiting a border space means to occupy a dimension of agency, questioning and exchange, in which binary oppositions related to gender, ethnicity or creed, and the narratives that support them, are contested while alternative narratives are developed. Also in the short story, border-crossings and the inhabiting of a liminal dimension are relevant for a narrative in which dealing with the memory of a collective trauma becomes a way to oppose narratives that represent diverse South Asian groups in conflict each other.

"Defend Yourself Against Me" is set in Houston, where a group of South Asian expatriates meet for a dinner organised by Kishen, an Indian immigrant who has married a white American woman, Suzanne, and who has a large and varied group of Asian friends, which includes representatives from the Hindu and Muslim as well as the Sikh and Christian communities. During the dinner one of the hosts, Joy, meets by chance her childhood playmate, Mr. Sikander Khan. Both of them are Pakistanis and when they meet, Joy starts to remember the circumstances in which she and Mr. Khan had known each other. Thus, the narrative begins to move back and forth between two different times and places: the contemporary American house where, irrespectively of their faith, mother tongue and social background people join in a friendly and festive mood, and post-Partition Lahore where, as a child, Joy meets Sikander and his mother who have arrived in Pakistan as refugees. We later learn that they are the only survivors of a family killed when their village was attacked by a group of Sikh men. It is only during the dinner that Joy learns that during Partition Sikander's mother was among the women abducted, raped and sold in markets by men belonging to enemy groups. Later, the story moves to another dinner, this time organised by Mr. Khan himself, to welcome his mother, who is always referred to as Ammijee, as she arrives from Pakistan to reunite with her son. While the night seems to be set for a festive mood, the arrival of two young Sikh men, Pratab and Khushwant, rapidly changes the atmosphere. As the door is opened to let them enter in the house, the two, dressed as fakirs, lie down with their faces to the floor and repeatedly ask Ammijee to forgive them for their fathers' faults. The narration ends when the old woman, after an initial

---

[4]A. Hai, "Border Work, Border Trouble: Postcolonial Feminism and the Ayah in Bapsi Sidhwa's *Cracking India*," *Modern Fiction Studies* 46, no. 2 (2000): 387.

refusal to forgive them, tells them that she had had to forgive the perpe-trators of that violence many years before, as that was the only way for her to go on living.

In recent times, several studies have focused on the relationship between the South Asian diaspora and the issue of the Partition of India and Pakistan, claiming that the memories of that historical event can be read in transnational terms. These studies highlight that, just as for the people living in South Asia, for whom ethnic, religious and national belonging are central issues in the life of communities, this is also true for migrants. The events of 1947, their memory and the discourses developed around them were and still are crucial for the processes of national and ethnic identity construction. In 1947, certain migrant com-munities in the West had their own experience of Partition when they readjusted their relations with others, now defined as nationally Other, following the events that had brought about the creation of two nation states in their homeland.[5] Today the memory of Partition allows the diaspora to confront questions that arise from being individuals and communities that need to articulate their identities and their sense of belonging while they are far from their original home. Thus, Partition is for South Asian migrants part of what Vijay Mishra defines as "diaspora mythology", a complex imaginary where discourses converge around, among other things, the far homeland, the idea of return and ancient origins. Such an imaginary participates in the narratives that diasporic groups share and create about themselves: the idea that their community lives in a condition of displacement. According to Mishra, "for diasporas to face up their own ghosts, their own traumas, their own memories is a necessary and ethical condition."[6]

THE PLACE OF MEMORY

The relationship between memory and the constitution of both personal and community identity has been widely discussed within a wide range of fields, as diverse as literary criticism, psychology and sociology. One

---

[5] P. Ghosh, *Partition and South Asian Diaspora: Extending the Subcontinent* (London: Routledge, 2007), 10.

[6] V. Mishra, "The Diasporic Imaginary and the Indian Diaspora," *Asian Studies Institute Occasional Lecture* 2 (2007): 7.

fundamental issue is the distinction between individual and collective memory. As Astrid Erll writes, there are two levels of memory.[7] At one level, remembering is an individual cognitive process which contributes to the definition of personal identity while, on a different level, it is a sociocultural activity that allows groups to create themselves by developing a common identity rooted in a shared past. In the case of cultural memory, when remembrance is the product of a number of practices such as historical research, the collection and circulation of testimonies, and the creation of artistic expressions that promote discussions about certain events, the term memory acquires a metaphorical meaning. According to Erll, social memory-making is distinct from individual cognitive processes because it does not necessarily imply the recalling of facts directly experienced by the group or some part of it. At the same time, however, both kinds of memory share similar processes of reconstructing of the past. For example, in both cases the events brought back are selected and elaborated in a similar way, that is, "according to present knowledge and needs".[8] Also, as Erll points out, biological and social memory cannot be clearly distinguished as they influence each other. Indeed, it would be impossible to individuate a personal memory that is not influenced by the social context, just as a collective memory cannot be developed without people's individual participation.

For South Asians living far from the subcontinent as well as for those living where Partition took place, the collective revival of memory is also realised through the creation of works of art which comprise, among other things, a rich literary archive that started immediately after 1947 and continues up to the present. An example of recent fiction dealing with the relationship between Partition and the diaspora is Jhumpa Lahiri's *Interpreter of Maladies*. In this collection of short stories the author suggests the idea (one which Paulomi Chakraborty has pointed out to be questionable[9]) that there are similarities between the

---

[7] A. Erll, "Cultural Memory Studies: An Introduction," in *Media and Cultural Memory/ Medien und kulturelle Erinnerung*, ed. A. Erll and A. Nünning, 1–15 (Berlin: Walter de Gruyter GmbH & Co, 2008).

[8] A. Erll, "Cultural Memory Studies: An Introduction," 5.

[9] P. Chakraborty, "Refugee Women, Immigrant Women: The Partition as Universal Dislocation in Jhumpa Lahiri's *Interpreter of Maladies*," in *Partitioned Lives: Narratives of Home, Displacement, and Resettlement*, ed. A. G. Roy and N. Bhatia (New Delhi: Dorling Kindersley, 2008), 227–239 .

condition of Partition refugees and those who chose to migrate abroad: in both cases people find themselves in a state of displacement and exile from their homeland.[10] Yet, whether works deal with diasporic memories or focus on other Partition issues caused to many by their need to choose between India and Pakistan, whether or not the authors were direct or indirect witnesses to those facts, Partition fiction is always a literary representation of memory. Such works fall under the definition of what Brigit Neumann has called the "fictions of memory" a term which refers to "the stories that individuals or cultures tell about their past to answer the question 'who am I', or, collectively, 'who are we'".[11] Such narratives can be defined as "fictions of memory" because they recreate the past through a work of the imagination that mixes real facts and information with creations of literary fantasy that reflect the present needs of the author as well as of the society around her/him. It is through such literary works which remember and re-narrate Partition, these writers suggest, that "meaningful narratives do not exist prior to the process of remembering and narrating the past."[12] Creating a common narrative through such imaginative means is also a powerful way to develop and share a sense of belonging to a community.

Sidhwa's story focuses on how memory can participate in the creation of a community that is neither that of India nor that of Pakistan and which, even if inextricably related to what India and Pakistan have become after 1947, is still something other than that. Indeed, in the story, relocating difference can lead to its dissipation or reconfiguration. One such quality is *desi* clothing. This seems clear in passages like the following: "the sisters, hiding their smiles in their *dupattas*, start giggling. They have perked up in the presence of these young men who

---

[10] Chakraborty argues that Partition refugees and South Asians that migrate abroad do not share the same kind of experience. For example, they do not keep the same kind of relationship with the country they left. While migrants can think about returning to their land of origin, Partition refugees cannot go back after electing a new homeland. Furthermore, in her analysis Chakraborty points out that establishing this sort of similarity between those who choose between India and Pakistan and those who leave Asia to move to other, usually Western, countries, produces the effect of reducing the relevance of a traumatic event that is crucial in the history of South Asia.

[11] B. Neumann, "The Literary Representation of Memory," in *Media and Cultural Memory/ Medien und kulturelle Erinnerung*, ed. A. Erll and A. Nünning (Berlin: Walter de Gruyter GmbH & Co, 2008), 333–343, 334.

[12] B. Neumann, "The Literary Representation of Memory," 338.

speak their language and share their ways, their religious antagonism dissipated on American soil".[13] This suggests that even if the characters participating in the scene are Muslims and Sikhs, they share common cultural behaviours, such as the need for girls to show their modesty in front of the boys. Likewise, when Mrs. Khan and Khushwant talk about finding him a wife, the boy does not stress that there is a religious difference between them but says that the woman should find him "A girl who knows our ways".[14] In another scene the narrator says: "I make a polite conversation with Mrs Khan's sisters in hesitant Punjabi. They have just emigrated. The differences from our past remain: I, an English-speaking scion of Anglican Protestants from Lahore; they, village belles accustomed to drawing water to the rhythm of Punjabi lore".[15] Thus, when Joy stresses the differences between the women she is talking to and points out what distinguishes them, it is the difference in their social and cultural background that she emphasises: Joy is a well-educated woman from the city while the others are village women. This moves their sense of commonality and difference to a different location.

The recognition among the characters that they share the same background unites them and functions to contrast them with the American society in which they live, even if there are only vague references to the context outside the community of migrants. One reference to it is constituted by Suzanne, the only white person in the group. However, while other white American women are referred to as "white-washed memsahib(s)" it is said of Suzanne that "she is one of us"[16] because after marrying Kishen, she learns the customs and behaviours of her in-laws to such an extent that hers is "the very image of dutiful Brahman wifedom".[17] The house where Kishen lives with his family is located in an American suburb, but it reproduces an atmosphere that induces the narrator to think that in that place a person could forget for a moment that they were in the USA: "Perhaps it is this house, so comfortably possessed by its occupants and their Indian bric-a-brac. It takes an effort to

---

[13] B. Sidhwa, "Defend Yourself Against Me," in *And the World Changed: Contemporary Stories by Pakistani Women*, ed. M. Shamsie (New York: The Feminist Press, 2008), 27–52, 43.

[14] B. Sidhwa, "Defend," 43.

[15] Ibid., 30.

[16] See note 14 above.

[17] See note 15 above.

remember that we are in the greenly shaven suburbs of an American city in the heart of Texas".[18] This could be considered an attempt to appropriate an American space, giving it an Indian identity. However, the fact that the characters are aware of being in a place distant and different from the subcontinent is confirmed when Khushwant and Pratab meet Ammijee. In that circumstance, Joy comments that the scene seems, "incongruous and melodramatic in this pragmatic and oil-rich corner of the Western world".[19]

Throughout "Defend Yourself Against Me" the author associates the process of remembering with that of moving to a distant place, both metaphorically and physically. Describing the connection of two processes that she puts in practice as a writer, Joy states: "Since childhood memories can only be accurately exhumed by the child, I will inhabit my childhood. As a writer, I am already practiced in inhabiting different bodies; dwelling in rooms, gardens, bungalows, and space from the past; zapping in time".[20] The recall and narration of memories is here equated with the inhabitation of a space, the space of the past. According to Neumann's understanding of the "fictions of memory", the process of remembering is frequently represented through spatial metaphors that represent both individual and collective memory. A reference to space thus "serves to symbolically mediate past events, underlining the constant, physical presence of the multilayered cultural past, which is even inscribed in the landscape or in the architecture".[21] In Sidhwa's short story, the characters inhabit several spaces of the past and present that are inscribed, respectively, in the landscapes of an American and South Asian context. Therefore, references to distant physical places provide a means of invoking the concrete division of a tangible place, and with it the memories that are inscribed in that broken landscape. These are then radically localised in a new environment.

Jennifer Yusin points out that the border between India and Pakistan is both a geographical separation and the site of an ungraspable trauma; for this reason it can be understood as a physical entity as well as a symbol. She uses the expression "geography of trauma" to convey the idea

---

[18] B. Sidhwa, "Defend," 32.

[19] Ibid., 48.

[20] Ibid., 34.

[21] B. Neumann, "The Literary Representation of Memory," 340.

that "the borders created during the Partition exist at once as geographical separations and as a spatial, temporal figure for the unspeakable experience of that history, and as such become the site where the knowable realities of history become inextricably bound up with the problem of grasping trauma".[22] The geographical border established on the eve of the subcontinent's Independence thus becomes a visible mark of a trauma which is impossible to express through words. In the fiction discussed here, we also see references to other, mainly symbolic, borders and spaces. During the narration of her memories Joy describes a place that provides the locus for her memories as well as those of Mr. Khan and Ammijee. It is Race Course Road in Lahore, where the characters' houses were. It is there that Joy and Sikander meet first, observing each other through the cracks in the wall separating their compounds. This space, which is symbolically characterised by the failing of a physical barrier separating the houses and which allows the two children to become friends, is also the place where, to the woman, the memory of Partition is related to two elements. One is trauma, known in the form of the visible scars on her friend's body: "The sun-charred little body is covered with scabs and wounds [...] as he turns away I see the improbable wound on the back of his cropped head. It is a raw and flaming scar, as if the bone and flesh had been callously gouged out, and my compassion ties me to him".[23] Even if, as a child, Joy is unaware of the causes of those wounds, through Sikander's marked body she has her only direct contact with the violence generated by the clashes between opposing groups. However, whilst seen through the eyes of a young girl those marks of violence cause a feeling of compassion, and at the same time are signs of acts so brutal that for her they are "improbable". The other element that the narrator associates with Partition is an account of a violence that is both vague and unbelievable:

Sikander had described some of the details of the attack and of his miraculous survival. His account of it, supplied in little, suddenly recalled snatches—brought to mind by chance associations while we played—was

---

[22] J. Yusin, "The Silence of Partition: Borders, Trauma, and Partition History," *Social Semiotics* 19, no. 4 (2009): 459.

[23] B. Sidhwa, "Defend," 37.

so jumbled, so full of bizarre incident, that I accepted it as the baggage of truth-enlivened-by-fantasy that every child carries within.[24]

While, on the one hand, it emerges that the pieces of the story narrated by her playmate contain elements so "bizarre" they induce her to simply classify them as children's fantasies, on the other, Sikander's narration, which is at times detailed but always fragmentary, makes "no mention at all of Ammijee's ordeal".[25] In this way, for Joy, Race Course Road functions as a private memory that also saves and symbolises her memory of a public event. Yet that site is like the border in Yusin's definition of the geography of trauma, acting as both a concrete place associated with a historical event and a figure of an experience that is so overwhelming, because of its traumatising nature, that it cannot be fully understood and expressed while it appeals for testimony.

The mother and son fulfil a fundamental role within the narrative. They act as living testimonies to the consequences of Partition and of the unspeakable nature of that trauma. The image that the narrator retains of Ammijee in Lahore is blurred. This seems to be a way to associate the representation of the woman with the fact that her fate during Partition will remain vague:

I search my memory. I dimly perceive a thin, bent-over, squatting figure [...] The ragged cotton chador always drawn forward over her face, the color of her form blended with mud, the ash, the utensils she washed, the pale seasonal vegetables she peeled. This must be Ammijee: a figure bent perpetually to accommodate the angle of drudgery and poverty. I don't recall her face or the color of her dusty bare feet; the shape of her hands or whether she wore bangles.[26]

The narrator does not remember Ammijee's face or any detail about her aspect, and she is presented as the unremarkable figure of a woman only associated with her daily domestic routine. Nevertheless, this person, so little characterised by the author, seems to be a symbol representing all the women who are victims of the violence. From the scant information provided by other people, Joy speculates on has happened to Ammijee

---

[24] Ibid., 39–40.
[25] Ibid., 40.
[26] Ibid., 39.

during Partition but the accounts she hears do not say what exactly the woman went through. Before stating that "Ammijee never talks about it",[27] Mr. Khan's wife talks about the moment when the village was attacked and all the women, who had planned to kill themselves before falling in the enemy's hands, had no time to fulfil their plan. "Ammijee says she went mad!" Mrs. Khan tells the group of listeners: "She would have killed herself if she could. So would you: So would I. ... She heard her eleven-year-old daughter screaming and screaming ... she heard the mullah's sixteen-year-old daughter scream: Do anything you wish with me, but don't hurt me. For God's sake don't hurt me!"[28] Later Mr. Khan adds further information "Ammijee heard street vendors cry: '*Zenana* for sale! *Zenana* for sale!' as if they were selling vegetables and fish. They were selling women for 50, 20, and even 10 rupees!"[29] Like the image that Joy associates with the woman, her story emerges in a way that is so vague and fragmented that it is impossible to gather a clear picture of Ammijee's past. Furthermore, it seems that the bits of information that the old woman has shared say more about what she personally experienced.

ENACTING TRAUMA

Trauma can be defined as a deeply negative experience that leaves behind long-term problems for the people who are forced to deal with it mentally and emotionally. Cathy Caruth's work on trauma, memory and narrative takes as its starting point the awareness of the unresolved nature of trauma, where a traumatic event is so overwhelming that when it happens the consciousness is unable to understand it totally. Because a traumatic event cannot be assimilated to any other kind of experience due to its paradoxical nature, the mind will not treat it in the way it treats all other past events. As a result, the traumatic fact will repeatedly come back to the person's consciousness as an unresolved past. The event that has not been assimilated tends to emerge continuously, showing

---

[27] Ibid., 41.

[28] Ibid., 41.

[29] Ibid., 45.

the "repeated possession of the one who experiences it".[30] At the same time, the person possessed by the traumatic memory tries to produce a testimony of the trauma, but language fails to express it. Caruth's study highlights the ways in which the narration of a trauma can function so as to allow the experience to be integrated into an individual as well as a collective narrative. All too often, the attempt to verbalise the experience is unsuccessful because the narrator realises that "there are never enough words or the right words" to express it. As a consequence, when put into words the narration of the past trauma seems to be less precise and intense than the trauma as it is retained in the mind of the person that experienced it. "Defend Yourself Against Me" seems to illustrate this problem, as each character struggles to give voice to the experience of Partition. In the case of Ammijee and Sikander, the failure of language seems also to reveal an attempt to put aside the memory of what they experienced, as a strategy for survival. Sikander, for example, is reticent about his past: "They noticed Mr Khan's reticence on the subject and stopped asking questions ... but they suspect she (Ammijee) has been through something terrible"[31] and this also shows that he does not want to recall his story. Likewise, Sikander hides the most visible physical signs left on his body using a wig and thus tries to cover the marks of his trauma in a concrete way: "passing a hand down the back of his head, [he] dryly says, 'I am wearing a wig. The scar is still there'".[32] That Sikander and his mother choose to put aside the past is confirmed by Ammijee's face, which shows no sign of suffering or bitterness.[33] Above all, this is expressed by Mr. Khan when he says that he refuses to treat Khushwant and Pratab as enemies because "they weren't even born" and especially because he acknowledges that all the groups were guilty in the same way for what happened: "We Muslims were no better...we did the same...Hindu, Muslim, Sikh, we were all evil bastards".[34]

Following distinct paths of memory, Joy and the Sikh boys carry out the processes of recalling an event that has not affected them directly.

---

[30] C. Caruth, *Trauma: Explorations in Memory* (Baltimore: Johns Hopkins University Press, 1995), 4.

[31] B. Sidhwa, "Defend," 39.

[32] Ibid., 38.

[33] Ibid., 46.

[34] Ibid., 45.

By doing so they show that the effects produced by events of such enormous dimensions as Partition have also touched those who did not experience them in person and have been handed down to the next generation. Thus, Sikander and Ammijee's experiences are a trauma that, as such, comes back as an unresolved issue. Because Pratab and Khushwant were born many years after the events took place, they belong to what Marianne Hirsch has called "the generation of postmemory". The defining characteristic of the people belonging to this generation is that even if they were not born when the violent event happened, it has been transmitted to them in a way so profound that they have been affected by it anyway. They have been touched by the traumatic fact in a manner so impressive that what they store in the mind can be defined as memory, even if it does not derive from a direct experience but is a consequence of an image associated to the event which they have acquired while they were growing up. Consequently, that memory is different from the memory of witnesses. A consequence produced by the acquisition of postmemory is that the younger generation's identity is "shaped, however indirectly, by traumatic events that still defy narrative reconstruction and exceed comprehension".[35] Usually, the transmission of memory takes place within the family but it is not restricted to this context; in fact, postmemory also contributes to the formation of a collective cultural identity. At the same time, Sikander could be identified as belonging to what has been defined "the 1.5 generation". This definition, like that of "the generation of postmemory" was originally developed with reference to the experience and the memory of the Holocaust. To Susan Rubin Suleiman, the 1.5 generation is that of the children who survived the Holocaust but who, even if they were direct witnesses of the events, were too young to understand what was happening.[36]

RELOCATING MEMORY

Proceeding through distinct paths, Joy, Pratab and Khushwant and Ammijee and Sikander fulfil a role in recalling and relocating South Asian memory in the West. The narrator both talks about her own memories

---

[35] M. Hirsch, "The Generation of Postmemory," *Poetics Today* 29, no. 1 (2008): 111.

[36] S. R. Suleiman, "The 1.5 Generation: Thinking about Child Survivors and the Holocaust," *American Imago* 59, no. 3 (2002): 277–295.

and is the first person to lead the community to remember. When she recognises Sikander and associates him with what, for her, is his defining trait, that of being a survivor of the 1947 violence, the group's attention is turned to Mr. Khan and his mother's story. Associating her knowledge with other people's, Joy's function is that of making the narration of memory a collective act. While Joy inhabits a space of memory through narrative, Pratab and Khushwant choose to embody the memory of what their ancestors did by symbolically acting in their place. The narrator describes the scene: "The fakirs lie face down across the threshold, half outside the door and half in the passage, their hands flat on the floor as if they were about to do pushups. Their faces are entirely hidden by hair. Suddenly, their voices are moist and thick, they begin to cry, "*Maajee! Maajee!* Forgive us".[37] And later, when the woman initially refuses to forgive them, they add ""*Maajee*, forgive us: Forgive the wrongs of our fathers'".[38] Through the scene that they produce to ask for forgiveness, they adopt a studied appearance that is meant to allow them to embody their ancestral identity, as they seek redemption. In these actions and embodiments, they act as a sort of link between the past and present and between South Asia and America. Through an almost silent act, which is dense with meaning and reaffirms the difficulty of putting trauma into words, they produce the most effective form of recalling, through performance. Indeed, the atmosphere in the house changes as well as Ammijee's behaviour. Her voice becomes fearful and her face shows signs of "the bitterness, the horror, the hate".[39] Suddenly the past is back and "the behaviour of the Sikhs, so incongruous and flamboyant before, is now transcendentally essential, consequential, fitting".[40] Their act obliges the old woman as well as all the others to participate in an act of recalling that acquires a physical form and which, because of its visible presence, cannot be ignored. The boys have acquired a memory that is not their own, in a way so profound that it seems to be theirs.

The presence of Mr. Khan and his mother in Houston is what starts the personal and collective process of remembering. As they move

---

[37] B. Sidhwa, "Defend," 48.

[38] Ibid., 49.

[39] Ibid.

[40] Ibid.

between 1948 Lahore and contemporary Houston they become the most evident sign of the relocation of a memory that thus establishes itself in a space that is unrelated to the Partition. The private spaces constituted by the American houses where the community reunites to build and maintain its identity become the physical spaces where remembering contributes to the characterisation of the community of migrants. Detached culturally and historically from those facts, the American space in which the memory of the Partition emerges is a liminal one and thus it gives to the people that inhabit it the possibility of acting in order to realise their own process of self-definition. According to Homi Bhabha "in-between spaces provide the terrain for elaborating strategies of self-hood—singular or communal—that initiate new signs of identity, and innovative sites of collaboration, and contestation, in the act of defining the idea of society itself".[41] In Bapsi Sidhwa's short story, personal and collective identities cannot be defined through silencing the past; however, the acts of remembering and narrating Partition appear to be relevant for the shaping of the identity of a diasporic community that needs to recall an unresolved common past, in order to define itself as united regardless of the ethnic and religious differences among its members.

WORKS CITED

Antze, P., and M. Lambek *Tense Past: Cultural Essays in Trauma and Memory.* New York and London: Routledge, 1996.

Assman, Jan. "Collective Memory and Cultural Identity." *New German Critique* 65 (1995): 125–133.

Bhabha, Homi. *The Location of Culture.* New York: Routledge, 1994.

Caruth, C. *Trauma: Explorations in Memory.* Baltimore: Johns Hopkins University Press, 1995.

Cilano, C. *Contemporary Pakistani Fiction in English: Idea, Nation, State.* London: Routledge, 2013.

Erll, A. "Cultural Memory Studies: An Introduction". In *Media and Cultural Memory/Medien und kulturelle Erinnerung*, ed. A. Erll and A. Nünning, 1–15. Berlin: Walter de Gruyter GmbH & Co, 2008.

Ghosh, P. *Partition and South Asian Diaspora: Extending the Subcontinent.* London: Routledge, 2007.

---

[41] H. Bhabha, *The Location of Culture* (New York: Routledge, 1994), 1–2.

Hai, A. "Border Work, Border Trouble: Postcolonial Feminism and the Ayah in Bapsi Sidhwa's *Cracking India*." *Modern Fiction Studies*, 46, no. 2 (2000): 379–426.

Hirsch, M. "The Generation of Postmemory." *Poetics Today*, 29, no. 1 (2008): 103–128.

Kanwal, A. *Rethinking Identities in Contemporary Pakistani Fiction: Beyond 9/11*. London: Palgrave MacMillan, 2015.

Mann, H.S. "Cracking India: Minority Women Writers and the Contentious Margins of Indian Nationalist Discourse." *The Journal of Commonwealth Literature* 24, no. 2 (1994): 71–94.

Mishra, V. "The Diasporic Imaginary and the Indian Diaspora." *Asian Studies Institute Occasional Lecture 2*, 2007.

Neumann, B. "The Literary Representation of Memory". In *Media and Cultural Memory/Medien und kulturelle Erinnerung*, ed. A. Erll and A. Nünning, 333–343. Berlin: Walter de Gruyter GmbH & Co, 2008.

Roy, A.G., and N. Bhatia, eds. *Partitioned Lives: Narratives of Home, Displacement, and Resettlement*. New Delhi: Dorling Kindersley, 2008.

Sidhwa, B. *Cracking India*. Minneapolis: Milkweed, 1991.

_____. "Defend Yourself Against Me." In *And the World Changed: Contemporary Stories by Pakistani Women*, ed. M. Shamsie, 27–52. New York: The Feminist Press, 2008.

Suleiman, S.R. "The 1.5 Generation: Thinking About Child Survivors and the Holocaust," *American Imago* 59, no. 3 (2002): 277–295.

Yusin, J. "The Silence of Partition: Borders, Trauma, and Partition History." *Social Semoitics* 19, no. 4 (2009): 453–468.

CHAPTER 8

Poetics of Pain: Writing the Memory of Partition

Anne Castaing

This chapter explores the use of emotive narration as a strategy within Partition literature which encourages subaltern expression. The recent development of Affect Studies and of the "affective turn" in different fields and disciplines (notably history) offer new perspectives in the comprehension of tragedies as at once individual and collective experiences.[1] This sheds new light on how memory is constructed in Partition narratives, especially when personal experience can often remain subservient (as was particularly the case for Partition) to ideological "grand" narratives, within which individual, and even more so collective emotions, have been considered as interfering in (or "troubling" to, in Alok

---

[1] See notably Ramsey MacMullen, *Feelings in History, Ancient and Modern* (Claremont: Regina Books, 2015); Anne Vincent-Buffault, *Histoire des larmes: XVIIIe-XIXe siècles* (Paris: Rivages, 1986); and Pernau Margrit and Jordheim Helge, eds., *Civilizing Emotions. Concepts in Nineteenth Century Asia and Europe* (Oxford: Oxford University Press, 2015).

A. Castaing (✉)
CNRS/Centre for South Asian Studies, Paris, France
e-mail: annecastaing@yahoo.fr

© The Author(s) 2018
C. Mahn and A. Murphy (eds.), *Partition and the Practice of Memory*,
https://doi.org/10.1007/978-3-319-64516-2_8

155

Bhalla's words) more "objective" narratives.[2] Highlighting the imbricated practices of emotion and memory, this chapter will discuss how literature can offer a creative insight into the experience of collective tragedy that should and can be considered alongside the official archive of Partition history.

FICTION AS A (SUBALTERN) MEMORY OF PARTITION

Both the memory of Partition and its aporia—which are more significant today than ever as we are about to celebrate the seventieth anniversary of Pakistan and India's Independence—are the preoccupation of most recent historical writings on Partition. In *The Pity of Partition* (2013), Ayesha Jalal underlines the limits of memory as a way of investigating Partition, since it both mingles with the crucial issue of guilt while being vulnerable to manipulation, and "ends up folding communitarian remembrances into the straitjacket of official nationalist narratives."[3] While stressing these limits of memory is quite common practice—in the words of Urvashi Butalia, "working with memory is never simple or unproblematic"[4] —historians such as Ayesha Jalal also distance themselves from Partition's "traditional" archives, which they rightly consider as subservient to colonial or nationalist political agendas. On the other hand, historians who regularly resort to interviews with survivors or witnesses, such as Ian Talbot in *The Epicentre of Violence* (2006) or Urvashi Butalia in *The Other Side of Silence* (1998), have promoted memory as a way of shaping a social history of Partition, arguing as Butalia has done that "the way people choose to remember an event, a history, is at least as important as what one might call the 'facts' of that history, for after all, these

---

[2] In his interview with Bhisham Sahni, titled "Objectifying Troubling Memories. An Interview with Bhisham Sahni," in *Inventing Boundaries: Gender, Politics and the Partition of India*, ed. Mushirul Hasan (New Delhi: Oxford University Press, 2000), 338–350.

[3] Ayesha Jalal *The Pity of Partition. Manto's Life, Times, and Work across the India-Pakistan Divide* (Princeton: Princeton University Press, 2013), 13.

[4] Urvashi Butalia, *The Other Side of Silence. Voices from the Partition of India* (Durham: Duke University Press, 1998), 10. See also Ananya Jahanara Kabir, *Partition's Post-Amnesias* (New Delhi: Women Unlimited, 2013); Sukheshi Kamra, "Engaging Traumatic Histories. The 1947 Partition of India in Collective Memory," in *Partition. The Long Shadow*, ed. Urvashi Butalia (New Delhi: Zubaan, 2015), 155–177.

latter are not self-evident givens; instead, they too are interpretations, as remembered or recorded by one individual or another."[5]

Others have elected to draw on fiction as a means to shed light on Partition and to use it to elaborate an alternative, popular history. As is well known, Partition has given rise to a number of stories, novels or films, most of which were written (or directed) between 1948 and 1955—in the "Heat of Fratricide" as Jason Francisco writes—fictional works which convey intense basic emotions, such as pain, anger, surprise or fear.[6] Since the 1990s, these fictional works dealing with the aftermath of Partition have been both intensively mobilised and re-examined. The publication of three anthologies of Partition fictions within two years (Alok Bhalla's *Stories about the Partition of India* in 1994, three volumes; Mushirul Hasan's *India Partitioned: The Other Side of Freedom*, two volumes, 1995; Saros Cowasjee and K.S. Duggal's *Orphans of the Storm*, 1995), bears witness to the necessity of both invoking the memory of Partition and imposing its memorialisation through literary media, as also shown by the publication of interviews with "partitioned" writers (such as in Bhalla 2006) or collections of essays on theirs and other authors' fictions (Hasan 2000). Such works promise to allow us, in Bhalla's words, to find "coherent explanations for the irrational passions", and in Hasan's, to provide authors with "a voice in the inconclusive debates on Independence and Partition."[7]

As reported by Jason Francisco, what arises in these works is the expression of vivid emotions on the one hand, and the striking differences between works written in the aftermath of Partition, and more recent, post-traumatic creations, on the other. If the former works convey raw emotions such as pain, anger, stupefaction, hatred or sadness, the most recent are inhabited by a feeling of nostalgia, an insatiable quest for the "Lost Home", testifying to what Urvashi Butalia has identified

---

[5] Butalia, *The Other Side of Silence*, 10.

[6] Jason Francisco, "In the Heat of Fratricide: The Literature of India's Partition Burning Freshly," in *Inventing Boundaries: Gender, Politics and the Partition of India*, ed. Mushirul Hasan (New Delhi: Oxford University Press, 2000), 371–393.

[7] Alok Bhalla, *Stories about the Partition of India*, 3 vols. (New Delhi: Indus, 1994), xxv; Mushirul Hasan, *India Partitioned: The Other Side of Freedom*, 2 vols. (New Delhi: Roli Book, 1995), 9.

as "the Long Shadow" of Partition.[8] These works, where the quest for
a lost space is crucial and where the recurrence of the metaphor of rootlessness is striking, offer a route into understanding the key place of literature in commemorating Partition in a landscape absent of physical
memorials. Trauma here is immediate and visceral, and memory located
in the body and in experience, expressed in a literary form.

REMEMBERING WOMEN

How do we approach the history of women in the context of the project of remembering and understanding Partition? The methods and
approaches discussed thus far have been central to this task: *The Other
Side of Silence* by Urvashi Butalia alternates between memory and
archives, constituted by both interviews and a number of historical
documents, while *Borders and Boundaries* (published in 1998, as was
Butalia's work) represents a feminist rereading of Partition by historians
Ritu Menon and Kamla Bhasin, to shed light on the role of women during Partition but also on their symbolic function in the construction of
the nation. Kamla Bhasin and Ritu Menon, in *Borders and Boundaries*,
both stress the ability of fiction to highlight the hidden histories of
Partition and to shape its social history: "Partition fiction has been a
far richer source both because it provides popular and astringent commentary on the politics of Partition and because, here and there, we
find women's voices, speaking for themselves."[9] These works encourage inquiry into the contribution of fiction to this history of women
and the ability of literature to take part in the elaboration of an alternative history of Partition. At the same time, Veena Das' *Life and Words*
(2006) has shown the way literature can contribute to the abstraction
of violence against women by conveying the metaphor of woman-as-
nation. This task is therefore a delicate one if one considers, like Veena
Das (or like Menon and Bhasin), that the representation of women
in Partition fictions is subservient to the great narrative of the nation,
and that the abductions, rapes and mutilations these works portray have

---

[8] See discussion, Urvashi Butalia, ed., *Partition: The Long Shadow* (New Delhi: Zubaan,
2015), ix.

[9] Kamla Bhasin and Ritu Menon, *Borders and Boundaries. Women in India's Partition*
(New Delhi: Kali for Women, 1998), 12.

been deprived of their realism in order to "reinstat[e] the nation as a pure and masculine space."[10] Besides, the prism of the history of women allows us also to qualify the capacity of fiction to become the privileged place for a popular history of Partition, as this so-called "popular" narrative remains dominated by male voices, while women are still represented as passive receptacles of violence. The popular history of Partition as shaped by fiction thus remains a history of the elites that should also be read against its grain. The issue of women during Partition also allows us to qualify the issue of the "Lost Home", which is a common place in Partition fiction. Indeed, much research has brought to light the complex relationship between woman and the notion of "home" and land in South Asia, where women are "owned" before they can own and belong themselves and where, consequently, the issue of exile and rootlessness is transformed.[11]

How can one thus articulate the history of women and a gendered memory of Partition through fiction? If the history of women is revealed in the popular memory of Partition explored in the historical material presented by Kamla Bhasin and Ritu Menon, how is this memory expressed in literature, which remains subservient to a masculine narrative of Partition? Which narrative or linguistic strategies may encourage this expression? In other words, can fiction really formulate a subaltern memory through a direct and empowered voice, that tells rather than being told?

In this regard, considering that most female characters in Partition fictions have not been given a subjective and independent voice,[12] I have prioritised women's narratives themselves, drawing on two texts written by female writers, both of whom have a more or less autobiographical dimension, both written in the aftermath of the Partition, both at the threshold of history as "romanticised" experiences. The first text is a novel, *Pinjar* (*The Skeleton*), written by Amrita Pritam and published in 1950, which recounts a history of Punjab from 1930 until about early 1948, through the stories of women who are

---

[10] Veena Das, *Life and Words. Violence and the Descent into the Ordinary* (Berkeley: University of California Press, 2006), 427.

[11] See in particular Ritu Menon, *No Woman's Land* (New Delhi: Woman Unlimited, 2004).

[12] See notably Jill Didur, *Unsettling Partition: Literature, Gender, Memory* (Toronto: University of Toronto Press, 2006).

victims of male violence; the second is Anis Kidwai's memoirs *Azadi ki chaon men* (translated into English as *In Freedom's Shade*, 2011), which were written in Urdu in 1949 but published only in 1974 (as is widely known, Anis Kidwai was a social worker who took an active part in the women's recovery campaign led by Mridula Sarabhai). Kidwai's memoirs, which open in September 1947 with her husband's death, narrate her commitment to Gandhi's campaigns and her actions in Delhi refugee camps, and are accompanied by a number of referential elements, such as (at least, in the English translation) original photographs of refugees, refugee camps and of some of the major political figures of Partition (Gandhi, Nehru, Mridula Sarabhai), as well as photographs of symbolic places or events connected with Partition: refugee camps, Nizamuddin Dargah in 1946, Maulana Azad's 1948 address at Jama Masjid and so on.

WRITING AN EMOTIONAL PARTITION

The depiction of the experience of Partition as a painful, even traumatic event can be considered as a common thread that guides us through these two accounts, in which the expression of emotions both inhabits and modifies the narration. The issue of the complex relationship between memory and history has of course been widely discussed by historians, notably in order to emphasise not so much the limits of memory as its contribution to the elaboration of an alternative and social history.[13] In *Remembering Partition* (2001), Gyanendra Pandey observes that regarding Partition, "historians' history works to produce the 'truth' of the traumatic, genocidal violence of Partition and to elide it at the same time" (45). Indeed he refers to the "denial" of the official histories of Partition that, according to him, need to be deconstructed, and stresses the urgent need for a "different History" to be written. Similarly, in "The Prose of Otherness" (1994), he identifies a "language problem" raised by the historian's representation of Partition, which fails to describe pain and suffering. He thus discusses the issue

---

[13] See notably Paul Veyne, *Comment on écrit l'histoire?* (Paris: Seuil, 1971); Paul Ricoeur *La Mémoire, l'histoire, l'oubli* (Paris: Seuil, 2000); and Hayden White, *Metahistory. The Historical Imagination in Nineteenth-Century Europe* (Baltimore: John Hopkins University Press, 1973).

of the historian's analytical position: how can one be objective while also properly depicting this violence?

Pandey is centrally concerned with the issue of objectivity, as are a number of historians, as what is at stake is the description of the experience of thousands of men and women whose lives were brutally disrupted by Partition. He suggests that "historiography has been loath to examine the massive violence that accompanied (and constituted) Partition, and the experiences and emotions of the people involved in or affected by it."[14] He decries the disinterest within historical writings in the popular construction and thus the social history of Partition, and argues that violence and brutality are only taken into consideration in the field of fiction, in literature and films. Pandey writes: "That there are, however, other ways of constructing the memory of Partition and other themes that have been suppressed and (at least, publicly) forgotten is evidenced by a whole range of writings, fictional and non-fictional", where one may hear "marginal voices and memories, forgotten dreams and signs of resistance."[15] And notably, he suggests, the expression of emotions is a crucial component of the narration of the experience of Partition.

Indeed, Pandey does resort to fiction as it can supplement and qualify historians' history: Saadat Hasan Manto's stories, as well as Anis Kidwai's *Azadi ki chaon men* can shed light on the "truth of Partition", as Pandey shows. He draws on Kidwai's memoirs for informational purposes, as a historical archive. Although he doesn't take into account the emotional aspect of these texts, he uses them to counterbalance the principle of rationality which governs the "scientific" writing of history, quoting Manto's story *Toba Tek Singh*. Similarly, this question of rationality is at the heart of Kidwai's discourse, notably regarding the recovery of abducted women.

MONTAGE AND METAPHORS AS A TESTIMONY

As Pandey highlights, emotion is a device that is commonly used in literature and film to convey great human tragedies and to design a popular history that is too often left aside by historians. Everyone has in mind the visual or poetic strategies and the imaginary associations

---

[14] Pandey, *Remembering*, 205.

[15] Pandey, *Remembering*, 215, 214.

elaborated by fiction or cinema to allow the reader/spectator to experience in some way the tragic destiny of refugees, of separated families, of the victims of collective tragedies. The analysis of images as an emotional vehicle of history is at the heart of Georges Didi-Huberman's seminal work, and notably in the last volume in his series *The Eye of History* (*L'Oeil de l'histoire*), entitled *Peoples in Tears, Peoples in Arms* (*Peuples en larmes, peuples en larmes*, 2016), in which one immediately identifies the close articulation between emotion and historical narrative. Analysing Sergei Eisenstein's films, and more specifically *Battleship Potemkin* (1925) which portrays the Russian Revolution of 1905, Georges Didi-Huberman shows the way in which the use of "montage" (editing) allows the viewer to "reach pathos through movement",[16] quoting Eisenstein himself. "Tragedy", Didi-Huberman writes, "is possible in cinema because images themselves are gifted with pathos, can fraternize together and lift together, and this is what we call editing". For Eisenstein, Didi-Huberman argues, "the historical facts never go without concomitant social affects that can be supported only by formal editing specifically built for this: the pathos of the event is strengthened, multiplied by the pathetic construction." He concludes that editing is not the negation of the phenomenon, but on the contrary "the best method to make it sensitive, recognize and promote it."[17]

In her article "Transactions in the Construction of Pain" (1996), Veena Das also underlines the way editing strategies can be used to formulate what history does not tell. Referring to "Fundanen", a story written by Saadat Hasan Manto in the aftermath of Partition, she shows that metaphors can be used to express the unspeakable of both violence and its effects. In this story, a woman sitting in front of her mirror draws incoherent sketches on her body that accompany equally incoherent speech: both language and images fail to capture the reality of violence, but the scene itself as a metaphor of this violence can formulate an intimate history of Partition. As Veena Das writes in the concluding section of this fascinating article:

> It was on the register of the imaginary that the question of what could constitute the passion of those who occupied this unspeakable and

---

[16] Georges Didi-Huberman, *Peuples en larmes, peuples en larmes* (Paris: Editions de Minuit, 2016), 235.

[17] Ibid, 236.

unhearable zone was given shape. The zone between the two deaths that the women had to occupy did not permit of any speech, for what 'right' words could be spoken against the wrong that had been done them.[18]

She thus skilfully justifies the use of metaphors as the only appropriate language with which to tell of both violence and the experience of violence. The metaphor becomes an efficient historiographical device which validates and draws on fiction and "poetics" as a vehicle of an historical experience—something historians' history does not allow.

Similarly, Partition's violence in Amrita Pritam's *Pinjar* is mainly expressed through images and comparisons. Like in Manto's story, these images bear witness to the internalisation of suffering in the female body which, in Amrita Pritam's words, has become the paper on which the history of the nation is written: "My story is the story of women in every country, and many more in number are these stories which are not written on paper, but are written on the bodies and minds of women".[19] *Pinjar* tells the tragic story of Pooro, a young Hindu woman who was abducted a few years before Partition and then forcibly married to a Muslim boy as a result of a vendetta between their families. Throughout its heartbreaking narrative, the novel follows the tragic story of Punjab's women, told to Pooro by the victims themselves: Kammo, an orphan exploited by her aunt; Taro, married by her parents to a man who was already married to another woman; the "Mad Woman", who dies in childbirth and whose baby is adopted by Pooro; a young Hindu girl, who has been the victim of multiple rapes during the Partition riots; and Lajo, Pooro's brother's wife, who is abducted, and then saved by Pooro, who manages to bring her back to her family. At the end of the novel, Pooro defies national and religious boundaries: although she has been "found" by her Hindu family, she decides to stay in Pakistan with her husband, her abductor, and the novel ends with the following words pronounced by Pooro: "Whether one is a Hindu girl or a Muslim one, whosoever reaches her destination, she carries along my soul also" (50).

The expression of pain accompanies Pooro's story in a series of metaphors that makes the female body a place of both suffering and disgust,

<hr />

[18] Veena Das, "Language and Body: Transactions in the Construction of Pain," *Daedalus* 125, no. 1, Social Suffering (Winter, 1996): 87.

[19] Amrita Pritam, quoted in Susie Tharu and K. Lalitha (ed.), *Women Writing in India. Vol II: The Twentieth Century* (New Delhi: Oxford University Press, 1993), 162.

two intense emotions that govern the novel. For instance, Pooro perceives and experiences her pregnancy as an unbearable event, comparing the foetus to a worm inside a rotten fruit: "If only she could take the worm out of her womb and fling it away! Pick it out with her nails as if it were a thorn, pluck it off as if it were a maggot or a leech!" (1).

This section follows another where, peeling beans, Pooro suddenly finds a worm on her finger. Disgusted by this worm, she shakes her hand to get rid of it and then presses her hands on her heart. The feeling of disgust is thus internalised and embodied in Pooro's unborn child (alternately compared to a thorn, a leech and a maggot) and her own body carrying this child, as the "result" of her forced marriage to her abductor.

Similarly, the rise of violence is experienced by Pooro as an intimate experience, in another sequence:

> Then it began in her own village. The Hindus moved into one home for safety. They hoarded grain and provisions in the courtyard and no man or woman stirred out. They were like animals in a cage. Only the Muslims roamed about free. They broke into the homes of the Hindus and occupied them [...] Pooro's village looked deserted. The only non-Muslim left in it were the three charred corpses in the street. In two days, the crows and pie-dogs had torn away the flesh. Only the skeletons remained in front of the burnt-down house.

> That was not all. Pooro felt like glass splinters in her eyes. She saw a band of a dozen or more goondas pushing a young girl before them. She had not a stitch of clothing on her person. The goondas beat drums and danced about the naked girl. Pooro could not find out where they came from and where there were going.[20]

Here, emotions arise from the internalisation of violence and pain. This section opens with a number of referential elements: a precise date (15 August 1947), a precise place (Gujrat district), precise elements belonging to the collective imaginary of Partition ("the Hindus in the villages next to theirs began to flee"; "They left their cows tethered"; "Others were found murdered many miles away"). In the second section, the space is gradually reduced to that of Pooro's village ("In her own village"), and

---

[20] Amrita Pritam, *The Skeleton, Followed by That Man* (New Delhi: Sterling Publishers, [1950] 1987), 85, 86.

violence is replaced by fear and threat ("They were like animals in a cage"; "They broke into the homes of the Hindus and occupied them"), in other words a more subjective expression of violence. Moreover, fear and threat are accompanied by a series of images that aim at amplifying them: the deserted village, the crows and the dogs as necrophagous animals, the skeleton. Starting with the expression "That was not all", the third section seems to announce the paroxysm of violence, but interestingly, this violence is metaphoric and concerns Pooro's body: the unbearable pain in the narrative of Partition's violence is internalised ("Pooro felt like glass splinters in her eyes"), and gives rise to a feeling of guilt and shame ("It was a crime to be born a girl"), which intensifies the sense of that violence.

In order to tell the history of the margins of Partition, Amrita Pritam, who felt concerned about both the tragic destiny of Punjab overall and the equally tragic condition of women during Partition, promotes a language of the margins: the rhetorics of emotions, metaphors and allegories.[21] In other words, this is a language that does not partake in the scientific rhetoric of history, but in the literary rhetoric of fiction.

ANIS KIDWAI: PARTITION, SELF-NARRATIVE AND EMOTIONS

In a different vein altogether, Anis Kidwai's memoirs appear to provide a detailed account of historical events with a large amount of referential information. Her work, however, combines a referential narrative with an intimate exploration and the spontaneous expression of emotions, as if the latter might allow her to retrieve the "truth" of history. This "truth" has received considerable reconsideration: a range of theorists have proposed that history acts as a narrative based on a regime of fictionalisation.[22] Jenkins proposes, in *Re-Thinking History*, that "history is a discourse, a language game: within it 'truth' and similar expressions are devices to open, regulate and shut down interpretation [...] such truths

---

[21] See notably her well-known poem "Aaj Aakhan Waris Shaah nu" ("Today I call Waris Shah") where, addressing the Punjabi poet Waris Shah, she refers to "a million daughters" of Punjab: Amrita Pritam, "Today, I Call Waris Shah, Speak from Your Grave," in *Memories of a Fragmented Nation. Rewriting the Histories of India's Partition*, ed. Mushirul Hasan (Edinburgh: Edinburgh University Press, 1998).

[22] Ricoeur's *Histoire et vérité* (2001), Paul Veyne's *Comment on écrit l'Histoire?* (1974) and Hayden White's *Metahistory* (1973).

are really 'useful fictions' that are in discourse by virtue of power (some-body has to put and keep them there) and power uses the term 'truth' to exercise control: the regimes of truth."[23] This has a direct relevance to the representation of Partition; Pandey has argued that the historian's history of Partition "works to produce the 'Truth' of the [...] violence of Partition and to elide it at the same time."[24] The "truth" of Kidwai's work, therefore, is found elsewhere.

Whereas Kidwai's narrative is a historical account, it nevertheless does not follow a protocol of objectivity. As a matter of fact, in the English translation, the first chapter is entitled: "I gather once again the pieces of my shattered heart". On the sidelines of referential information, the narrative bears witness to the anxiety of both the Indian people facing Partition, and the author herself, whose husband, a local administrator based in Mussorie, bravely remained there in the midst of fire and blood. The intimate frame therefore mingles with the historical account, until Anis' husband's death at the end of the chapter; which, we understand, is the event that triggers her commitment to the movement led by Gandhi, as she recalls in a passionate mode:

> Now, when everything was over, my shattered heart imploded. For a moment, I was ablaze in a passion for vengeance but soon I regained control. Where thousands have lost their lives, he was just one. Was it not solace enough that he had died unsullied? He did not take another's life; he did not commit cruelty; he was not responsible for the destruction of another. Whatever God and faith asked of him, he submitted; whatever his dues in service of humanity, he settled. (16)

She thus describes both collective and personal feelings: collective, with a "we" that alternately refers to the people of the new Indian nation and to the Muslim community, for example in "anxieties and tribulations" of the Indian people (1); "anger mounted in our hearts" (4); "we were happy" (4). Examples of personal feelings include: "My heart would clutch with foreboding" (3); "Lifted my head with pride" (5); "I went searching for happiness", 6; "This was too painful" (6); "Anxiety about Mussorie consumed me" (9); "Whenever I think about those times, I want to take my own life" (11); "I tried unsuccessfully to quieten my

---

[23] Keith Jenkins, *Re-Thinking History* (London: Routledge, 1991), 32.
[24] Pandey, *Remembering*, 45.

anxious heart" (15); "The wound in my heart would fester forever" (16); and "The sorrow of my life" (18). Conditioned by this first chapter, the whole narrative is overwhelming because of the dual nature (both collective and individual) of the tragedy that Anis Kidwai narrates: she successively evokes feelings such as deep sadness, despair, doubt, shame, but also pity, joy, wonderment, hope, empathy and even love. She thus writes as a conclusion: "I had a heart that could feel" (288).

If, unlike Amrita Pritam, Anis Kidwai does not use metaphors, the expression of emotions circulates through emphatic expressions and participates in the development of the historical narrative. Besides, these emotions are accompanied, even nurtured, by numerous quotations from poems (by Mirza Ghalib, Mohammad Iqbal, Hafiz Shirazi, etc.), that emphasise them:

Charming young men with innocent faces left schools and colleges in search of matchsticks, kerosene, bricks and knives, as amassing these was more important than seeking knowledge. And then,

> *ghar jala saamne,*
> *aur ham-se bujhaya na gaya*
> The house was ablaze before our eyes
> But we could not douse the flames
>
> Mirza Ghalib

This was the India of 1947–48, and it is a portrait of this I wish to sketch for you. But not because I want readers to gaze upon these scenes in horrified fascination, but because:

> *taaza khwaahi dashtan gar daagh haye seena ra*
> *gaahe gaahe baaz khwan en qissa-e-pareena ra*
> If you wish the scars in your heart to remain fresh
> Then, from time to time, revisit this old tale afresh.
> Maulana Mohammad Ayyub Surti Qasmi in
Muqqadamah Tarikh-e-Gujarat[25]

---

[25] Anis Kidwai, *In Freedom's Shade* (New Delhi: Penguins, [1974] 2011), xvii.

I also touched my eyes to the takht Bapu used to sit on, the cloth that covered it. But there was no comfort, no solace, then or later. On the takht, leaning on the bolster was not Bapu but a large picture of him, but I couldn't summon the courage to look at it. In Iqbal's words:

> *zauq-e-huzoor dar jahaan rasm-e-sanamagri nihad*
> *ishq fareb mi dihad jaan-aummeedwar ra*
> Pleasure in presence has established the practice of idolatry
> Love deceives the desirous soul.
>
> Mohammed Iqbal[26]

These quotations certainly reflect a wish to make the historical account a literary one, but also to penetrate and touch the collective imaginary of Urdu speakers and, as Anis Kidwai writes, to provoke or share emotions with the reader through the reference to a well-known cultural heritage that promotes feelings and affects. The rhetoric of emotions, whether collective or individual, reflects Anis Kidwai's willingness to build an alternative history of Partition.

A SUBALTERN LANGUAGE

This alternative narrative of the history of Partition, as inhabited by emotions, can be perceived as women's sociolect as actors of history and not as mere objects. The rhetoric of intimacy and inner suffering should not be understood as an essential characteristic of female discourse, but rather as an attempt to narrate Partition through its *experience*, which, for women, was the experience of pain.[27] If, for women's history scholars such as Ritu Menon and Kamla Bhasin, the goal is to "restore women to history and to restore our history to women", as they write, quoting Joan Kelly, they also aim to show that this experience is specific and differs from men's, as women had to accommodate both real and symbolic violence on a major scale, as shown by the large-scale abduction of

---

[26] Ibid., 138.

[27] As it has been done in the 1970–1980, in the field of Women Studies. See notably Hélène Cixous, "Le rire de la Méduse" (Paris, *L'Arc 61*, 1975); Béatrice Didier, *L'Ecriture-femme* (Paris: Presses Universitaires de France, 1981).

women and the large women's-recovery campaigns.[28] In this regard, this history of women, highlighted by both Amrita Pritam and Anis Kidwai, strikingly bears witness to the exploitation, reification and commodification of female bodies, and of the appropriation of female voices and stories.

A subaltern narrative is thus constructed by means of an autonomous subaltern language, which stems from the minoritisation of an experience in history. The reappropriation of a stigma (pain) as a federative pattern in order to articulate contestation results from what Gyanendra Pandey has identified as a strategy for drawing on difference as a motif of oppression, the same one adopted by Dalit, Queer or "Negritude" movements, for example, in which the denomination of the group itself bears witness to this oppression:

> This is not a *politics* that flows from cultural difference (somehow already constituted), but rather a culture that flows from political difference—and an alternative political perspective. Consider the political claim that inheres in the very act of naming a political assemblage as 'dalit', 'black', 'African American', *adivasi*, aboriginal, First Nation, 'gay', 'lesbian' (not to mention LGBTQ), and for that matter even 'women'. What this signals is the history and politics of a *becoming*, and with that, the search of an ethics—a position from which to act without fear, to demand one's right, to live.[29]

Stigma thus allows a subaltern language and culture to be deployed. For Pandey, this reappropriation is of course undertaken through political mobilisation and the constitution of a social group on the basis of the denunciation of oppression, which was not the case for abducted and/or raped women during Partition. It remains, however, that the narrative of oppression is produced by these women, as it is produced in Dalit poetry for example, by highlighting both oppression and the pain that it causes, which becomes the heart of a rhetoric and a language of the oppressed. Interestingly, as Pandey shows, emotion and experience are located at the centre of this discourse and this language, and their formulation is perceived as an *appropriate*, relevant language with which to narrate the history of women during Partition.

---

[28] Bhasin and Menon, *Borders and Boundaries*, 9.

[29] Gyanendra Pandey, ed., *Subalternity and Difference. Investigations from the North and the South* (New York: Routledge, 2011), 16–17.

Works Cited

Bhalla, Alok. *Stories About the Partition of India*, 3 vols. New Delhi: Indus, 1994.

Bhalla, Alok. "Objectifying Troubling Memories. An Interview with Bhisham Sahni." In *Inventing Boundaries: Gender, Politics and the Partition of India*, edited by Mushirul Hasan, 338–350. New Delhi: Oxford University Press, 2000.

Bhalla, Alok. *Partition Dialogues*. New Delhi: Oxford University Press, 2006.

Bhasin, Kamla, and Menon, Ritu. *Borders and Boundaries. Women in India's Partition*. New Delhi: Kali for Women, 1998.

Butalia, Urvashi. *The Other Side of Silence. Voices from the Partition of India*. Durham: Duke University Press, 1998.

Butalia, Urvashi. *Partition: The Long Shadow*. New Delhi: Zubaan, 2015.

Cixous, Hélène. "Le rire de la Méduse." Paris, *L'Arc* 61, 1975.

Cowasjee, Saros, and Duggal, K. L. *Orphans of the Storm: Stories of the Partition of India*. New Delhi: UBS, 1995.

Das, Veena. *Life and Words. Violence and the Descent into the Ordinary*. Berkeley: University of California Press, 2006.

Das, Veena. "Language and Body: Transactions in the Construction of Pain," *Daedalus* 125, no. 1, Social Suffering (Winter, 1996): 67–91.

Didier, Béatrice. *L'Ecriture-femme*. Paris: Presses Universitaires de France, 1981.

Didi-Huberman, Georges. *Peuples en larmes, peuples en larmes*. Paris: Editions de Minuit, 2016.

Didur, Jill. *Unsettling Partition: Literature, Gender, Memory*. Toronto: University of Toronto Press, 2006.

Francisco, Jason. "In the Heat of Fratricide: The Literature of India's Partition Burning Freshly." In *Inventing Boundaries: Gender, Politics and the Partition of India*, edited by Mushirul Hasan, 371–393. New Delhi: Oxford University Press, 2000.

Hasan, Mushirul. *India Partitioned: The Other Side of Freedom*, 2 vols. New Delhi: Roli Book, 1995.

Hasan, Mushirul. *Inventing Boundaries: Gender, Politics and the Partition of India*. New Delhi: Oxford University Press, 2000.

Jalal, Ayesha. *The Pity of Partition. Manto's Life, Times, and Work across the India-Pakistan Divide*. Princeton: Princeton University Press, 2013.

Jenkins, Keith. *Re-Thinking History*. London: Routledge, 1991.

Kabir, Ananya Jahanara. *Partition's Post-Amnesias*. New Delhi: Women Unlimited, 2013.

Kamra, Sukheshi. "Engaging Traumatic Histories. The 1947 Partition of India in Collective Memory." In *Partition. The Long Shadow*, edited by Urvashi Butalia, 155–177. New Delhi Zubaan, 2015.

Kidwai, Anis. *In Freedom's Shade*. New Delhi: Penguins, [1974] 2011.

MacMullen, Ramsey. *Feelings in History, Ancient and Modern*. Claremont: Regina Books, 2015.

Menon, Ritu. *No Woman's Land*. New Delhi: Woman Unlimited, 2004.

Pandey, Gyanendra. "The Prose of Otherness." In *Subaltern Studies VIII*, ed. David Arnold and David Hardiman, 188–225. New Delhi: Oxford University Press, 1994.

Pandey, Gyanendra. *Remembering Partition: Violence, Nationalism and History in India*. Cambridge: Cambridge University Press, 2001.

Pandey, Gyanendra, ed. *Subalternity and Difference. Investigations from the North and the South*. New York: Routledge, 2011.

Pernau, Margrit, and Jordheim, Helge, ed. *Civilizing Emotions. Concepts in Nineteenth Century Asia and Europe*. Oxford: Oxford University Press, 2015.

Pritam, Amrita. *The Skeleton, followed by That Man*. New Delhi: Sterling Publishers, [1950] 1987.

Pritam, Amrita. "Today, I Call waris Shah, Speak from Your Grave." In *Memories of a Fragmented Nation. Rewriting the Histories of India's Partition*, edited by Mushirul Hasan. Edinburgh: Edinburgh University Press, 1998.

Ricoeur, Paul. *La Mémoire, l'histoire, l'oubli*. Paris: Seuil, 2000.

Ricoeur, Paul. *Histoire et vérité*. Paris: Seuil, 2001.

Talbot, Ian. *The Epicentre of Violence. Partition Voices and Memories from Amritsar*. Delhi: Permanent Black, 2006.

Tharu, Susie, and K. Lalitha ed. *Women Writing in India. Vol II: The Twentieth Century*. New Delhi: Oxford University Press, 1993.

Veyne, Paul. *Comment on écrit l'histoire?* Paris: Seuil, 1971.

Vincent-Buffault, Anne. *Histoire des larmes: XVIIIe-XIXe siècles*. Paris: Rivages, 1986.

White, Hayden. *Metahistory. The Historical Imagination in Nineteenth-Century Europe*. Baltimore: John Hopkins University Press, 1973.

PART III

Specters of Partition within the Lived Present

CHAPTER 9

The Gulbarg Memorial and the Problem of Memory

Heba Ahmed

Fifteen years after the anti-Muslim pogrom in Gujarat 2002, the Gulbarg Society massacre continues to generate significant political controversy. It has acquired a gruesome spectacle-like status, through the gory nature of the violence perpetrated, the profile of Ehsan Jafri and his brutal killing, the persecution of activists like Teesta Setalvad who have been involved in related legal claims and Zakia Jafri's continuing fight against Narendra Modi. The Gulbarg Society massacre was also the subject of a

This chapter has been written on the basis of fieldwork conducted in Ahmedabad and Surat over several weeks in 2016–2017. I am grateful to Nishrin Jafri, Najid Hussain, Tanveer Jafri, Duraiyya Jafri, Aniqua Jafri, Saira Sandhi, Salim Sandhi, Rupa Mody, Dara Mody, Imteyaz Khan Pathan, Shama Khan Pathan, Qasam Mansuri, Noorjehan and Shakila for sharing their testimonies with me. Special thanks to Nirjhari and Pratik Sinha for providing accommodation for my Ahmedabad stay. I am also deeply grateful to Dr. Anne Murphy and to Dr. Churnjeet Mahn for their input on the essay as it evolved. As always, I have eternal gratitude for my younger sister, Sana Ahmed, and my mother, Farah Anwar, for always being so generous with their help.

H. Ahmed (✉)
Jawaharlal Nehru University, Delhi, India
e-mail: heba.ahmed.1610@gmail.com

film, *Parzania*, which was temporarily banned in Gujarat; cinema owners refused to screen it. The film focuses on the Pithawala family, who are shown to be Parsi residents of a close-knit housing society which represents Gulbarg. The film shows how Parzan Pithawala disappears in the massacre which followed as a consequence of the Godhra train burning, and portrays his parents' struggle to find any trace of him. The Parsi family depicted in the film was based on Dara and Rupa Mody, who lost their son in the Gulbarg Society massacre. The end credits of *Parzania* included a missing-person notice for Azhar Mody, who remains missing to this day.

When *Parzania* was banned in Gujarat, the head of an association of multiplex owners said that now that there was peace in Gujarat, people should not be reminded of the "riots".[1] This reluctance to remember the pogrom was informed by a strong belief in the motif of development or *vikaas* in the aftermath of violence. The Chief Minister of Gujarat (now the Indian Prime Minister), Narendra Modi, presented his term of office as heralding a "Vibrant Gujarat" which promised a climate of investment and economic growth. The annual Vibrant Gujarat Summit was initiated in 2003 under his aegis. It was held in Ahmedabad and Surat—two cities that had been convulsed by violence in 2002—and received favourable responses and participation from industrialists and various chambers of commerce. This impulse to forget the large-scale killing and displacement of Muslims, as Leela Fernandes has said, "refers to a political discursive process in which specific marginalised social groups are rendered invisible and forgotten within the dominant national political culture."[2] As Fernandes also notes, "The politics of forgetting is not merely an inadvertent process of particular locations being left out of economic globalisation. It is a political project that seeks to produce a sanitised vision of the economic benefits of globalisation."[3] The urge to forget anti-Muslim violence does not arise from the rhetoric of development alone. It has also been effected through the cultural nationalism of Hindutva, which exculpated the conscience of

---

[1] Henry Chu, "Film about Massacre banned in India State: LA Director Had Friend Who Lost Son in Hindu Slaughter," *Los Angeles Times*, 25 February 2007, http://www.sfgate.com/politics/article/Film-about-massacre-banned-in-India-state-L-A-2646206.php.

[2] Leela Fernandes, "The Politics of Forgetting: Class Politics, State Power and the Restructuring of Urban Space in India," *Urban Studies* 41, no. 12: 2415–3240 (November 2004), 2416, http://citeseerx.ist.psu.edu/viewdoc/download?doi=10.1.1.502.3637&rep=rep1&type=pdf.

[3] Ibid., 2416.

Gujaratis by constant references to Gujarati collective pride or *asmita*. In this, the erasure of violence in 2002 parallels the treatment of the foundational violence of Partition in 1947, which was subsumed within the making of triumphant national imaginaries in both India and Pakistan.

But the politics of forgetting does not remain uncontested. The proposed Gulbarg Society memorial is a refutation of an amnesia imposed upon the majority, of a wilful forgetting of violence that was committed against the minority. Furthermore, the site of the Gulbarg Society has already been converted into a space for individual remembrance and an arena for the collective memory of survivors. The memorialisation of those Muslims killed in the Gulbarg Society parallels those practices associated with the making of Partition memories. The memorialisation of those who are killed in mass violence, especially minority lives, is a struggle against the state's attempts at the erasure of memories. To remember violence implies an acknowledgement of the vulnerability of minority lives, which is consistently denied by the majoritarian politics of the state. The purpose of narratives around people's memories of Partition is to show how the creation of nation states and the etching of borders leads to an incalculable loss of life. The Gulbarg Society massacre indicates the persistence of "borders" in locations where intercommunity relations have been deliberately antagonised by the state. In the nationalist discourse, those on the "other" side of the border are vilified, just as the nation on the other side of the international boundary line of India is hated. But the memories of those killed at Gulbarg lead to a questioning of the existence of borders and the permanence of Partition.

Locating the 2002 Pogrom within the Narrative of Partition Memories

Aata hai yaad mujhko, guzra hua zamana.
Woh baagh ki bahaare, woh sab ka chechahana.

[I remember those days of a lost past,
The spring of that garden, the songs of all the people.]
            Allama Iqbal, 'Ek Parinde ki Fariyaad' (A Bird's Plaint)[4]

The opening scene of *Parzania* shows Parzan in a classroom, where the teacher is giving a lecture about Partition and how it was followed

---

[4] Translation by author.

by the establishment of a secular democracy in India. This is immediately followed by a scene in which Muslims are shown to be celebrating the victory of the Pakistani cricket team against the Indians. Members of the "Parishad"[5] are then seen conspiring among each other. "They want to see fireworks? We'll show them fireworks!" Parzan himself is stopped on his way to school and asked if he is Hindu. The violence gradually building in the city is contrasted with the dream world which Parzan imagines with his sister, Dilshad: the world of "Parzania", where "the buildings are made of chocolate, the rivers are made of kheer, and the mountains are made of ice-cream". Parzan's imaginary arcadia is also reflected in the harmony of the neighbourhood in which he and his family live. Located in Behrampura, it is a cluster of houses with cordial, affectionate relations among its residents. When violence breaks out and armed mobs storm the gates of the housing society, it is a tragedy not just for individual Muslims and Parsis (both as religious minorities), but also a collective loss of shared living. The housing society of *Parzania*, located in Behrampura, is a symbol of the Gulbarg Society, in Asarwa-Chamanpura of Ahmedabad.

As Priya Kumar writes, "The ghost of Partition continues to haunt the collective memory of the subcontinent in the repeated instances of violence that are mirrored in 'other' places on the subcontinent."[6] Instances of anti-Muslim pogroms and massacres in post-Partition India always include a reference to Pakistan. The killings of Muslims in Gujarat in 2002 were sparked off by the burning of the S-6 coach on the Sabarmati Express on 27 February 2002 at Godhra. More than 50 *kar-sevaks*[7] who were aboard the train were killed; they were on their way back from Ayodhya. It was alleged by the Sangh Parivar[8] that this crime against the *kar-sevaks* was premeditated by Muslims in Godhra in collaboration with the ISI (the intelligence service) of Pakistan. Even Narendra Modi, then Chief Minister of Gujarat, delivered a speech

---

[5] The Parishad stands for the Vishwa Hindu Parishad, a right-wing Hindu organisation in India advocating the ideology of Hindutva, established in 1964.

[6] Priya Kumar, "Testimonies of Loss and Memory," *Interventions* 1, no. 2 (2006): 201–215; 215, http://dx.doi.org/10.1080/13698019900510311.

[7] A *kar-sevak* refers to someone who serves a religious cause (from the Hindi word seva meaning "service"). Hindutva activists in India are called *kar-sevaks*.

[8] The Sangh Parivar refers to the family of right-wing Hindu nationalist organisations which have been established by members of the Rashtriya Swayamsevak Sangh (RSS).

which was broadcast on television, in which he condemned those who were responsible for Godhra and warned that they would be punished.[9] The widespread killings of Muslims which followed was termed a "spontaneous" response to a heinous action. Narendra Modi popularised the action–reaction trope, thereby instigating a desire for revenge and legitimising its manifestation. However, even today, the exact details of how the Godhra fire was started remain shrouded in mystery. A report by Mohinder Singh Dahiya, then assistant director of the Forensic Studies Laboratory (FSL) at Gandhinagar, Gujarat, has debunked the narrative of the coach being set alight by an angry mob of Muslims which had gathered at Godhra railway station. The report concluded that the coach was set on fire by someone "standing in the passage of the compartment near seat number 72, using a container with a wide opening about 60 litres of inflammable liquid has been poured and then a fire has been started in the bogie."[10] In 2006, the Justice Banerjee inquiry report stated that the fire on the Sabarmati Express was the result of an accident, and not a deliberate act.[11] Despite the dubious nature of the crime, Modi described Godhra as "a pre-planned conspiracy of collective terrorism".[12] As Siddharth Varadarajan writes, "To blame terrorists for the Godhra attack was his less than subtle way of putting the blame on Muslims as a whole."[13] Many of the survivors of the 2002 pogrom have testified that Muslims were condemned as "Pakistanis" and asked to leave India and go to Pakistan. The documentary *The Final Solution* by Rakesh Sharma portrays this.[14] By identifying the Muslim as the

---

[9] Narendra Modi speech after Godhra incident, 2002, https://www.youtube.com/watch?v=4CiuBBKJ30Q.

[10] Mohan Guruswamy, "15 Years After Godhra, We Still Don't Know Who Lit the Fire," *Hindustan Times*, 27 February 2017, http://www.hindustantimes.com/analysis/15-years-after-the-godhra-we-still-don-t-know-who-lit-the-fire/story-vkeZowN2nhvVkAJP-ZAPntN.html.

[11] "Godhra Train Fire Accidental: Banerjee Report," *The Times of India*, 4 March 2006, http://timesofindia.indiatimes.com/india/Godhra-train-fire-accidental-Banerjee-report/articleshow/1437742.cms.

[12] Quoted in Siddharth Varadarajan, *Gujarat: The Making of a Tragedy* (New Delhi: Penguin Books), 7.

[13] Ibid.

[14] These statements of survivors, of being asked to go to Pakistan, have been narrated to the author, during interviews with survivors in Naroda Patiya. *The Final Solution*, dir. Rakesh Sharma (2004).

jihadi conspirator, the Hindutva regime created the figure of the unpatriotic, disloyal Muslim whose death was necessary to affirm Gujarati pride or *asmita*. But the urge to demand loyalty from Muslims in India and to highlight their putative disloyalty is not new; it has existed since Partition and the creation of Pakistan. As Gyanendra Pandey has argued in his essay, "Can a Muslim be an Indian?", Partition was "the moment of the congealing of new identities, relations, and histories, or of their being thrown into question once again."[15] Muslims were the numerical minority in independent India; but they were not seen as naturally loyal citizens. After all, Pakistan had been formed as a result of the Muslim demand for a separate state. Therefore, those Muslims who had remained in India would have to "demonstrate the sincerity of their choice: they had to prove that they were loyal to India and, hence, worthy of Indian citizenship."[16] However, this demand for proof of loyalty was not made of Hindus. As Pandey writes, "'Hindu' or 'Indian' was an irrelevant distinction; the terms were practically interchangeable."[17]

This commonsensical notion that Indian Muslims are insufficiently Indian, because they were responsible for the division of India, ignores one crucial fact: that India had been declared to consist of two nations by Veer Savarkar in his presidential address at the annual session of the Hindu Mahasabha in 1937.[18] This was three years before the Muslim League propounded its two-nation theory. Indian nationalist ideology has elided this fact. This selective memory of who was behind the demand for two nations has resulted in Muslims becoming perpetual scapegoats of patriotism. The stereotype of the unpatriotic, anti-national Muslim feeds into every occurrence of violence against Muslims. The majoritarian impulse to ask minorities to constantly prove their loyalty arises out of what Arjun Appadurai calls "predatory identities",[19] an idea

---

[15] Gyanendra Pandey, "Can a Muslim be an Indian?," *Comparative Studies in Society and History* 41, no. 4 (1999): 612.

[16] Ibid., 611.

[17] Ibid.

[18] Mohammad Mujeeb, "The Partition of India in Retrospect," in *India's Partition: Process, Strategy and Mobilisation*, 403–415, ed. Mushirul Hasan (New Delhi: Oxford University Press, 2001), 413.

[19] Arjun Appadurai, *Fear of Small Numbers: An Essay on the Geography of Anger* (Durham and London: Duke University Press, 2006), 50.

which he uses to explain the conundrum of how minorities—which by definition consist of small numbers—become "objects of fear and rage". The figure of the "other" is delineated through the dynamics of contrasting identities and stereotyping, as a necessary prerequisite to demarcate the notion of a "we". Appadurai uses the term "predatory identities" to refer to "those identities whose social construction and mobilisation require the extinction of other, proximate social categories, defined as threats to the very existence of some group defined as a 'we'".[20] The conversion of an "ethnos" into a modern nation state is premised upon the formation of predatory identities; predatory identities are usually majoritarian identities inasmuch as they are based on the claims of "a threatened majority". Appadurai suggests that every majoritarianism— Nazism in Germany, Hindutva in India, the "sons of the soil" ideology in Malaysia, exclusionary ideologies of citizenship in Europe—portends genocide, since it is ineluctably linked to singularity and the aspiration of national purity and wholeness.

The trauma of Partition in 1947 is only selectively remembered, but it is relived in every incident of mass violence that results in frenzied killings and displacement of minorities. Since Partition is remembered as the consequence of the culpability of Muslims and the role of the Congress and the Hindu Mahasabha in it is forgotten, genocidal violence against Muslims is seen as the unfinished business of Partition. As Suvir Kaul writes, "Partition remains the unspoken horror of our time. But not quite unspoken, for each time Indians are killed in the name of religion, each time a pogrom is orchestrated, memories of Partition resurface."[21] "Kaul continues, each time we teach the story of Partition in order to demonstrate Jinnah's guilt or the culpability of the Muslim League, and ignore the role played by religious chauvinists within the Congress or other political and social organisations, we tell a tale that deepens the divide signified by Partition."[22]

The question that arises, then, is how is Partition remembered? On the fiftieth anniversary of Partition, scholars like Mushirul Hasan argued that the official history of Partition had concerned itself only with the "high

---

[20] Ibid., 51.

[21] Suvir Kaul, ed., *The Partitions of Memory: The Afterlife of the Division of India* (New Delhi: Permanent Black, 2001), 3.

[22] Ibid., 5.

politics" of Partition: the men behind the transfer of power, mutual accusations about who was responsible for the division of India, relations between India and Pakistan following the transfer of power.[23] As Anjali Gera-Roy and Nandi Bhatia have written, "official histories have contributed tremendously to the 'forgetting' of the human dimension of Partition. On one level, such 'forgetting' has been enabled through the preoccupation with statistical analysis, dates and the 'bare truth' to produce narratives that suppress the terrible human experiences, and through such suppression engendered a 'collective amnesia' about the past."[24] Conventional historiography has not allowed the expression of the affective aspects of Partition, such as the loss and nostalgia for homeland, the trauma of crossing borders, the impossibility of return and the vicissitudes of trying to begin life anew. Works of fiction, films and oral histories have helped fill these lacunae by giving accounts of the human experience of witnessing Partition.[25] These accounts have helped to provide a "people's history" of Partition as opposed to the "official" history of two independent states. Therefore, the role of memory would be crucial to the task of writing a people's history of Partition. As Ritu Menon and Kamla Bhasin have written, "it is the collective memory of thousands of displaced families on both sides of the border that have imbued a rather innocuous word—partition—with its dreadful meaning: a people violently displaced, a country divided, a metaphor for irreparable loss."[26]

Remembering the affective dimensions of Partition also helps us to understand how Partition is re-enacted in every incident of mass violence. The massacre of Sikhs in 1984, the Bhagalpur massacre of 1989, the Moradabad massacre of 1980, the demolition of the Babri Masjid and the outbreak of countrywide violence in 1992, the Gujarat pogrom of 2002: all these are instances of a majoritarian impulse to exterminate the minority. Each incident of mass violence is followed by loss of home, difficulty of return and vagaries of legal justice. But the violence itself is

---

[23] Mushirul Hasan, ed., *Inventing Boundaries: Gender, Politics and the Partition of India* (New Delhi: Oxford University Press, 2000), 28.

[24] Anjali Gera-Roy and Nandi Bhatia, eds., *Partitioned Lives: Narratives of Home, Displacement and Resettlement* (New Delhi: Pearson, 2008), xiii.

[25] Tarun K. Saint, *Witnessing Partition: Memory, History, Fiction* (New Delhi: Routledge, 2010).

[26] Ritu Menon and Kamla Bhasin, *Borders and Boundaries: Women in India's Partition* (New Delhi: Kali for Women, 1998), xi.

forgotten: in other words, there is no acknowledgement of responsibility or guilt, no resolve to not let the violence be repeated. Thus, while the supposed guilt of Muslims for the 1947 Partition is invoked repeatedly, there is no accounting for the other partitions that are created *within* the country. As Urvashi Butalia has argued in *The Other Side of Silence,* there are partitions everywhere[27]; there is loss of life and home in every episode of mass violence.

Apart from works of fiction and autobiographical narratives, there is also a need for the public remembrance of anti-minority violence. In Tilak Vihar, a neighbourhood in West Delhi where many Sikh families affected by the anti-Sikh massacre of 1984 were resettled, there are three-day prayers held annually for those who were killed. In the gurudwara of Tilak Vihar, there are hundreds of framed photographs of the "martyrs" of 1984.[28] Many of the residents of Tilak Vihar are women who were widowed in 1984 and can give testimony about the massacre. Known as the "Widows' Colony", Tilak Vihar occasionally finds itself in the midst of media attention. In 2014, for example, there were demonstrations by Sikhs at Rahul Gandhi's refusal to apologise for the massacre that occurred under the watch of his father, Rajiv Gandhi.[29] In 2014, the Delhi Sikh Gurdwara Management Committee started the construction of a memorial for the victims of 1984. The decision to build the memorial had been made in 2013, after the Karkadooma court acquitted Congress leader Sajjan Kumar, who had faced allegations of being one of the perpetrators of the massacre in 1984.[30] Known as the "Wall of Tears", the memorial is "dedicated to the memory of thousands of

---

[27] Urvashi Butalia, *The Other Side of Silence: Voices from the Partition of India* (New Delhi: Penguin Books, 1998), 7.

[28] Naveed Iqbal, "Everyone in Tilak Vihar Has a Story," *Indian Express,* 3 November 2014, http://indianexpress.com/article/cities/delhi/everyone-in-tilak-vihar-has-a-1984-story/.

[29] Showkat Shafi, "In Pictures: Delhi's Widow Colony," *Al Jazeera,* 4 February 2014, http://www.aljazeera.com/indepth/inpictures/2014/02/pictures-delhi-widow-colony-20142381643420910.html.

[30] Press Trust of India, "32 Years Later, the 'Wall of Truth' Memorial in Delhi," 7 January 2017. https://www.scoopwhoop.com/32-Years-Later-The-Wall-Of-Truth-Memorial-In-Delhi-For-1984-Sikh-Riots-Victims-Finally-Complete/#.e6woh3vkx.

innocent Sikhs killed in the massacre and those who laid down their lives trying to protect them."[31]

But the process of memorialisation is not simply an endeavour by religious minorities that have faced large-scale killing. There are also majoritarian efforts to resignify a place by selectively commemorating the past. For example, after the Kachchh earthquake of 2001, as individual survivors came to terms with their loss, the Sangh Parivar moved in to rebuild post-earthquake Kachchh in such a way as to be reminiscent of Kachchh's ancient Hindu past. As Edward Simpson has written, villages that were rebuilt by the Sangh Parivar were given names such as "Keshav (Krishna) Nagar". Another village was named as "Indraprastha", alluding to the mythical village in the Mahabharata.[32] Thus, the earthquake clearly is "a break with the past, at least in the terms of personal memory; but, because of the renewed importance of the past in a more general sense, there is now more past in the present than there was before the disaster."[33] Previous Muslim and Dalit residents of Kachchh who were deemed as misfits in this sacralised landscape were physically prevented from occupying the reconstructed spaces; hence the shared living and cohabitation of earlier neighbourhoods became a thing of the past. Thus, the Hinduisation of Kachchh occurred at several levels: at the level of heritage, at the level of rebuilding villages and at the level of determining the identity of people who lived in the post-earthquake spaces. But the resignification of Kachchh as a Hindu site of memory had an immediate presentist concern. Kachchh had to be connected with the currents of right-wing Hindu nationalism within Gujarat and even in national politics. In October 2002, many of the leaders of the Vishwa Hindu Parishad in Gujarat visited Kachchh to attend one of the first inauguration ceremonies of this "post-earthquake village". Pravin Togadia, the international secretary of the VHP, chose the occasion to make a vitriolic speech against those detractors who had heavily criticised the Gujarat government for the pogrom of Muslims in early 2002. Kachchh was no longer

---

[31] "Memorial for 1984 to Come Up in Delhi," 1 November 2014, http://www.dnaindia.com/india/report-memorial-for-1984-anti-sikh-riot-victims-to-come-up-in-delhi-2031339.

[32] Edward Simpson and Stuart Corbridge, "The Geography of Things That May Become Memories: The 2001 Earthquake in Kachchh-Gujarat and the Politics of Rehabilitation in the Prememorial Era," *Annals of the Association of American Geographers* 96, no. 3, 566–585 (September 2006), 580, http://www.jstor.org/stable/4124433.

[33] Ibid., 581.

in isolation from the rest of Gujarat; it became another epicentre for hate speeches and election propaganda.

Jeffrey Olick has called memory "the handmaiden of nationalist zeal."[34] The memory of a Hindu past commemorated at Kachchh illustrates this. An "invented tradition" of Hindu rule had to be established at Kachchh so that it could become the epicentre for denying the violence of the anti-Muslim pogrom that had occurred at the hands of the VHP and the Bajrang Dal. But if the power of memory is unleashed by the forces of majoritarianism to impose an amnesia upon the testimonies of survivors of anti-minority pogroms, the need for a memory of the survivors becomes all the more exigent. This provides the context for understanding the Gulbarg Society memorial.

Gulbarg Society Massacre: Event and Aftermath

The Gulbarg Society was a cluster of about 20 buildings in the Chamanpura area in Ahmedabad; the people who lived there were mostly middle-class Muslims, except for one Parsi family, the Modys. On 28 February 2002, one day after the Sabarmati train-burning incident, violent mobs went on a rampage in Ahmedabad. Gulbarg Society was one of the flashpoints of violence. The house of former Congress MP Ehsan Jafri became a refuge for the other residents of Gulbarg as the mobs drew closer and closer. As other Muslims sought sanctuary with him, Jafri made several phone calls to high-ranking police officials, Congress colleagues and even the then Chief Minister Narendra Modi to seek protection. Jafri's pleas fell on deaf ears and he was dragged outside and brutally killed. As Rupa Mody has testified about her own recollections of that day,

> I thought that being burnt to death was worse than being cut into pieces since nothing would remain of us if we were burnt. So, we decided to run out of our third story flat and we found other people in our society who were also fleeing to safety. Everyone was running to Ehsan Jafri sahab's house. We too went to his place on the first floor. In front of me, he

---

[34] Jeffrey K. Olick, ed., *States of Memory: Continuities, Conflicts and Transformations* (Durham, NC: Duke University Press, 2003), quoted in J. Edward Mallot, *Memory, Nationalism and Narrative in Contemporary South Asia* (New York: Palgrave Macmillan, 2012), 6.

called Narendra Modi several times. We had asked him to call Modi. We had even asked him to call all the *gundas* if he could and convince them to spare our lives. Finally, Modi picked up the phone and used an abusive word for Jafri, and said he was surprised Jafri had not been killed already... I saw him being dragged away by the mob. They hacked him, poured petrol over him and set him on fire.[35]

As Amrita Shah writes, "by demonstrating Ehsan Jafri's vulnerability, his assailants had also shown the ineffectuality of an ideology and a party. Indeed, they had conveyed the message that, under the new dispensation, to be like him was to court trouble."[36] Jafri represented the socialist ideology of the Congress Party; but more than that, he embodied strength and fortitude for many Muslims belonging to the lower echelons of society. By making him their target, the mobs demonstrated the extent of vulnerability to which Muslims could be subjected.

In 2003, the Gulbarg Society massacre was one of the cases, apart from those such as Godhra, Best Bakery, Naroda Patiya and Sardarpura, which the National Human Rights Commission recommended should be shifted to Maharashtra or any other state, in order to avoid a miscarriage of justice.[37] In November 2007, the Gujarat High Court dismissed a petition by Zakia Jafri seeking the court's directive to the police to register a complaint against then Chief Minister Narendra Modi and sixty-two others for alleged involvement in the Gulbarg Society massacre.[38] In March 2008, the Supreme Court directed the Gujarat government to set up a Special Investigation Team (SIT) for a further investigation into the Godhra case and the cases of massacres which followed. Under the chairmanship of R.K. Raghavan, former CBI director, the SIT looked into the cases of Godhra, Sardarpura, Gulbarg Society, Ode, Naroda Patiya, Deepda Darwaza and a case involving British

---

[35] Suhas Munshi, "Ehsan Jafri Called Modi for Help, I Heard Modi Abuse Him: Gulbarg Survivor," *Catchnews*, 2 June 2016, http://www.catchnews.com/india-news/ehsan-jafri-called-modi-for-help-i-heard-modi-abuse-him-gulberg-survivor-1464888144.html.

[36] Amrita Shah, *Ahmedabad: A City in the World* (New Delhi: Bloomsbury, 2015), 21.

[37] J. Venkatesan, "Supreme Court Stays Proceedings in 10 Godhra-Related Cases," *The Hindu*, 22 November 2003, http://www.thehindu.com/2003/11/22/stories/2003112206210100.htm.

[38] "Gulbarg Society Massacre Case: Timeline," *The Hindu*, 2 June 2016.

nationals.[39] In 2012, citing lack of prosecutable evidence, the SIT filed a closure report in the probe case. But the Gulbarg Society massacre case continued, even as Zakia Jafri's petition in 2013 challenging the closure report filed by the SIT was dismissed. It was stated by the prosecution in the Gulbarg Society case that 39 persons had been burnt alive and 30 others, including Ehsan Jafri, had gone missing. He and others were presumed to be dead after the legal waiting period of seven years.[40]

When the verdict on the Gulbarg Society case was pronounced in June 2016, the charge of criminal conspiracy was ruled out and there were 36 acquittals, including those of top BJP leaders and police officials. It was declared by the court that the massacre was a result of Ehsan Jafri's having fired into the crowd. The witnesses of the case were declared to have forgotten his having done this. This is an instance of testimonial injustice. As Miranda Fricker has written, "testimonial injustice occurs when prejudice causes a hearer to give a deflated level of credibility to a speaker's word."[41] In the meanwhile, the Gulbarg Society itself was declared to be a "disturbed area", and efforts at building a memorial there were stalled.

The Gulbarg Society as Disputed Property

In the years following 2002, the Gulbarg Society has acquired the reputation of being scarred by violence and prone to conflict. In 2007, Gulbarg also became the site for a proposed memorial for 2002, which became the locus of further contentions.

Five years after the carnage in Gujarat, a proposal emerged to establish a memorial at the Gulbarg Society. Some of the former residents wished to sell their property at Gulbarg in order to be able to purchase housing elsewhere. But selling land in a place marked by a massacre was not easy. Instead of selling any of the Gulbarg properties at throwaway prices, the Society passed a resolution to put a stay on the sale of any property. The

---

[39] J. Venkatesan, "Notify SIT in 10 Days," *The Hindu*, 27 March 2008, http://www.thehindu.com/todays-paper/Notify-SIT-in-ten-days-court/article15191981.ece.

[40] "Trial Resumes in Gulbarg Society Case," *The Hindu*, 28 November 2014, http://www.thehindu.com/news/national/other-states/trial-resumes-in-gulberg-society-case/article6644132.ece.

[41] Miranda Fricker, *Epistemic Injustice: Power and the Ethics of Knowing* (Oxford: Oxford University Press, 2007), 1.

Society also appointed a government-approved valuer to undertake a survey and measure the valuation of the land at Gulbarg so that the market price of the property could be determined.[42] Then Teesta Setalvad, who had taken the responsibility of handling the Gulbarg cases, offered to buy the Gulbarg property through the Sabrang Trust which she runs with Javed Anand. She suggested that the land thus purchased would be used to set up a memorial to those Muslims who had been killed in 2002.

After a five-year hiatus, Setalvad announced in 2012 that the Sabrang Trust had been unable to collect sufficient funds to purchase the Gulbarg property at the market price. At this time, one of the former residents of Gulbarg, Feroz Khan Pathan, filed a police complaint against Setalvad alleging misappropriation of the funds collected for the purpose of setting up the museum. This allegation was also echoed by the BJP. Purushottam Rupala, the national vice-president of the BJP, demanded that the Foreign Contributions Regulations Act (FCRA) registration of Setalvad's NGO should be cancelled (the FCRA registration is mandatory for every NGO). Rupala also demanded that criminal charges should be initiated against the trustees of Citizens for Justice and Peace (CJP), the NGO run by Setalvad.[43] Setalvad denied the charges levelled against CJP, and said that these attempts by the BJP to malign her were a tactic of intimidation.[44] After this, the stay upon the sale of individual properties by former residents was lifted and Setalvad announced that the owners were free to sell their land to any prospective buyer. But in 2013, any sale of property at Gulbarg was stalled because the government of Gujarat brought it under the extended ambit of the Disturbed Areas Act.

The Gujarat Prohibition of Transfer of Immovable Property and Provision for Protection of Tenants from Eviction from Premises in Disturbed Areas Act, or the "Disturbed Areas Act" was enacted in 1986.[45] It was first introduced as an ordinance for a temporary duration

---

[42] Tanveer Jafri, interview with the author on 7 March 2017.

[43] "BJP MP Seeks Action against Setalvad," *Indian Express*, 2 February 2013, http://archive.indianexpress.com/news/bjp-mp-seeks-action-against-setalvad/1068267/.

[44] "Intimidation by Foisting False Cases against Teesta Setalvad and Javed Anand: Statements by Sabrang and CJP," *South Asia Citizens Web*, 5 January 2014, http://www.sacw.net/article7161.html.

[45] Full text of the Act available on http://www.lawsofindia.org/pdf/gujarat/1986/1986GUJARAT30.pdf.

by the Congress government of Madhavsinh Solanki. The law prohibits a Muslim from selling, leasing or transferring his property to a Hindu, or a Hindu to a Muslim in a "disturbed area"[46] unless permission is granted by the district collector. The list of disturbed areas is notified by the state government, based on inputs provided by the home department. The law intends to prevent neighbourhoods from becoming ghettoised in the event of communal violence. It seeks to prevent Hindus and Muslims from selling their property in mixed neighbourhoods at depreciated rates, so as to ensure that the neighbourhood can retain a semblance of interreligious cohabitation. But instead of remaining as a temporary measure in post-conflict urban locations, the Act has become permanent. Successive governments have passed additional notifications such that more and more areas have been brought under the jurisdiction of the Act. Ayesha Khan writes,

> In 2009, the Gujarat government amended the Act, giving sweeping powers to the district collector to ensure what it termed was the effective implementation of the Act. The district collector now has been empowered to hold inquiry suo moto or based on an application by anyone if the provisions of the Act are felt to be violated in any manner. The penalty clause was introduced for the first time while making the violation of any of its provisions a cognisable offence. It also empowers the district collector to seize any property temporarily and restrain the transfer as well as alterations in the property if he construes it as a violation of the Act. In reality, officials, builders and activists admit that the Act has made it more difficult as well as more expensive for Muslims to buy property than Hindus.[47]

The Act has now become a tool in the hands of the state revenue department, along with the powerful real estate lobby, to promote

---

[46] Section 3 of the 1986 Act defines a "Disturbed Area" as follows: "Where the State Government, having regard to the intensity and duration of riot or violence of mob and such other factors in an area is of opinion that public order in that area was disturbed for a substantial period by reason of riot or violence of mob during the period commencing on the 18th March, 1985 and ending on the day immediately before the commencement of this Act, it may, by notification in the *Official Gazette*, declare such area to be a disturbed area."

[47] Ayesha Khan, "How to Profit from a Disturbed Area," *Ink*, 3 October 2013, http://fountainink.in/?p=2784&all=1.

"homophily—the tendency of like-minded people to congregate in the same places."[48] The restrictions of the Act remain the same: Hindus and Muslims in a disturbed area cannot undertake property transactions with each other without attestation by the District Collector. But now, the existence of the Disturbed Areas Act perpetuates mistrust and fear of the "Other" and prevents intercommunal living. The Act has resulted in more ghettoisation. The moniker of a "Disturbed Area" is today attached to predominantly Muslim localities, such as Kalupur, Shahpur, Dariyapur, Raikhad and Paldi. These places are locally referred to as mini-Pakistans, revealing how legislative regimes result in evoking the imagery of Partition. Critics say the Act's continued enforcement and the addition of new districts covered by it—about 40% of Ahmedabad is now governed by the law—means it is effectively being applied as a tool of social engineering.[49]

In fact, in 2014, Praveen Togadia of the Vishwa Hindu Parishad was reported to have incited the residents of Bhavnagar to forcefully evict a Muslim who had purchased a property there.[50] The imposition of the Act has spelled doom for Gulbarg Society, which is the lone Muslim-dominated housing colony in the predominantly Hindu neighbourhood of Asarwa.[51] The sale of the Gulbarg Society has effectively been halted, since Muslims cannot purchase property in Asarwa, and Hindus are discouraged from undertaking transactions with the Muslim members of the Gulbarg Society. The former residents allege that this has been done simply to harass the primary eyewitnesses against Modi and to thwart the creation of a memorial.[52]

---

[48] Raheel Dhattiwala, "Next-Door Strangers: Explaining 'Neighbourliness' between Hindus and Muslims in a Riot-Affected City," in *Indian Muslims: Struggling for Equality of Citizenship*, ed. R. Hassan(Melbourne: Melbourne University Press, 2016), 147.

[49] John Chalmers, "In Narendra Modi's Gujarat, a Case of Rule and Divide," *Livemint*, 14 May 2014, http://www.livemint.com/Politics/xDcv5reXXuzWlCMdDBtstI/In-Narendra-Modis-Gujarat-a-case-of-rule-and-divide.html.

[50] Ibid.

[51] Aarefa Johari, "Stuck in Time: Why Gulbarg Society Survivors Are Finding It Impossible to Sell Their Abandoned Homes," *Scroll*, 20 June 2016, https://scroll.in/article/810220/stuck-in-time-why-gulbarg-society-survivors-find-it-impossible-to-sell-their-abandoned-homes.

[52] As stated by Tanveer Jafri, Saira Sandhi and Rupa Mody, in personal interviews with author.

The Gulbarg Society as a Memorial Site

It feels very lonely, to hold that truth, because we can't talk about this to everyone. A memorial will help conversations about it. There were so many victims of the pogrom, like my father, whose bodies could not be traced. It was not possible to trace the remains of his body, but we insisted that there should be a grave, which Ammi can visit. But what about people who don't even have a marked grave? At least a memorial can give a place to those victims. A memorial for Gulbarg Society will also impel people to remember that pogrom.[53]

Nishrin Jafri

The present survivors of the Gulbarg Society remember their past life as idyllic. Memories of that imagined idyll are made even more vivid by the tragic way in which it was terminated. Qasam Mansuri says, "*Ye society kitna achcha tha. Andar aane se lagta tha, jannat mein aayein hain*" (The Society was so beautiful. If you would come here, you would feel that you have entered paradise).[54] Despite the fact that there are rifts within the Society today, regarding the sale of property and the involvement of Teesta Setalvad, members remember a time when they lived in mutual harmony. Saira Sandhi reminisces, "My father-in-law, Sharief's father Nasruddin Khan (he was known as 'bhaijaan', he died before the *toofan*), Jafri *sahab*, they were all like brothers to each other. They had all bought the land together and built the society."[55]

The physical site of Gulbarg consists of a cluster of houses. However, as Paul Connerton has argued, a house is not simply a building in which people live; "it provides more than a shelter and spatial disposition of activities, a material order constructed out of walls and boundaries. It is a medium of representation, and, as such, can be read as a mnemonic system."[56] Even today, the mnemonic codes of the housing society are fresh in the minds of survivors, as they remember 28 February 2002. They point out the room where they hid from the mobs, the rooms that they witnessed being burnt down, the office of Ehsan Jafri, where

---

[53] Nishrin Jafri, interview with the author, 26 February 2017.

[54] Qasam Mansuri, interview with author, 6 March 2017.

[55] Saira Sandhi, interview with author, 2 March 2017.

[56] Paul Connerton, *How Modernity Forgets* (Cambridge: Cambridge University Press, 2009), 19.

he attempted to telephone for help. Each survivor narrates a detailed account of how he or she escaped from the mobs—across houses and rooms and corridors—or how he or she witnessed relatives and neighbours falling prey to sword and fire.

A house provides a coherent unit of belonging to its inhabitants, not only for their individual selves but also for their material possessions; it provides regularity for the everyday experience and regular functions of life. In this case, the remnants of Gulbarg Society are a stark spectacle of how that regularity was ruptured and has not been resumed. Since this is the only site of violence in Ahmedabad that has not been reclaimed by resettlement and human habitation, the abandoned and damaged houses still bear traces that show how the pogrom of 2002 was a disruption of the ordinary. Stanley Cavell has pondered if the "manifestation of a society's internal, intimate and absolute violence are comprehensible as extreme states, or suddenly invited enactments, of a pervasive fact of the social fabric that may hide itself, or one might also say, may express itself, in everyday encounters."[57] The rupture of peoples' everyday lives is therefore a form of violence. At Gulbarg Society, there has been no restoration of that ruptured "ordinary" texture of people's lives; as explained above, the inability to either dispense with the Gulbarg property or to resume human habitation there has mired Gulbarg Society in perpetual distrust. Veena Das has noted that "life was recovered not through some grand gestures in the realm of the transcendent but through a descent into the ordinary."[58] In other words, there occurs "a mutual absorption of the violent and an ordinary", such that the event is always "attached to the ordinary as if there were tentacles that reach out from the everyday and anchor the event to it in some specific ways."[59] In this case, the "ordinary" has been expurgated from Gulbarg, while allowing the "violent" to hold sway.

The remains of former habitation that still mark the premises of Gulbarg Society remind the visitor of the impossibility of the return and resettlement of its original residents. Since there has been no "descent into the ordinary", Gulbarg Society stands out as a place perpetually

---

[57] Stanley Cavell, foreword to Veena Das, *Life and Words: Violence and the Descent into the Ordinary* (Berkeley and Los Angeles: University of California Press, 2007), xiii.

[58] Veena Das, *Life and Words*, 7.

[59] Ibid.

scarred. The rubble of the houses is overgrown with weeds; a stagnant carpet of leaves covers the empty staircases; the windows have cracked panes and there are thick cobwebs in the doorways. The ceilings are all blackened by soot, reminding one of the fire that engulfed them years ago. There is a smashed commode in what was once a bathroom. The walls bear traces of attempts to break them down, while the mouldy plaster is coming off them. There is a rusty bicycle in a corner, there are damaged air conditioners, there are compact discs and matchboxes strewn around: in a nutshell, the flotsam and jetsam of abandoned life. In Amrita Shah's description, "All signs of life—and there must have been plenty of it here once: the colour of wet clothes on a line, the warbling of a television set, the shrieks of children at play—have been stamped out. There is only the sound of crushed leaves underfoot."[60] Locals refer to the buildings as *bhoot* or "ghost" bungalows owing to the dread the sight of them induces.[61]

But if the afterlife of Gulbarg Society is one marked by scars of violence, its past life is characterised by resilience and resistance. Nishrin Jafri narrates a poignant tale of how her parents were very young and she was only a four-year-old child when their family witnessed their house being burnt down in the communal violence of 1969.[62]

We used to live in a rented house in the very same area where Gulbarg Society is located today. My entire family comprising six adults and five children shifted to the relief camp at Shah Alam dargah where we lived for six months. Even after having witnessed violence and the killings of Muslims, Abba still had the courage to build his new house in the same place from which he had been forced to move. Abba would say, '*Ye mere hi log hain*' [I am one of these people]. Thus he trusted his Hindu neighbours enough to build a housing society in their midst. His belief in secular ideals was very tenacious. Abba had hundreds of books at home; books on law, literature, poetry, philosophy. So many of those books were burnt that day! Today, when I return from the United States, I don't have any home in Gujarat to return to. I won't be allowed to buy any property in

---

[60] Amrita Shah, *Ahmedabad*, 20.

[61] Syed Khalique Ahmed, "Gulbarg Society Beyond Recognition Seven Years After Carnage," *Indian Express*, 28 February 2009, http://archive.indianexpress.com/news/gulbarg-society-beyond-recognition-seven-years-after-carnage/429106/.

[62] Nishrin Jafri, interview with author, 26 February 2017.

Ahmedabad. But I still consider Gulbarg as my home. I grew up there. But whenever I visit my house at Gulbarg, I take off my shoes. What if I step on a spot where the remains of my father's dead body had lain? I want the memorial to be built in my father's home.[63]

But apart from cobwebs and weeds, the empty houses at Gulbarg also contain dusty belongings and traces of people who were killed or are missing. On 28 February 2017, the survivors got together at Gulbarg to observe the fifteenth year of the massacre. I accompanied Rupa Mody as she made her way to her flat on the first floor of a building. The wall beside the staircase still bore traces of her son's handwriting. The partially damaged door of the flat had stickers of sports personalities which Azhar Mody had pasted on it. Inside the house, Rupa stopped at the sight of an open briefcase with its contents spilling out. She could see an old drawing book with sketches made by her daughter, an old school diary that had belonged to her son. There was also an old school cardigan and other sundry pieces of cloth lying in the dirt, their colour indistinguishable from it. On the wall of the room, there was a school timetable that Azhar had put up. There was also a poster of the Hindu god Krishna in a corner of a wall; Rupa Mody told me that when the mob had invaded her home, they had refrained from burning it down because the image of Krishna seemed to indicate that the house belonged to a Hindu family.[64] Rupa broke down as she saw all the objects lying on the floor. Before leaving, she picked up the school diary and the drawing book, dusted them and put them in her bag. Rupa and Dara Mody live in Thaltej now, a part of Ahmedabad which is quite far from Asarwa.

The abandoned buildings at Gulbarg are infested with many stray dogs and monkeys, and their corpses are often found lying around. Qasambhai Mansuri deeply resents the fact that the erstwhile vibrancy of Gulbarg Society has now been overcome with the stench of the rotting corpses of dogs. Qasambhai is the only survivor of the massacre who has returned to Gulbarg. Since his house is located in front of the main entrance of Gulbarg, it has borne maximum damage. He narrates his story: "I stayed in the relief camp at Dariya Khan dargah for

---

[63] Nishrin Jafri, interview with author, 26 February 2017.

[64] Rupa Mody, interview with author, 28 February 2017.

six months in 2002. After that, I returned to Gulbarg. I have rebuilt my house even after it was burnt down. I have even fixed the lights here. *Pura hindustan bhi laake do mujhe, mein phir bhi apna ghar nahi doonga. Mujhe agar kahin rehna hai, toh mein yahin rahunga.* [Even if someone brings me the whole of India, I will still not give up my home. If I have to stay anywhere at all, it will be only at my own house.] When the *haadsa* [tragedy] happened, I was not here at Gulbarg. But I lost nineteen members of my family that day. My sons, Aslam and Rafique, were young then. They don't want to remember the past now. My sons have even fought with me. They asked me how I can go back to a place where so many of our family and other families were killed. But I was determined to live here. My sons live in Bapunagar and Naroda and have a business of mattress-making. But I stay here. Only here. Even if I visit my sons' homes, I won't be able to sleep peacefully there. I can't sleep unless I am here at my home in Gulbarg. I guard and look after this place. Some years ago, a few locks from the house doors were stolen. I got them replaced. Why don't the other people of Gulbarg come and stay here? They should! I am the only one who stays here. There are dead dogs found in the houses. But why don't people come here and clean their houses? Why do they come only on the 28th of February? I spent the money given to me as compensation in rebuilding my house. This is my house. I have lived here for more than 45 years. It was built in 1970. I refuse to sell my house, even for the proposed memorial. There is another house here, building number 13, which belonged to my mother. I intend to rebuild even that. Other people don't bother about their old homes, everyone is ready to sell them. But I am not like them. Look at the victims of Naroda Patiya, didn't they return to stay at the very place where they witnessed the massacre? If people rebuild their houses, others can come and stay there on rent. Look at this other house beside mine. There are daily wage earners staying there. They pay a rent of a thousand rupees. There are five or six of them. They work in the bakeries nearby, and then they come to sleep here at night. They are all Mohammedans. They have been staying here for seven or eight years. Their families live elsewhere. If other houses are rebuilt, more such workers will come. There are also *namaazis* who come to the mosque for *namaaz*. I also contributed to getting the mosque repaired. I spend my time here or at a small dargah near this place. It is the dargah of the saint Sheikh Jalaluddin. His blessings are upon me."[65]

In *The Comfort of Things,* David Miller writes that "people's lives take place behind the closed doors of private homes. The person in that living room gives an account of herself by responding to questions. But every object in that room is equally a form by which they have chosen to express themselves."[66] Miller explores the material things according to which people make sense out of their lives. For both Rupa Mody and Qasambhai Mansuri, Gulbarg Society is a memorial site not only because it reminds them of their loved ones who were killed or have been missing; it also helps them to express loss and recovery in material terms. For Rupa, objects that belonged to her children fifteen years ago must be retrieved from the dusty flotsam in which they lie in her abandoned house. For Qasambhai, every detail of his reconstructed house evokes a sense of resilience for him: the lights, the water pipeline, the paint on the wall which distinguishes it from the grey surroundings of Gulbarg, the few sacks of groceries which neighbouring shopkeepers sometimes keep in his room. Each of these details convinces him that he was right to return to Gulbarg and resume his life there even after losing nineteen members of his family in 2002. Rupa and Qasambhai belong to the collective of the Gulbarg Society, but their individual memories of loss and recovery are linked to the material things which are present in their homes. Qasambhai repeatedly asked me, *"Aapko sukoon hai na yahaan?"* (You are feeling at ease here, right?) when I visited his home. It is essential for him to ensure that visitors to his home should feel *sukoon,* or peace and relaxation. This allows the absorption of the violent into an the ordinary, and a resumption of an ordinary way of living.

Despite differences among themselves with regard to details of the sale of property, the members of the Gulbarg Society have a common desire to embody their memories of violence so that future generations can relate to them. Nishrin Jafri says,

> The memorial should be built in a way which can engage everyone, not just Muslims. It should be a place for history, like the Holocaust Museum in Washington. There should also be a *yaadgaar* (memorial) for the long history of communal violence in Ahmedabad. Most of the people in

---

[65] Qasambhai Mansuri, interview with author, 6 March 2017.
[66] David Miller, *The Comfort of Things* (Cambridge: Polity Press, 2008), 1–2.

Gujarat have forgotten the long history of violence in the city. So there needs to be a room, a room somewhere, not just for the images of victims, but also for recordings of the hate speeches of people like Togadia which were uttered in those days. The process of rehabilitation and the giving of compensation after the pogrom has already allowed a certain measure of amnesia to set in. But doesn't this community also need a sense of history, to impress upon the country what had happened?[67]

Imteyaz Khan Pathan says that a memorial is needed "so that there is a space for Muslims to express the crimes that have been done against them, so that the coming generations of both Muslims and non-Muslims can have some '*ehsaas*'" (sensitivity).[68] Saira Sandhi says that if and when a memorial is built, it can contain the possessions which belonged to those who were killed. "For example, my son's bike can be kept there. His birthday was on 9th February, and he got killed on 28th February. *Hum howe na howe, humari aane wali peedi aate jaate dekhegi* [Even if I am not there, the coming generations will see that memorial]. My daughter's children will be able to see and remember how their uncle was killed."[69] Saira adds, "The government does not want a memorial at Gulbarg because Modi is directly responsible for the 2002 pogrom. *Memorial bane toh peedi par peedi usko yaad karena? Jaise Hitler ko kaise abhi yaad karte hain sab.* [The memorial will be a direct indictment of Modi and the coming generations will remember his role in engineering the pogrom, just like Hitler is remembered today for the Holocaust.] That is why the government does not want a memorial to be built at Gulbarg Society."

Enacting Memory at the Gulbarg Society

What is the significance of a damaged site for people who once called it home? It provides a space for mourning. There is considerable debate as to whether mourning should be imbued in the ordinariness of life, as suggested by Veena Das, or whether it should take place as an expression or act *outside* the realm of everyday life and on a site demarcated for this purpose, as a reminder of the extraordinary brutality of violence. In the case of the Gulbarg Society, it is surely the latter. Mourning and

---

[67] Nishrin Jafri, interview with the author, 26 February 2017.

[68] Imteyaz Khan Pathan, interview with the author, 2 March 2017.

[69] Saira Sandhi, interview with the author, 2 March 2017.

remembering violence together with people who have been fellow victims constitutes a community of care; as Paul Connerton points out, the
etymological meaning of the word "to mourn" is closely connected to a
notion of care. He observes that "caring was once connected to memory through the idea of mourning"; this etymological connection of the
verbs "to care" and "to mourn" has been rendered obsolete now.[70]

In 2012, ten years after the Gujarat carnage, about 45 voluntary
organisations gathered a group of people at the Gulbarg Society and
led them through the abandoned buildings, recounting the horrors of
the tragedy ten years ago.[71] Saira Sandhi narrates, "There was a huge
programme done in memory of 10 years of the Gulbarg Society massacre. Even invitation cards were printed. Everyone got to see what the
museum would look like. Shobha Mudgal was invited by Teesta ma'am.
My husband worked in the municipality then; he and a few others got
together to get the whole of Gulbarg cleaned. There were some houses
in which there were bodies of dead dogs. They had to be removed. The
stench was terrible."[72] There was a display of photographs of those who
had been killed. Photographs of faces of those who have been exter-
minated evoke an affective connection with the dead, especially when
these are displayed at the site of extermination itself. Susan Sontag has
described the role of the photograph:

> To remember is, more and more, not to recall a story but to be able to call
> up a picture. People remember only the photographs. This remembering
> through photographs eclipses other forms of understanding, and remem-
> bering. The concentration camps—that is, the photographs taken when
> the camps were liberated in 1945—are most of what people associate with
> Nazism and the miseries of the Second World War. Narratives can make us
> understand. Photographs do something else: they haunt us.'[73]

---

[70] Paul Connerton, *The Spirit of Mourning: History, Memory and the Body* (Cambridge:
Cambridge University Press, 2011), 20.

[71] Manas Dasgupta, "A Decade After, Memories Haunt Godhra, Gulbarg," *The Hindu*,
28 February 2012, accessed 29 June 2016 at 15:24, http://www.thehindu.com/news/
national/a-decade-after-memories-haunt-godhra-gulberg/article2939332.ece.

[72] Saira Sandhi, interview with the author, 2 March 2017.

[73] Susan Sontag, *Remembering the Pain of Others* (New York: Picador, 2003), 70–73.

Sontag observes that the gaze of the photograph of massacred victims is often an ordeal for viewers, but it is one that must be undertaken to perceive the "face" of the other:

> Submitting to the ordeal should help us understand such atrocities not as the acts of 'barbarians' but as the reflection of a belief system … that by defining one people as less human than another legitimates torture and murder. But maybe they *were* barbarians. Maybe *this* is what most barbarians look like. (They look like everybody else.)[74]

The survivors of the Gulbarg Society massacre come together annually on 28 February to hold a *Quran-khaani* at Gulbarg.[75] The women get together in Saira Sandhi's house, while the men assemble in the mosque. Copies of the Quran are read by the people present. The reading of the Quran is interrupted by conversation, as individual survivors greet each other, and reminisce about the time when they used to live together. This is the one day of the year when the Society meets as a collective and observes a ritual of collective memory. After the reading of the Quran has been completed, a small snack is distributed among the members. Saira lights incense sticks in her house and lets the incense smoke waft through the rooms. The men offer *namaaz* for the dead in the mosque. After these rituals are over, people visit their abandoned homes.

Saira Sandhi says, "The *Quran-khaani* has happened every year since 2002. I have never missed even a year. Earlier there were many people who used to come here to join us. But after the FIR was filed against Teesta, and the Disturbed Areas Act was imposed, people don't come in large numbers. People are scared." Rupa Mody says, "For everyone at Gulbarg, 28th February is a marked day. We go to Gulbarg and put flowers in our houses, we light the *agarbatti* there, as a *shraddhanjali*. It is important for everyone to come together to hold the *Quran-khaani*. In a way, we always remember those whom we lost in the *dhamaal*. We can't forget them even for a day. But on [the] 28th, we remember them collectively, we remember the time when we had all lived together. Anyone can come to Gulbarg, but they will leave. The media comes every year. The media people tell us that they know everything about the past, and ask us

---

[74] Ibid.

[75] I was part of the *Quran-khaani* at Gulbarg Society this year.

what is new there. But for us, the new does not matter. When Sairaben and I meet, we inevitably talk about the *dhamaal*, we talk about our sons. Everyone else has forgotten."[76] Imteyaz Khan Pathan says that he goes to Gulbarg sometimes even during Ramzan or *shab-e-baraat*. He also goes to the Kalandhari Kabristan to offer prayers. The Kalandhari Kabristan has mass graves where the dead of Gulbarg Society and Naroda Patiya lie buried. But his wife, Shama Khan Pathan says that she has stopped going to the *Quran-khaani*. "I haven't been going there for a couple of years because I have been unwell. I feel too upset whenever I go to Gulbarg, and my children cry. Instead, I read the Quran at home."[77]

The Muslim practice of reading the Quran to observe remembrance of the dead is a commonplace religious practice (although the doctrinal validity of this practice has been contested in different schools of Islamic theology and jurisprudence). But in the context of Gulbarg Society, this practice assumes a special salience. It registers the identity of the victims as Muslims. This identification is important to the mourners. It is not enough to mourn a photograph or a name; participating in a collective recitation of Quranic verses enunciates an affective link between the living and the dead. The reading of the Quran and the offering of *dua* (prayer) also takes place at the Kalandhari Kabristan. Saira Sandhi says, "My son has been buried at the Kalandhari Kabristan. That is why I live there at Dariyapur at the relief colony, close to the grave where my son lies buried. *Iske Pappa wahaan Juma ke din jaawe namaaz padhne, aur hum jumraat ke din jaate phool chadhane. Yahaan ghar se bhi woh kabrein dikhti hain.* [My husband goes to the Kabristan on Friday to offer *namaaz*. I go there on Thursdays, and put flowers on the grave. Here the graves are visible even from my home.]"[78]

Maurice Halbwachs offered the following observations on why a survivor feels the urge to remember the past.

That faraway world where we remember that we suffered nevertheless exercises an incomprehensible attraction on the person who has survived it and who seems to think he has left there the best part of himself, which

---

[76] Word agarbatti translates as incense sticks, shraddhanjali translates as homage to the dead. Dhamaal translates as "commotion" or "confusion," but refers specifically to the massacre in this context. Rupa Mody, interview with the author, 1 March 2017.

[77] Shama Khan Pathan, interview with the author, 2 March 2017.

[78] Saira Sandhi, interview with author, 2 March 2017.

he tries to recapture. This is why, given a few exceptions, it is the case that the great majority of people more or less frequently are given to what one might call nostalgia for the past.[79]

The individual sufferer/survivor has an inevitable impulse to remember "things as they once were." But as Halbwachs has enjoined, "no memory is possible outside frameworks used by people living in society to determine and retrieve their recollections."[80] This is how the "collective" emerges: within frames of memory employed by individual memory-makers. But the notion of the collective is also inherent in each individual, since individual remembering is always done as part of a group. The "collective" not only signifies individual memories, it also determines the nature and form of memorials that emerge. Thus the individual and the collective are intertwined within the process of memorialisation. The creation of a formal memorial at Gulbarg Society has been put on hold by the legislative regimes of the state, internal rifts within the Society itself and the exorbitant market prices of land. The proposal has been further jeopardised by the charges of misappropriation of funds levelled against Teesta Setalvad. Setalvad herself had proposed the idea of a memorial along with the members of Gulbarg Society, but the allegations against her have compelled her to give up this endeavour. Therefore, the prospects of establishing a memorial at Gulbarg Society look rather bleak. Even though there are impediments to the creation of a formal memorial with the help of NGO funds, the survivors of the Gulbarg Society massacre have already converted Gulbarg into a memorial site. While Qasambhai Mansuri has tenaciously refused to leave his house at Gulbarg, the other survivors are unable to return. Imteyaz Khan Pathan says, "I lost ten members of my family in the massacre. How can I return? Gujarat is a place where riots happen all the time. How can we trust that there will be no violence in Gulbarg again? Even the police had fired at people there. We are afraid, we will not be able to sleep there. And we don't have the money to rebuild the damaged house at Gulbarg. We can't return there."[81] Despite these differences between individual members and disagreements arising therefrom, the society of survivors

---

[79] Maurice Halbwachs, *On Collective Memory*, ed. and trans. Lewis Coser (Chicago: University of Chicago Press, 1992), 49.

[80] Ibid., 43.

[81] Imteyaz Khan Pathan, interview with the author, 2 March 2017.

gathers every year on 28 February to collectively pray and mourn. Each of them affirms that if the future brings further attempts to establish a memorial, they will give it their full support. But even if the establishment of a "formal" memorial has been deferred indefinitely, Gulbarg Society stands as reminder of the brutality of violence engineered by the state. It signifies how hatred towards the "other" can permanently tear apart the fabric of social living. But Gulbarg also demonstrates the courage of individual survivors, and what it takes to mend the broken threads of an injured life.

In Lieu of a Conclusion

How should the outside world regard Gulbarg Society as a memorial? How should the rest of us perceive the stories that cohere therein? Perhaps it would be apt to recognise how Gulbarg Society demonstrates the mournability of life. As Judith Butler writes, "the frames through which we apprehend or, indeed, fail to apprehend the lives of others as lost or injured (lose-able or injurable) are politically saturated. They are themselves operations of power."[82] Butler has outlined an ethical perspective for adumbrating the mournability of human beings:

> Without grievability, there is no life, or, rather, there is something living that is other than life. Instead, 'there is a life that will never have been lived', sustained by no regard, no testimony, and ungrieved when lost. The apprehension of grievability precedes and makes possible the apprehension of precarious life. Grievability precedes and makes possible the apprehension of the living being as living, exposed to non-life from the start. The differential distribution of grievability across populations has implications for why and when we feel politically consequential affective dispositions such as horror, guilt, righteous sadism, loss, and indifference.[83]

Butler argues for the recognition of the precariousness and vulnerability of one and all. But precariousness itself is often made invisible by discourses of power which regulate how we see the "Other". The "Other" is often deemed to be unmournable; hence, we refuse to establish any affect of solidarity or empathy. But the mournability of the Other must

---

[82] Judith Butler, *Frames of War: When Is Life Grievable?* (London: Verso Books, 2009), 1.
[83] Ibid., 25–26.

be acknowledged, as an ethical imperative. Avishai Margalit speaks of "a moral duty of remembrance". He insists that everyone has a moral obligation to remember "gross crimes against humanity, especially when those crimes are an attack on the very notion of a shared humanity."[84] Margalit says that the responsibility to remember is central to the notion of care. This is an ethics that has driven Partition studies: the drive to remember, to hear, and to speak.

The memories of survivors at Gulbarg Society constitute evidence of the pogrom which consolidated the majoritarian politics of Hindutva in Gujarat. This in turn catapulted the BJP and Narendra Modi to power in the general elections of 2014. But the collective memory of those who have survived violence engineered by the state is a testament against the ruthlessness of that power. The Gulbarg Society massacre is reminiscent of the violence of Partition in 1947, which saw the simultaneous concentration of the power of ruling elites and the annihilation of masses. Such incidents of mass violence are germane to the foundational violence of the nation state. But the violence of the state requires the agency of individuals and the complicity of society. The events that befell Muslims in Gujarat in 2002 are today denied to have occurred by the majority of people. When there is failure to acknowledge the voices and memories of survivors of violence, there is also a failure to condemn violence. Therefore, in order to halt the iterative violence instigated by the state, in order to forestall the state from killing with impunity, there needs to be a recognition of those who have been affected by that violence. And Gulbarg Society beckons us to remember and to care, in order to abjure the horrors of violence. It is an embodiment of memory against the amnesia of the state. Paying heed to the memories of those who survived the Gulbarg Society massacre is a palliative to the pitilessness of right-wing Hindutva nationalism that exists in India today.

APPENDIX: IMAGES FROM GULBARG

See Figs. 9.1, 9.2, 9.3, 9.4, 9.5, 9.6, 9.7 and 9.8.

---

[84] Avishai Margalit, *The Ethics of Memory* (Cambridge, MA: Harvard University Press, 2002), 9.

Fig. 9.1 Salma Jafri (right) and Duraiyya Jafri (left) reading the Quran at a *Quran-khaani* in Gulbarg Society on 28 February 2017 *Source* Copyright Heba Ahmed

Fig. 9.2 Distribution of food at the *Quran-khaani Source* Copyright Heba Ahmed

Fig. 9.3 Saira Sandhi lighting an incense stick in her home at Gulbarg Society *Source* Copyright Heba Ahmed

Fig. 9.4   The mangled body of a dead dog at Gulbarg Society *Source* Copyright Heba Ahmed

Fig. 9.5 Door of Rupa Mody's flat at Gulbarg Society, showing stickers pasted by Azhar, her son who has been missing since 2002 *Source* Copyright Heba Ahmed

Fig. 9.6 A school timetable stuck on the wall by Azhar Mody, before the massacre 15 years ago *Source* Copyright Heba Ahmed

Fig. 9.7 Saraspur Roza, where the remains of Ehsan Jafri's body have been buried *Source* Copyright Heba Ahmed

Fig. 9.8 Qasambhai Mansuri, at the dargah near Gulbarg Society *Source* Copyright Heba Ahmed

Works Cited

Ahmed, Syed Khalique. "Gulbarg Society beyond recognition seven years after carnage." *Indian Express.* February 28, 2009. http://archive.indianexpress.com/news/gulbarg-society-beyond-recognition-seven-years-after-carnage/429106/.

Appadurai, Arjun. *Fear of Small Numbers: An Essay on the Geography of Anger.* Durham and London: Duke University Press, 2006.

"BJP MP seeks action against Setalvad." *Indian Express.* February 2, 2013. http://archive.indianexpress.com/news/bjp-mp-seeks-action-against-setalvad/106826/.

Butalia, Urvashi. *The Other Side of Silence: Voices from the Partition of India.* New Delhi: Penguin Books, 1998.

Butler, Judith. *Frames of War: When is Life Grievable.* London: Verson Books, 2009.

Cavell, Stanley. Foreword to Veena Das. *Life and Words: Violence and the Descent into the Ordinary.* Berkeley and Los Angeles: University of California Press, 2007.

Chalmers, John. "In Narendra Modi's Gujarat, a case of rule and divide." *Livemint.* May 14, 2014. http://www.livemint.com/Politics/xDcv5reXXuzWlCMdDBtstI/In-Narendra-Modis-Gujarat-a-case-of-rule-and-divide.html.

Chu, Henry. "Film about massacre banned in India state/L.A. director had friend who lost son in Hindu slaughter." *Los Angeles Times.* February 25, 2007. http://www.sfgate.com/politics/article/Film-about-massacre-banned-in-India-state-L-A-2646206.php.

Connerton, Paul. *How Modernity Forgets.* Cambridge: Cambridge University Press, 2009.

Connerton, Paul. *The Spirit of Mourning: History, Memory and the Body.* Cambridge: Cambridge University Press, 2011.

Das, Veena. *Life and Words: Violence and the Descent into the Ordinary.* Berkeley and Los Angeles: University of California Press, 2007.

Dasgupta, Manas. "A Decade After, Memories Haunt Godhra, Gulbarg." *The Hindu.* February 28, 2012. Accessed June 29, 2016 at 15:24. http://www.thehindu.com/news/national/a-decade-after-memories-haunt-godhra-gulberg/article2939332.ece.

Dhattiwala, Raheel. "Next-door Strangers: Explaining 'Neighbourliness' Between Hindus and Muslims in a Riot-affected City." In *Indian Muslims: Struggling for Equality of Citizenship*, edited by R. Hassan. Melbourne: Melbourne University Press, 2016.

Fernandes, Leela. "The Politics of Forgetting: Class Politics, State Power and the Restructuring of Urban Space in India." *Urban Studies* 41, no. 12 (November, 2004): 24152430. http://citeseerx.ist.psu.edu/viewdoc/download?doi=10.1.1.502.3637&rep=rep1&type=pdf.

Fricker, Miranda. *Epistemic Injustice: Power and the Ethics of Knowing*. Oxford: Oxford University Press, 2007.

"Godhra Train Fire Accidental: Banerjee Report." *The Times of India*. March 4, 2006. http://timesofindia.indiatimes.com/india/Godhra-train-fire-accidental-Banerjee-report/articleshow/1437742.cms.

"Gulbarg Society Massacre Case: Timeline." *The Hindu*. June 2, 2016.

Guruswamy, Mohan. "15 Years After Godhra, We Still Don't Know Who Lit the Fire." *Hindustan Times*. February 27, 2017. http://www.hindustantimes.com/analysis/15-years-after-the-godhra-we-still-don-t-know-who-lit-the-fire/story-vkeZowN2nhvVkAJPZAPntN.html.

Halbwachs, Maurice. *On Collective Memory*. Edited and translated by Lewis Coser. Chicago: University of Chicago Press, 1992.

Hasan, Mushirul, ed. *Inventing Boundaries: Gender, Politics and the Partition of India*. New Delhi: Oxford University Press, 2000.

"Intimidation by Foisting False cases Against Teesta Setalvad and Javed Anand: Statements by Sabrang and CJP." http://www.sacw.net/article7161.html.

Iqbal, Naveed. "Everyone in Tilak Vihar has a Story." *Indian Express*. November 3, 2014. http://indianexpress.com/article/cities/delhi/everyone-in-tilak-vihar-has-a-1984-story/.

Johari, Aarefa. "Stuck in Time: Why Gulbarg Society Survivors Are Finding it Impossible to Sell Their Abandoned Homes." *Scroll*. June 20, 2016. https://scroll.in/article/810220/stuck-in-time-why-gulbarg-society-survivors-find-it-impossible-to-sell-their-abandoned-homes.

Kaul, Suvir, ed. *The Partitions of Memory: The Afterlife of the Division of India*. New Delhi: Permanent Black, 2001.

Khan, Ayesha. "How to Profit from a Disturbed Area." *Ink*. October 3, 2013. http://fountainink.in/?p=2784&all=1.

Kumar, Priya. "Testimonies of Loss and Memory." *Interventions* 1, no. 2 (2006): 201–215. http://dx.doi.org/10.1080/13698019900510311.

Margalit, Avishai. *The Ethics of Memory*. Cambridge, MA: Harvard University Press, 2002.

"Memorial for 1984 to come up in Delhi." November 1, 2014. http://www.dnaindia.com/india/report-memorial-for-1984-anti-sikh-riot-victims-to-come-up-in-delhi-2031339.

Menon, Ritu, and Kamla Bhasin. *Borders and Boundaries: Women in India's Partition*. New Delhi: Kali for Women, 1998.

Miller, David. *The Comfort of Things*. Cambridge: Polity Press, 2008.

Mujeeb, Mohammad. "The Partition of India in Retrospect." In *India's Partition: Process, Strategy and Mobilisation*, edited by Mushirul Hasan. New Delhi: Oxford University Press, 2001.

Munshi, Suhas. "Ehsan Jafri called Modi for Help, I Heard Modi Abuse Him: Gulbarg Survivor." *Catchnews.* June 2, 2016. http://www.catchnews.com/india-news/ehsan-jafri-called-modi-for-help-i-heard-modi-abuse-him-gulberg-survivor-1464888144.html.

Pandey, Gyanendra. "Can a Muslim be an Indian?" *Comparative Studies in Society and History* 41, no. 4 (1999): 608–629. http://www.jstor.org/stable/1794.

Parzania. Directed by Rahul Dholakia (2007).

The Final Solution. Directed by Rakesh Sharma (2004).

Press Trust of India. "32 Years Later, the "Wall of Truth" Memorial in Delhi." 7 January 2017. https://www.scoopwhoop.com/32-Years-Later-The-Wall-Of-Truth-Memorial-In-Delhi-For-1984-Sikh-Riots-Victims-Finally-Complete/#.e6woh3vkx.

Roy, Gera, Anjali and Nandi Bhatia, ed. *Partitioned Lives: Narratives of Home, Displacement and Resettlement.* New Delhi: Pearson, 2008.

Saint, Tarun K. *Witnessing Partition.* New Delhi: Routledge, 2010.

Shafi, Showkat. "In Pictures: Delhi's Widow Colony." *Al Jazeera.* February 4, 2014. http://www.aljazeera.com/indepth/inpictures/2014/02/pictures-delhi-widow-colony-20142381643420910.html.

Shah, Amrita. *Ahmedabad: A City in the World.* New Delhi: Bloomsbury, 2015.

Simpson, Edward, and Stuart Corbridge. "The Geography of Things That May Become Memories: The 2001 Earthquake in Kachchh-Gujarat and the Politics of Rehabilitation in the Prememorial Era." *Annals of the Association of American Geographers* 96, no. 3 (September, 2006): 566–585. http://www.jstor.org/stable/4124433.

Sontag, Susan. *Remembering the Pain of Others.* New York: Picador, 2003.

"Trial resumes in Gulbarg Society Case." *The Hindu.* November 28, 2014. http://www.thehindu.com/news/national/other-states/trial-resumes-in-gulberg-society-case/article6644132.ece.

Venkatesan, J. "Notify SIT in 10 Days." *The Hindu.* March 27, 2008. http://www.thehindu.com/todays-paper/Notify-SIT-in-ten-days-court/article15191981.ece.

Venkatesan, J. "Supreme Court stays Proceedings in 10 Godhra-related cases." *The Hindu.* November 22, 2003. http://www.thehindu.com/2003/11/22/stories/2003112206210100.htm.

CHAPTER 10

The Shahbag Protest and Imagining an "Ideal" Bangladesh

Sanchari De

The "Shahbag protest" refers to the mass gathering that took place in Shahbag Square in Dhaka, Bangladesh, on 5 February 2013. This gathering came about after the International Crimes Tribunal (ICT) sentenced the war criminal Abdul Kader Mollah to life imprisonment instead of death. In 2009 the Awami League Government in Bangladesh had formed the ICT to investigate and prosecute suspected perpetrators of the genocide that took place in the region during Bangladesh's struggle for independence in 1971. The formation of the ICT in Bangladesh is significant because unlike other war crime trials, which have mainly been initiated by the United Nations, the ruling government of Bangladesh formed this ICT in their own country. Thousands of people gathered at Shahbag Square on 5 February 2013 and demanded capital punishment for Kader Mollah.[1] Rapidly the protest spread to other

---

[1] Sanchari De, "Debates About Religion and Secularism Turn Lethal in Bangladesh: The Case of The Shahbag Movement," *Religion Going Public Blog*, Last modified January 29, 2017, http://religiongoingpublic.com/archive/2017/debates-about-religion-and-secularism-turn-lethal-in-bangladesh-the-case-of-the-shabag-movement.

S. De (✉)
Jadavpur University, Kolkata, India
e-mail: sancharide.ju@gmail.com

© The Author(s) 2018
C. Mahn and A. Murphy (eds.), *Partition and the Practice of Memory*,
https://doi.org/10.1007/978-3-319-64516-2_10

211

parts of Bangladesh and continued for several months. The Blogger and Online Activist Network (BOAN) played an important role in initiating the protest demonstrations at Shahbag Square.

Although the Shahbag protest started with the demand for the capital punishment of war criminals from the 1971 Bangladesh Liberation War, this protest also demonstrated a broader struggle to conceptualise social justice in relation to the constitution of the Bangladeshi nation, especially in the face of the ongoing legacy of Partition. This struggle took its inspiration from the Bangladeshi Language Movement (1948–1952), which had challenged the adoption of Urdu as a national language and which was at the core of the articulation of an independent Bangladesh. Through this later social justice movement, a longer history of language, culture, identity and self-determination was invoked. The demonstrations themselves explicitly referenced the 1971 war and struggle through songs, slogans, recitation and street dramas, as well as other forms of cultural expression. The online sphere was active in archiving materials which were often personal and not easily available through mainstream sources. Pro-Shahbag Bengali language blogs such as *Mukto-mona* were popular as an alternative to the official sources of history, which glossed over the complexities of the Liberation War. Glorified accounts of the Liberation War were challenged and interrogated at this time, as past conflicts resurfaced in the events and discourses of the Protest.

The Liberation War and the birth of Bangladesh problematise the "two-nation theory" which initiated the partition of India and Pakistan. Although the Liberation War of Bangladesh was a result of unrest between East and West Pakistan, the memory and trauma of the India–Pakistan partition played an important role during the 1971 Liberation War.[2] The liberation of Bangladesh also underlines the complexities of constructing "nations" based on a homogeneous European ideal within heterogeneous South Asian contexts. The Bengali nationalism of 1971 was an outcome of the complexities in, and differences between, South

---

Accessed 8 May 2017. The demand for the capital punishment in the name of justice seems to be very decisive one in the case of the Shahbag protest. While the demand for death might seem to be inhumane, in the context of Bangladesh it remains a legal demand which the activists term as "highest punishment."

[2] Bina D'Costa, *Nationbuilding, Gender and War Crimes in South Asia* (Oxon, NY: Routledge, 2011), 41.

Asian nation-building projects. Amena Mohsin argues that the West Pakistani model of nationhood was an imposition upon the entire population of the state of Pakistan.[3] Mohsin argues that "this imposition resulted in the alienation of the Bengalis of East Pakistan who sought to counter it through Bengali nationalism."[4] In this regard, to counter a form of nationhood (Pakistani), another form of nationhood (Bengali) was conceptualised, and it was understood to be based on language and culture, rather than on religion. The Shahbag protest therefore demonstrates the imagination of an 'ideal' Bangladesh in close proximity to the underlying conceptual underpinnings of Bengali nationalism.

At the same time, the Shahbag protest opens up possibilities of addressing the complexities to be found within a new nation derived from a post-Partition state. Although the new nation of Bangladesh was formed after the Liberation War, the nation-building process encountered new complications. For example, as Amena Mohsin notes, "The Bangladesh which was carved out of the eastern half of Pakistan in 1971, has a homogeneous population of 98 percent, yet she too faces an integrational challenge".[5] The Bengali language and culture which was the basis of Bengali nationalism could not be all-inclusive, according to Mohsin's research. Bangladeshi nationalism, which came after the coup in August 1975 and was notable for "move on towards Islamization",[6] could not be all-inclusive either. As a result, twocompeting forms of nationalism developed in the new nation.

The birth of Bangladesh through the Liberation War and the genocide of almost 3 million people during the 1971 Liberation War took place in what was then East Pakistan, itself a legacy of the 1947 Partition of the subcontinent.[7] Indeed, the Liberation War in 1971 can be seen

---

[3] Amena Mohsin, *The Politics of Nationalism: The Case of the Chittagong Hill Tracts Bangladesh* (Dhaka: The University Press Limited), 25.

[4] Ibid., 26.

[5] Ibid., 3.

[6] Ibid., 67.

[7] Navine Murshid, "The Genocide of 1971 and the Politics of Justice," in *Routledge Handbook of Contemporary Bangladesh*, ed. Ali Riaz and Mohammed Sajjadur Rahman (Oxon, NY: Routledge, 2016). Navine Murshid notes that the number of people killed during the genocide is disputed. It is estimated that between 300,000 and 3 million people were killed.

to emerge from a series of protests and unrest that date from that time. Rounaq Jahan notes:

> Though the liberation war in Bangladesh lasted only nine months, the nationalist movement that preceded the war spanned the previous two decades. Indeed, the seeds of the Bangladesh nationalist movement were planted very soon after the creation of Pakistan in 1947.[8]

Although East Pakistan was liberated in 1971 through a nine-month long war, the consequences of this second partition has rippled through the decades. The Shahbag protest, it is argued here, is another manifestation of that struggle. A recent series of assassinations of bloggers in Bangladesh has led the international media to focus on the contribution of the digital Bengali language sphere in debating freedom of expression and interrogating religious controversies.[9] Since blogs in Bangladesh played an active role in organising and facilitating the Shahbag protest in Dhaka, such online political expression is at the centre of our concern here.

This chapter discusses how this protest about justice for the victims of genocide became a political struggle that involved a return to the moment of Bangladesh's independence—itself a violent conflict—to interrogate the ways in which partition has produced unstable contexts which propagate violence, trauma and ultimately a form of failure. The question addressed is as follows: how did the memories of the Liberation War and war crimes inform the consciousness of the generation that took part in the protest? The essay examines how individuals attempted to construct an "imagined community" of the nation through pro-Shahbag blogs. Further to this, I discuss the emergence of Bengali blogs in which individual accounts of national belonging received a platform for expression in Bangladesh, articulating new ideas of an "ideal" Bangladesh. How does the imagination of this "ideal" Bangladesh help to create the momentum necessary to organise resistance? Touching on the work of

---

[8] Rounaq Jahan, "Genocide in Bangladesh," in *Century of Genocide: Critical Essays and Eyewitness Accounts*, 3rd ed., ed. Samuel Totten and William S. Parsons (New York: Routledge, 2009), 245.

[9] De, "Debates About Religion and Secularism."

Keightley and Pickering,[10] this chapter will suggest ways in which the past represents a point of tension between the state and contemporary protest. I argue that references to glorious past movements and the idea of an "ideal" Bangladesh have been used to point out dissatisfaction with the present democratic state and to validate the current demands and protest of the Shahbag movement. This chapter also points out how the issue of freedom of expression was reflected in the *Mukto-mona* blog through the imagining of an "ideal" Bangladesh, which was constituted as a politically and culturally challenging act.

Background to the Study

This paper is related to my PhD project, which is based on research material gathered from interviews with 22 activists/bloggers directly associated with the Shahbag protest. The interviews were conducted through Skype and transcribed and translated for coding, allowing for thematic analysis. Apart from the interviews, this research also gathers data using some aspects of digital ethnography and visual analysis. I used these methods, for example, to study the *Mukto-mona* blog. Started in 2001 by the late blogger, writer and activist Avijit Roy, *Mukto-mona.com* was turned into a blog in 2004. It became a platform for free thinking and writing about science, and scientific, as opposed to religious, explanations of the universe; it also provided a space for an intimate history of the 1971 Liberation War alongside the idea of a secular Bangladesh, which was revisited by many bloggers. The assassination of Dr. Avijit Roy and the attack on Roy's wife, Rafida Ahmend Bonya on 26 March 2015, brings forward the issues of human rights and freedom of expression, and of the plight of this group of bloggers in present-day Bangladesh. This incident forced many bloggers in Bangladesh to flee the country and seek political asylum in different parts of the world. However, Roy's murder is not the first incident of the curbing of the freedom of expression of bloggers in Bangladesh. During the Shahbag protest in 2013 the blogger Ahmed Rajib Haider was murdered in the same way Roy was— hacked to death. These two incidents and an exodus of bloggers are some of the consequences of the Shahbag protest.

---

[10] Emily Keightley and Michael Pickering, *The Mnemonic Imagination: Remembering as Creative Practice* (New York: Palgrave Macmillan, 2002).

I will use the data gathered from my interviews to reflect here on two features which underpinned the Shahbag protest: the aspiration to connect with memories of struggle and the demand for democratic freedom. The interview data will be compared to blog posts to examine whether the above-noted aspirations were mediated through the blogosphere and if individual aspirations corresponded with the digital sphere of protest. While discussing the blog posts, some interview data will be used to elaborate on how blog posts correspond to the individual reflections of people who participated in the interviews I conducted. Finally, in the data analysis I will discuss the process of remembering and the issue of memories of struggle and protest, especially around Partition, in order to understand the working of cultural and political memory in the context of the Shahbag protest.

Media Censorship and Rise of Bengali Blogs

There is a long history of censorship in Bangladesh—dating from before its liberation from Pakistan—and it was this "heavily regulated framework" for traditional media that was so important in the rise of the Bengali blogs, where people could freely express their thoughts.[11] The introduction of the internet in Bangladesh in 1996 opened up possibilities for creating an alternative to these highly controlled media sources and the media censorship of political, cultural and rational debates; initially blogs were not regulated like the traditional media.[12] As a result, Bengali-language blogging communities emerged. Within a decade, Bangladeshi blogs had become very popular platforms on which internet users could participate in political as well as sociocultural discussions.[13] Blogging soon emerged as an alternative platform on which to express

---

[11] A.B.M. Hamidul Mishbah, "Media Law in Bangladesh," in *Bangladesh's Changing Mediascape: From State Control to Market Forces*, ed. Brian Shoesmith, Jude William Genilo, and Md. Anisuzzaman (Bristol, UK: Intellect, 2013); Naeem Mohaiemen, "Fragile Fourth Estate: A History of Censorship in Bangladesh (1972–2012)," in *Bangladesh's Changing Mediascape*, ed. Shoesmith et al.

[12] Naeem Mohaiemen, "Fragile Fourth Estate: A History of Censorship in Bangladesh (1972–2012)," in *Bangladesh's Changing Mediascape*, ed. Shoesmith et al.

[13] Fahmidul Haque, "Bangla Blog Community: Opinion, Virtual Resistance or the Hunger for Creating Community of the Detached People," *Yogayog* 10 (2011).

opinions about politics and other issues such as religion, atheism and homosexuality that had been targeted for censorship in other venues.

Moiyen Zalal Chowdhury's research on "The Internet as a Public Sphere" examines discussions about the Liberation War and radical Islamist issues on popular blogs.[14] He found that such issues generated active and interactive participation among users. Civic issues were a prime concern of these blogs. In some cases, blogs even outperformed traditional media coverage in terms of their swiftness in communicating a piece of information.[15] However, the popularity and practice of blogging were limited to the educated and urban middle class as a result of the digital divide and socio-economic configuration of the country. Many bloggers, within their small community, tried to address the issue of secularism and often took part in various street demonstrations prior to the Shahbag protest. While talking about secularism, they often researched and investigated the history of the Bangladesh's emergence, and they came to claim that secularism and freedom of cultural expression were the main ideas behind the liberation struggle of 1971.

As a way of investigating history, the pro-Shahbag bloggers' community also often referred to a significant mock trial that occurred in 1992. In that year, Jahanara Imam, who is known as the "mother of the martyr", set up a symbolic mock trial under the name of the "Ghatak Dalal Nirmul Committee" (the committee to exterminate the killers and collaborators), following accused war criminal Ghulam Azam's ascension to the post of 'Amir' ('leader') of the Jamaat-e-Islami (the largestconservative Islamist party in Bangladesh) in 1991. In 1992, the Committee led by Jahanara Imam set up a "Gano-adalot" (mass court) in which accused war criminals were "tried" and "sentenced". In retrospect, Nazin Tithi writes that:

> When Nirmul Committee's statement was published in newspapers, it was met with huge support from the public. Many organisations such as Muktijoddha Sangsad (Mahfuz-Kabir), *Shaheed Lieutenant Selim*

---

[14] Moiyen Zalal Chowdhury, "The Internet as a Public Sphere: Blogging 'Liberation War vs Jamaat' Issue in Somewherein … Blog, a Case Study," *The Academis.edu* (2012), last modified June 25, 2012, http://www.academia.edu/2241606/The_Internet_as_a_public_sphere_Blogging_Liberation_war_vs_Jamaat_issue_in_somewherein...blog_a_case_study. Accessed 8 May 2017.

[15] Ibid.

Mancha, Projonmo '71, Gram Theatre and many socio-cultural organisations expressed solidarity with the committee. Pro-liberation political parties and progressive student organisations expressed their support for the movement.[16]

Jahanara Imam's image was held high during the Shahbag protest.[17] Tithi describes Imam's symbolic presence in the Shahbag protest thus:

> Young people from all across the city joined the protest, demanding that he receive the death sentence. They chanted slogans: Jahanara Imamer rokto amader dhomonite (Jahanara Imam's blood flows through our veins), as they carried Shaheed Janani's portraits in their hands. Three years earlier, in March 2010, the International Crimes Tribunal had been formed and the trial of war criminals began. Jahanara Imam became a symbol of their movement.[18]

There are several layers to Imam's representation that are worth noting. Firstly, Jaharana Imam is known by the title "mother of the martyr", as her son Rumi died during the Liberation War. Rumi was a young man whose glorious martyrdom was portrayed by Jahanara Imam in her memoir of the Liberation War, *Ekattorer Dinguli* (1986). Rumi was a source of inspiration for many contemporary young activists, who were too young to have participated in the Liberation War but felt deeply moved by it. One interviewee says that "The Character of Rumi actually inspired a lot... I used to think myself as Rumi, a young freedom fighter who died for his country."[19] Here the young activist's image of a freedom fighter is inspired by the heroic sacrifices of Rumi, Imam's son. Jahanara Imam's symbolic presence at the Shahbag protest on this level thus suggests the unfinished achievements of the Liberation War. Secondly, her role as a woman and mother is striking in this regard. The slogan "Jahanara Imam's blood flows through our veins" extends this

---

[16] Nazin Tithi, "Gano Adalot: The Rallying Cry of the Masses for Justice," *The Daily Star*, last modified January 23, 2016, http://www.thedailystar.net/in-focus/gano-adalot-205765. Accessed 8 May 2017.

[17] Online Desk, "22nd Death Anniversary of Jahanara Imam Sunday," *The Daily Samakal*, last modified June 25, 2016, http://www.samakal.net/2016/06/25/6810. Accessed 8 May 2017.

[18] Tithi, "Gano Adalot."

[19] Interviewee 3, in discussion with the author, 16 April 2016.

metaphorical portrayal of Imam as mother, and is indicative of how people chose to conceptualise an "ideal" Bangladesh through her. Thirdly, the primary aim of the Committee was to try the people they convicted. It thus sought out a concrete goal, in pursuit of justice through existing legal means. The protest was mainly a non-governmental initiative by many intellectuals in Bangladesh, but it did not challenge the authority of the courts. A young martyr; female (and maternal) leadership; and intellectuals expressing their willingness to try the war criminals through existing legal channels; all of these components contributed to a new image of an "ideal" Bangladesh. The Committee's activity was not acknowledged by the then government and Jahanara Imam was convicted with treason, although her conviction was dropped in 1996. To many, this conviction of treason, and later the verdict of life in prison instead of capital punishment for Kader Mollah, were proof that the state was not providing for justice.

The interviewees directly refer to the symbolic trial of Mollah, which created the scope for the mass mobilisation. As the trial did not materialise in reality, the Shahbag protest became a means for continuing mass protest to force the realisation of the Committee's demands for justice. A blogger/activist says that "in 1992 Jahanara Imam created the Ghatak Dalal Nirmul Committee … so it [the Shahbag protest] is a continuation".[20] In this regard, the Shahbag protest is seen by the interviewees as another chapter of the ongoing struggles in Bangladesh that had started with the language movement of 1952; at this time, language and culture became the means for resisting religion. For example:

> In 1952 Pakistan declared that Urdu will be the state language. Why Urdu should be the state language? Because Urdu is written in Arabic Script. So they are bringing religion here… In 1971 when our people killed us they were convinced that freedom fighters are half Muslims… The political game was to denounce us as the atheist. It is justified in Islam to kill the atheists. So, if someone is marked as an atheist, then things become easier in a country where 90% of the people are the followers of the Islam.[21]

An important aspect of this comment is the connection of the present struggle with memories of previous political upheavals and the resistance

---

[20] Interviewee 12, in discussion with the author, 9 June 2016.

[21] Interviewee 3, in discussion with the author, 16 April 2016.

movement for linguistic and cultural freedom. In another interview, an interviewee recalls how culture was used to resist political oppression:

> In '71 Bengali nationalism and Bengali culture became prominent because of politics. Pakistan tried to impose Pakistani culture as Islamic culture to establish their power. So we needed a strong foundation to establish ourselves against them. So our foundation was based on language, culture, for example songs. We used to protest against Pakistanis singing Tagore songs. We used to observe Bengali cultural festivals. They used to say these are Hindu culture. So we started practicing our Bengali culture as a form of protest against Pakistani forces.[22]

In both of these comments, we see an attempt to reconstruct history through the imagination. As these interviewees did not witness those political movements, however, their retellings of the historical struggle are a blend of imagined memory and fact. In the blogosphere, this blend is used as a resource for the reconstruction of memories out of history.

From the interview data, it is evident that apart from the available historical material at hand, this young generation was fed by stories of this Liberation War, its dreams and the horrors people faced to gain freedom. The medium of expression was through personal remembrance in the form of storytelling from the family members or social acquaintances of earlier generations. On the one hand, the interviewees had internalised the glorified account of a struggle which they had not witnessed and wanted to be part of that glory. A blogger activist comments:

> I was born in '71. [...] my family helped freedom fighters. My home was the centre... this is why my nickname means 'revolution'... I felt bad that my father could not go to war, because of me. So I wanted to do something... There was an urge in me to do something ... So, when I got the scope, I started.[23]

On the other hand, the present critical condition of the nation means that the bloggers were experiencing deprivation in the socio-economic

---

[22] Interviewee 2, in discussion with the author, 17 April 2016.

[23] Interviewee 7, in discussion with the author, 4 June 2016.

sphere. This sense of deprivation was further aggravated by the rise of fundamentalist religious groups. According to one interviewee:

> I was a student of Chittagong University... first they come to the halls [university accommodation] as good boys and then there is *dawat* [which] means welcoming and inviting others ... Through the 'dawat' I talked about, they brainwash people. I saw this personally. These are relevant. So Shibir terrorism along with communalism, anti-India propaganda which Ziaur Rahman used as a weapon during from the 1970s, and following Middle Eastern practices, spread strict Wahhabism in the name of Islam. These emerged horribly, and they never confessed their alliance with 1971's genocide.[24]

This sense repeatedly comes across in the writings of the pro-Shahbag blogs. Cultural practices become a means of commemorating history in the case of The Shahbag protests—according to another interviewee, "it is true that [the] Shahbag protest fetched out aspects of Bengali culture, Bengali people had started to forget their own cultural self and the uniqueness of that culture in the flow of Arab culture."[25]

The issue of cultural expression here seems to be intrinsically related to the strategy and meaning-making process evident in the blog posts quoted so far. When the blog posts repeatedly refer to war criminals as the "Rajakars",[26] they evoke the history which, the interviewees claim, was suppressed in official accounts:

> During the era of dictatorship what happened?... for example I read in [...] childhood that on March 25, 1971, a group of invaders attacked the Bengali people. Who are those invaders? It was not written if they were Pakistanis... I came to know about it from my family. My elder brother wrote against dictator Ershad from a small city called Jessore. So he was

---

[24] Interviewee 7, in discussion with the author, 4 June 2016.

[25] Interviewee 1, in discussion with the author, 27 February 2016.

[26] The Rajakar force also known as Razakar was formed by the Pakistani Army during the 1971 Liberation War. In the post-liberation context, the word "Rajakar" refers to those East-Pakistani people who collaborated with the Pakistani Army. "Rajakar" is used pejoratively to mean "traitor."

abducted and kept in secrecy for two years. He died the day after he was released. So, the anti-Ershad[27] movement is in my blood.[28]

In this regard, the blogosphere becomes a space for the articulation of a "suppressed" history. As a result, the protests become a visible reference to a personalised mnemonic version of history. In this process of demonstrations and the recalling of history, contrasting versions of events co-exist, clash and contest one another.

IMAGINING THE PAST

The loss of an imagined "ideal" Bangladesh is a common theme that is evident in the blog posts. This sense of loss is further aggravated by the sense of deprivation of democratic rights. A blogger with the screen name Oippapotyik Oikyapatya comments:

> Sometimes it feels that Ganajagoron Mancha [the platform for mass uprising] was a fallacy. Why should people come to the street and protest for months in demand for the punishment for Rajakars who did not even want this country? Why should we have to ask for their punishment through a protest movement? Why should we be splashed by hot water and beaten by the police if we demand the same, a second time? Is it still East Pakistan? Is it still Yahya Khan in power?[29]

This sense of loss, frustration and deprivation hints at what Emily Keightley and Michael Pickering term "an active synthesis of remembering and imagination."[30] This active synthesis is indicative of the creative aspect of memory:

---

[27] Hussain Muhammed Ershad was the tenth president of Bangladesh; he was in power from 1982 to 1990 and imposed martial law. He became president through a bloodless coup against President Abdus Sattar on 24 April 1982. Later he founded a political party named the Jatiyo Party. In 1989, during Ershad's presidency, Islam was made the state religion. The Anti-Ershad movement, a series of popular protests, was led by Begum Khaleda Zia and Sheikh Hasina, and was active from 10 October 1990 to 4 December 1990.

[28] Interviewee 8, in discussion with the author, 11 June 2016.

[29] Oippapotyik Oikyapatya, "Sayeedir Raay," trans. Sanchari De, *Mukto-mona* blog, last modified September 25, 2014, https://blog.mukto-mona.com/2014/09/25/42687/. Accessed 8 May 2017.

[30] Keightley and Pickering, *The Mnemonic Imagination*, 7.

Memory is mobile and formative, not merely repetitive; it is this which gives memory its creative potential, but the potential is only realized through the productive tension that arises between memory and imagination. The creative quality of these interactions has a cross-temporal resonance, with memory necessary in thinking of the future, and imagination necessary in thinking of the past.[31]

However, to understand the relationship between past, present and future, "an active synthesis of remembering and imagining"[32] is needed:

> It is through the mnemonic imagination that our engagements with the past move through a series of interactive dualities: the constitution of selfhood and the commission of social action; the interplay between experience and expectation, memory and possibility; the relations between lived first-hand experience and mediated or inherited second-hand experience.[33]

Personal recollections of loss and deprivation, in this regard, coalesce in the blog posts and blend with an imagined history; the collective memory becomes individualised when it is compared and contrasted with present lived experiences. A comment from Interviewee 2 hints at the connection between history and democracy in the present, where the ascent to power of war criminals symbolises the loss of democratic rights and deprivation for citizens:

> In 1975 father of the nation [Sheikh Mujibur Rahman] was killed. Then the Rajakars came to power... Bangladesh started walking backwards. Again the Rajakars came to the power. ... then the discussions about the Liberation War were completely banned.[34]

The sense of frustration and deprivation created by the denial of history leads to calls for justice and demands to know the truth. Since the state-sponsored memorialisations often fail to acknowledge the individualised and personalised struggles related to that history, the digital sphere in

---

[31] Ibid., 7.

[32] Ibid.

[33] Ibid.

[34] Interviewee 5, in discussion with the author, 16 April 2016.

conjunction with physical protest can create possibilities for articulating such personalised accounts. Blogging, in this context, seems to widen the political sphere to the public sphere by investigating a history which is often personal and never acknowledged by the state:

> Many bloggers try to bring out the unpublished history of Bangladesh so an urge for knowing the history is being created. The official versions of the history, which are often informed by the government, are often biased and half true. It is a half-truth, because they say only in part. For example: BNP says it was Ziaur Rahman who announced the Liberation on 26th March. Awami League says it was Sheikh Mujib. Both are true. Actually Ziaur Rahman announced it on the behalf of Sheikh Mujib. Awami League says Bangabandhu (Sheikh Mujib) announced it. But they do not say that there were 8 other people who announced it, on the behalf of Bangabandhu. So, one has to take personal initiative to know about history.[35]

The digital sphere creates a context which helps to mobilise personalised articulations of political memory and imagination, an alternative history of this past, and that past's present impact on national narratives of identity and justice. According to another blogger:

> Blog posts are read by 1000[s] of people … There is a lot of propaganda on behalf of Jamaat … This is spread and accepted internationally. And the blogs countered it. In the contemporary Bangladesh, it is said that the highest circulated daily is *Prothom alo*. They have their web versions as well. So altogether, according to them, it is read by 100 million people. Facebook users in Bangladesh number around 500 to 700 thousand people. So when something is written on Facebook and it is circulated and shared on blogs, many people are influenced.[36]

The perceived loss of democratic rights, which is a prevalent theme in the studied blog posts, has been balanced with the individual recollection of anecdotes. While the frustration in these posts over the loss of democratic rights calls to mind historical figures associated with both the ideal of democracy and its loss, personalised recollections bring forward

---

[35] Interviewee 2, in discussion with the author, 17 April 2016.

[36] Interviewee 10, in discussion with the author, 5 June 2016.

the "ignored" people whose contribution could be important for the reshaping of historical events. This whole process indicates the existence of "prosthetic memory" which makes one remember something beyond one's personal experiences.[37]

PERSONAL DISSATISFACTION AS REFERENCE FOR THE FUTURE

This vision of an "ideal" Bangladesh, conjured up through reference to the glories of struggle and resistance in the Liberation War, was not homogeneous everywhere in Bangladesh during the Shahbag protests. Many instances of street violence by Islamist groups took place during this time, in several parts of Bangladesh. One of the significant acts of violence was the murder of blogger Ahmed Raijib Haider on 15 February 2013 near his residence in Pallavi, Dhaka. Rajib, whose pen name was "Thaba Baba" (Saint Claw), was (in)famous for his attitude towards religious fundamentalism. He was also vocal about the crimes committed by war criminals during the 1971 Liberation War. Blogs like *SonarBangladesh* (later banned by the government) in fact published posts criticising Thaba Baba's "anti-Islamic" stand. On 15 February, the day "Thaba Baba" was murdered, a post on Sonarbangladesh.com announced "this 'Thaba baba' is one of the key initiators of the Shahbag protest."[38] The post summarised the "anti-religious" activities of the Shahbag protestors, specifically those of Rajib Haider. The later imprisonment of the bloggers Subrata Shuva, Rasel Pervez, Mashiur Rahman Biplob and Asif Mahiuddin for "blasphemous" posts,[39] which was coupled with a massive counter-demonstration demanding the introduction of anti-blasphemy laws,[40] highlights a close connection between online activism, secularism and the Shahbag protest.

---

[37] Keightley and Pickering, *The Mnemonic Imagination*, 92.

[38] Sparsher Baire, "Shahbag Anodoloner Pichhoner Manushgulo: Parbo 1," *SonarBangladesh*, last modified February 15, 2013, http://www.mediafire.com/view/?ycsyrn4auinbqc7. Accessed 8 May 2017.

[39] Reporters Without Borders, "Four Bangladeshi Bloggers Arrested for 'Blasphemous' Posts," *ifex*, last modified April 4, 2013, http://www.ifex.org/bangladesh/2013/04/04/bloggers_arrested/. Accessed 8 May 2017.

[40] The Associated Press, "Hard-Line Muslim Rally Demands Anti-Blasphemy Laws in Bangladesh," *The New York Times*, last modified April 6, 2013, http://www.nytimes.com/2013/04/07/world/asia/rally-demands-anti-blasphemy-laws-in-bangladesh.html. Accessed 8 May 2017.

Rajib's death represents a very important point of transformation for the narrative structure of the pro-Shahbag blogs. From its emergence, the Shahbag protest tried to articulate the aspiration for a secular nation state. Rajib's death opened up the wider debate of religion vs. atheism. If we pay close attention to the cultural practices and performances in the physical sphere of the Shahbag protest, we notice how Shahbag Square was exploited as a space in which the "ideal" secular Bengali identity could be sketched out. The idea of a Bengali identity over a religious identity is in fact intermingled with the history of the nation itself. The ideals of the 1971 Liberation War for Bangladesh could be traced back to Bangladesh's Language Movement. The notion of the secular nation of Bangladesh, therefore, is linked to speaking the the Bengali language. The death of Rajib underlines this struggle with cultural identity. His murder was justified as an act of revenge against the propagation of atheist thoughts. After his murder his blogs and writings were circulated as PDF copies through anti-Shahbag blogs like the banned site *Sonarbangla*.

In the contemporary context of the Shahbag protest, the Liberation War is no longer simply a historical event that marked the birth of a new nation, "Bangladesh". This war appears now as a symbol which a younger generation connects to and internalises in relation to present struggles. The engagement of pro-Shahbag activists can be traced back to a network of larger cultural and political practices within the history of Bangladesh; the blogospheres gathered the different elements of this network and facilitated a space for discussion and value-creation out of its existing materials. However, after the death of Rajib, as the debate between atheism and religion gained in prominence, the singularity of the idea of a "nation" called Bangladesh came to be problematised. On the one hand, online blogs, instead of upholding the initial demand for justice, mixed it with a debate about religion and atheism. Many religious groups who were actually opposed to extremist practices were part of the Shahbag protest. On the other hand, religious minorities also used the sphere of Shahbag as a space for freedom.[41]

However, after the debate between religion and atheism commenced, one could see disengagement within the Shahbag sphere. This disengagement was considered a "failure" by many bloggers. This "failure"

---

[41] De, "Debates About Religion and Secularism."

in turn created scope for further discussion on the definition of democracy. On the *Mukto-mona* blog, a blogger with the screen name Khaledur Rahman Shaqil went on to explore the reason behind the "failure" in Shahbag's organisational structure:

> We named the 'Shahbag protest' 'Ganajagoron Mancha' … this 'Ganajagoron Mancha' received its first blow on March 26 … where 100,000 people gathered once during our meeting, there were only less than 1000 people on that day. The people who used to say and assume that Ganajagoron Mancha was created by the Awami League and was controlled by Chhatra League [the student wing of Awami League] were very happy on that day. This assumption was wrong, because I myself witnessed the democratic practices in the core committee meetings of Ganajagoron Mancha.[42]

This comment suggests that the participation of "less than 1000" people was evidence of people's disengagement with democracy. Here the concept of democracy is considered something beyond the ruling government party. As a result, any involvement with or association between the Awami League party and the protest is considered undemocratic. Indeed, one of the demands of the Shahbag protest was to ban the Islamic party Jamaat-e-Islami and its student wing, Chhatra Shibir. As the government did not fulfil this demand, the bloggers suspected that the government was mobilising Jamaat-e-Islami for votes. The demand for the outlawing of this party can be understood as a call for an "ideal" Bangladesh. When this did not materialise, it was seen as a form of injustice, caused by the government:

> At the very beginning of the Shahbag protest, the demand was to ban Jamaat-Shibir by March 26. […] After the murder of Rajib Haider, the prime minister uttered that 'Jamaat-Shibir have no right to do politics.' Everyone thought that now their expectations will be fulfilled. But when the protest wave was a little pacified, we read in the newspaper that 'The government is not thinking to ban Jamaat.' Then everyone understood everything. The public is not that foolish. We know what game is being played.[43]

---

[42] Khaledur Rahman Shaqil, "Shahbag Kon Pothey?," trans. Sanchari De, *Mukto-mona*, last modified September 30, 2014, https://blog.mukto-mona.com/2014/09/30/42857/. Accessed 8 May 2017.

[43] Avijit, "Jara Bhor Anbe Boley Pratigjna Karechhe," trans. Sanchari De, *Mukto-mona*, last modified March 29, 2013, https://blog.mukto-mona.com/2013/03/29/34609/. Accessed 8 May 2017.

While this apparent public disengagement was deemed problematic by Shahbag's activists, the end of the Shahbag protest in the physical sphere created scope for further online engagement. This engagement now directly questioned the government, which the earlier physical Shahbag protests had not done:

> But the latest news is that four members on hunger strike are seriously ill and were sent to the hospital. One of them is Niloy and his condition is critical. At the time of writing this, that is, at midnight on the 31st, no one from the government has come to the Shahbag to enquire about him.[44]

This comment was made about a hunger strike by members of the Sahid Rumi Squad who sought the banning of Jamaat-e-Islami. The dissatisfaction with the government that is evident in this comment connects the Shahbag protest to the wider history of political activism and consciousness in Bangladesh.

CONCLUSION

In this chapter I have discussed how blog writings created a discursive space in which individual and collective memories could be articulated in the context of the Shahbag protest. Since the Language Movement, cultural identity has been almost synonymous with national identity in Bangladesh. Amena Mohsin notes that:

> The Language movement of the Bengalis (1948–1952) had sown the seeds of Bengali nationalism. As such it drew its primary ingredients from cultural and linguistic factors. It accepted the total cultural heritage of Bengal which included the works of both Hindu and Muslim writers as its own. This secular orientation denoted a major shift from the 'two-nation' theory of Pakistan where religion alone constituted the base of a nation. In the new construction of the Bengalis, language and culture became predominant; these were the Bengalis from the population of West Pakistan.[45]

---

[44] Athithi Lekhak, "Shahbag Anodoloner 'Carnival Mood' Sesh, Ebar Mukhosh Khule Jabar Pala," trans. Sanchari De, *Mukto-mona*, last modified April 1, 2013, https://blog.mukto-mona.com/2013/04/01/34723/. Accessed 8 May 2017.

[45] Amena Mohsin, *The Politics of Nationalism: The Case of the Chittagong Hill Tracts Bangladesh* (Dhaka: The University Press Limited), 50.

This comment suggests that cultural traditions formed the basis of Bengali nationalism, and these traditions were merged together to form a secular culture. The Shahbag protest constructs this idea of secular cultural nationalism and identity in a number of different ways. In this construction, mnemonic practices hint at a past "ideal" conception of a free democratic nation that, through the protest, was to be realised in the present. This articulation of alternative memories of the Liberation War and related war tribunals and mock trials facilitated a politicised debate and rehearsal of justice in the public and digital spheres. Bloggers reflected on the end of the street protests and the continuation of the broader political and cultural struggle for modernity. The Shahbag protest opened up the possibility of talking about human rights and freedom of expression along with hope for more active public involvement in politics in the future. After the re-emergence of the debate on religion and secular identity in Bangladesh through the Shahbag protest, the blogger activists showed active engagement in talking about secularism and human rights in Bangladesh.

Works Cited

The Associated Press. "Hard-Line Muslim Rally Demands Anti-Blasphemy Laws in Bangladesh." *The New York Times*. Last modified April 6, 2013. Accessed 8 May 2017, http://www.nytimes.com/2013/04/07/world/asia/rally-demands-anti-blasphemy-laws-in-bangladesh.html.

Athithi, Lekhak. "Shahbag Anodoloner 'Carnival Mood' Sesh, Ebar Mukhosh Khule Jabar Pala." *Mukto-mona*. Last modified April 1, 2013. Accessed 8 May 2017, https://blog.mukto-mona.com/2013/04/01/34723/.

Avijit. "Jara Bhor Anbe Boley Pratigjna Karechhe." *Mukto-mona*. Last modified March 29, 2013. Accessed 8 May 2017, https://blog.mukto-mona.com/2013/03/29/34609/.

Baire, Sparsher. "Shahbag Anodoloner Pichhoner Manushgulo: Parbo 1." *SonarBangladesh*. Last modified September 15, 2013. Accessed 8 May 2017, http://www.mediafire.com/view/?ycsyrn4auinbqc7.

D'Costa, Bina. *Nationbuilding, Gender and War Crimes in South Asia*. Oxon, NY: Routledge, 2011.

De, Sanchari. "Debates About Religion and Secularism Turn Lethal in Bangladesh: The Case of The Shahbag Movement." *Religion Going Public*. Last modified January 29, 2017. Accessed 8 May 2017, http://religiongoingpublic.com/archive/2017/debates-about-religion-and-secularism-turn-lethal-in-bangladesh-the-case-of-the-shabag-movement.

Haque, Fahmidul. "Bangla Blog Community: Opinion, Virtual Resistance or the Hunger for Creating Community of the Detached People." *Yogayog*, 10 (2011).

Jahan, Rounaq. "Genocide in Bangladesh." In *Century of Genocide: Critical Essays and Eyewitness Accounts*, edited by Samuel Totten and William S. Parsons, 245–265. NY: Routledge, 2009.

Keightley, Emily, and Michael Pickering. *The Mnemonic Imagination: Remembering as Creative Practice.* NY: Palgrave Macmillan, 2002.

Mishbah, A.B.M. Hamidul. "Media Law in Bangladesh." In *Bangladesh's Changing Mediascape: From State Control to Market Forces*, edited by Brian Shoesmith, Jude William Genilo, and Md. Anisuzzaman, 133–149. Bristol, UK:*Intellect*, 2013.

Mohaiemen, Naeem. "Fragile Fourth Estate: A History of Censorship in Bangladesh (1972–2012)." In *Bangladesh's Changing Mediascape: From State Control to Market Forces*, edited by Brian Shoesmith, Jude William Genilo, and Md. Anisuzzaman, 113–132. Bristol, UK: Intellect, 2013.

Mohsin, Amena. *The Politics of Nationalism: The Case of the Chittagong Hill Tracts Bangladesh.* Dhaka: The University Press Limited, 2002.

Murshid, Navine. "The Genocide of 1971 and the Politics of Justice." In *Routledge Handbook of Contemporary Bangladesh*, edited by Ali Riaz and Mohammed Sajjadur Rahman, 52–61. Oxon, NY: Routledge, 2016.

Oippapotyik Oikyapatya. "Sayeedir Raay." *Mukto-mona.* Last modified September 25, 2014. Accessed 8 May 2017, https://blog.mukto-mona.com/2014/09/25/42687/.

Online Desk. "22nd Death Anniversary of Jahanara Imam Sunday." *The Daily Samakal.* Last modified June 25, 2016. Accessed 8 May 2017, http://www.samakal.net/2016/06/25/6810.

Reporters Without Borders. "Four Bangladeshi Bloggers Arrested for 'Blasphemous' Posts." *Ifex.* Last modified April 4, 2013. Accessed 8 May 2017, http://www.ifex.org/bangladesh/2013/04/04/bloggers_arrested/.

Shaqil, Rahman Khaledur. "Shahbag Kon Pothey?" *Mukto-mona.* Last modified September 30, 2014. Accessed 8 May 2017, https://blog.mukto-mona.com/2014/09/30/42857/.

Tithi, Nazin. "Gano Adalot: the Rallying Cry of the Masses for Justice." *The Daily Star.* Last modified January 23, 2016. Accessed 8 May 2017, http://www.thedailystar.net/in-focus/gano-adalot-205765.

CHAPTER 11

Remembering a Lost Presence: The Spectre of Partition in the Stories of Lahore-Based Punjabi-Language Author Zubair Ahmed

Anne Murphy

Zubair Ahmed, a Punjabi-language author living in Lahore, visualises the passage of time in this way:

> The beginning of our sojourn on this earth is like a blue sky. Time turns it grey. But remembrance turns that ash color into a deep smoky blue. This is the place between dreams and reality, where we live and die.[1]

---

[1] Anne Murphy, with Zubair Ahmed, trans. "Dead Man's Float," *South Asian Ensemble: A Canadian Quarterly of Literature, Arts & Culture* 7, nos. 1 & 2 (Winter and Spring 2015): 159.

An extended version of this paper, translated into French, will appear in *Raconter La Partition: Litterature, Cinema, Arts Plastiques* (*Telling the Partition: Literature, Cinema, Arts*), edited by Anne Castaing. Forthcoming.

A. Murphy (✉)
Department of Asian Studies, University of British Columbia, Vancouver, BC, Canada
e-mail: Anne.Murphy@ubc.ca

C. Mahn and A. Murphy (eds.), *Partition and the Practice of Memory,*
https://doi.org/10.1007/978-3-319-64516-2_11

Here, memories bring colour and depth to that which is lost in the grey advance of time, allowing for something in between life and death, within which memory resides. Remembrance brings the return of the rich blue colour of youth to a spent grey sky, as the promise of a kind of (almost) life. This is what is in between. Through it, past and present are tied, the past enriching the present, even as the passage of time denudes the sky of colour.

Partition is joined to the present through its enduring impact, extending out from the time of 1947 like a hand, grasping the present as a form of ongoing structural violence and loss. In causing a fundamental rupture to the social landscape, it is also a part of a reconfigured continuing political present. This idea and experience of the continuing loss of Partition speaks through Ahmed's stories, in which words such as those given above reflect on the passage of time and the role of memory in rendering the colour of the world. It is one of the ways in which our understanding of Partition as representation must also be configured, in appreciation of the ways that, in Bhaskar Sarkar's words, "the event we call Partition stretches all the way to the present moment", alongside the immediate testimonial mode that dominates in fiction explicitly and directly linked to it.[2]

While historical exploration of the experience of Partition violence was late in arriving, the same was not true in creative forms of expression; as Laurel Steele puts it, "the fictional and poetic response was immediate and significant."[3] The violence associated with Partition was such that, in the words of Ayesha Jalal in her recent study of the life and times of Urdu short story writer Saadat Hasan Manto (1912–1955), "even the coolest of Indian minds had no time to think."[4] Manto was renowned for his unrelenting and searing representations of Partition violence

---

[2] Bhaskar Sarkar, *Mourning the Nation: Indian Cinema in the Wake of Partition.* (Durham: Duke University Press, 2009), 14–15. Sarkar thus treats Partition as "a particularly harrowing moment within a larger trauma of the Indian modern," (ibid., 5) but here the definition of the legacy of and connection to Partition is more specific.

[3] Laurel Steele, "Patriotic Pakistanis, Exiled Poets, or Unwelcome Refugees? Three Urdu Poets Write of Partition and its Aftermath," in *The Indian Partition in Literature and Films: History, Politics, and Aesthetics,* 89–106, ed. Rini Bhattacharya Mehta and Debali Mookerjea-Leonard (London, Routledge, 2015), 92.

[4] Ayesha Jalal, *The Pity of Partition: Manto's Life, Times and Work Across the India–Pakistan Divide* (Princeton: Princeton University Press, 2013), 13.

and its impact, as well as his striking attention to women's experiences; as Aamir Mufti puts it, "his greatest achievement is to have asked how language itself is partitioned."[5] But the literary response to Partition, too, was varied, in ways that were determined by Partition itself. Safir Rammah has noted that Partition did not only divide Punjabis politically and socially, but also in literary and linguistic terms.[6]

While Urdu has dominated as the language of literature in the postcolonial state of Pakistan overall and English literature produced there has been the subject of interest and study, Punjabi-language literature in Pakistan has remained largely under the international and scholarly radar.[7] Most of the literature produced in Punjabi is, according to UK-based Punjabi-language poet and critic Amarjit Chandan, a "literature of lamentation."[8] Poetry has and continues to dominate in the

---

[5] Amir Mufti, *Enlightenment in the Colony: The Jewish Question and the Crisis of Postcolonial Culture* (Princeton: Princeton University Press, 2007), 202. On the role of narratives about women's experiences in destabilising nationalising closure in Partition-related literature, see Jill Didur, *Unsettling Partition: Literature, Gender, Memory* (Toronto: University of Toronto Press, 2006).

[6] Safir Rammah, "West Punjabi Poetry: From Ustad Daman to Najm Hosain Syed," *Journal of Punjab Studies* 13, nos. 1 & 2 (2006): 215–216.

[7] On Pakistani English writing, for example, see a special issue of the *Journal of Postcolonial Writing* 47, no. 2 (2011); yearly accountings of English-language work in Pakistan in the *Journal of Commonwealth Literature*; Tariq Rahman, *A History of Pakistani Literature in English* (Lahore: Vanguard Books, 1991); and the recent David Waterman, *Where Worlds Collide: Pakistani Fiction in the New Millennium* (New York: Oxford University Press, 2015).

The Punjabi language stories translated and included in Alok Bhalla's important three volume collection of stories about Partition are by three India-based authors: Kulwant Singh Virk, "Weeds," 203–208, vol. 1; Kartar Singh Duggal, "Kulsum," 91–94, vol. 3, & "The Abandoned Child" by Gurmukh Singh Musafir, 181–190. See Alok Bhalla, ed., *Stories about the Partition of India,* vols. 1–3 (New Delhi: Indus, 1994). See also: Neena Arora and R.K. Dhawan, eds., *Partition and Indian Literature: Voices of the Wounded Psyche,* vol. 1 (New Delhi: Prestige, 2010). Punjabi and other South Asian vernacular works are addressed in the first volume; English works and film are addressed in the second. See also the very important collection of Punjabi short stories: Nirupama Datt, ed. & trans., *Stories of the Soil* (New Delhi: Penguin Books India, 2010). For interviews with fiction writers about the portrayal of Partition, see: Alok Bhalla, ed., *Partition Dialogues: Memories of a Lost Home* (Delhi: Oxford University Press, 2006).

[8] Amarjit Chandan, "Punjabi Literature on Partition: Some Observations," paper presented to the British Association of South Asian scholars conference held in Bath, England, 11–13 April 1997. Online document available at: http://amarjitchandan.tripod.com/id8.html. Accessed 24

Pakistani Punjabi literary world, and this is where we see some representation of Partition experience.[9] Narrative fiction is a less popular medium of representation, countering the important role of the short story in Urdu, both in general and in representing Partition, where Mufti has argued it offered an important "ambivalent and ironic relationship to the narrative forms of national culture."[10] Punjabi-language literature is thus not simply a mirror or lesser cousin of Urdu representations, but represents a separate domain that requires attention in its own right. Both are deeply connected to the political, however.[11] But Punjabi's very different status in Pakistan vis-à-vis Urdu has defined such a role in its own terms, as Ahmed's work reveals.

PUNJABI IN PAKISTAN

To understand Punjabi-language literary production in the post-colonial period in both India and Pakistan we must register its emergence within colonial-period vernacular literary production in South Asia. As Farina Mir has made clear in an important study of what she calls the "Punjabi literary formation" in the colonial era, Punjabi thrived in that period, but did so outside of the ambit of colonial governmental support; the period saw the flourishing of a wide range of Punjabi literary works, from reformist tracts to the large numbers of inexpensive *qisse* or stories that were shared across religious communities.[12] The modern Punjabi literary formation in the post-colonial period both counters and mirrors the complicated position of Punjabi language and literature

---

May 2016. Thanks to Zubair Ahmed for making me aware of the essay, which provides a valuable overview of literature on Partition written by Punjabis, both in the Punjabi language and not.

[9] Rammah, "West Punjabi Poetry," 218 ff. Rammah notes the work of Ahmad Rahi (1929–2002), with his 1953 collection entitled *Triṅjhaṅh* (Girls' Gathering), which focused in almost half of its poems on the experience of women at Partition (ibid., 221).

[10] Mufti, *Enlightenment in the Colony*, 185.

[11] Christina Oesterheld, "Urdu Literature in Pakistan: A Site for Alternative Visions and Dissent," *The Annual of Urdu Studies* 20 (2005): 82. Oesterheld notes the use of Punjabi in an otherwise Urdu work, lending it a "homely touch"; further work is needed on how Punjabi features in Urdu language literature in Pakistan (ibid., 93).

[12] Farina Mir, *The Social Space of Language: Vernacular Culture in British Colonial Punjab* (Berkeley: University of California Press, 2010).

under the British that Mir describes—with, until recently, uncertain or non-existent state support—with the addition of deep ties to progressive/leftist politics that is typical of modern vernacular literary production in the late colonial period overall.[13] The Punjabi language has been implicated in the post-colonial state of India in the search for a platform for the expression of Sikh interests. This was most dramatically visible in the fight for a linguistically (and culturally) defined Punjabi *sūba* or province, which, as Paul Brass rightly noted early on, can only be understood in the context of the post-colonial state of India in relation to agitation for Hindi, and already existing issues around the imbrication of language and religious identity in the colonial-period Hindi/Urdu controversy.[14] Today, Punjabi's position in India is more secure, but still politicised.[15] In contrast, in Pakistan, the post-colonial state continued British policies in favour of Urdu. There, the language has been famously neglected, such that as Tariq Rahman has noted, any "effort to teach Punjabi [has] floundered on the rock of cultural shame and prejudice."[16] Instead, Urdu dominates and the state resists implementation of pre-collegiate education in and other forms of state support, for the language.[17]

Alyssa Ayres has highlighted a depoliticised role for Punjabi in Pakistan as a uniquely non-nationalist and symbolic linguistic project, such that "although this movement bears the surface features of a classical nationalist formation—insistence upon recovering an unfairly oppressed history and literature, one unique on earth and uniquely

---

[13] This is discussed at length in Anne Murphy, "Writing Punjabi Across Borders" South Asian History and Culture, special issue on "Scripts and Identity: The Politics of Writing Systems in South Asia," ed. Pushkar Sohoni and Carmen Brandt (forthcoming). Some of the material in this paragraph is drawn from this publication.

[14] Paul Brass, *Language, Religion, and Politics in North India* (New York: Cambridge University Press, 1974), 287.

[15] See Murphy, "Writing Punjabi."

[16] Tariq Rahman, *Language, Ideology and Power: Language-Learning Among the Muslims of Pakistan and North India* (Oxford/New York: Oxford University Press, 2002), 401.

[17] Parts of this paragraph and the following are based on background material presented in Anne Murphy, "A Diasporic Temporality: New Narrative Writing from Punjabi-Canada," in *Towards a Diasporic Imagination of the Present: An Eternal Sense of Homelessness*, ed. Tapati Bharadwaja, (Bangalore: Lies and Big Feet Press, 2015), 9–30. See also Murphy, "Writing Punjabi"; Rahman, *Language, Ideology and Power*; and Christopher Shackle, "Pakistan," in *Language and National Identity in Asia*, ed. Andrew Simpson (London, Oxford University Press, 2007), 100–115.

imbued with the spirit of the local people and the local land—the structural features of this process differ markedly from those we have come
to understand as classical nationalisms."[18] Punjabis in Pakistan, in
short, do not advocate for the language as a means to gain power, since
Punjabis dominate numerically in Pakistan, as well as in terms of access
to power and resources. Quite simply, however, as Kalra and Butt per-
suasively assert, "it is a lack of an analysis that takes into account class,
which misdirects much of the research on the Punjabi movement in
West Punjab", where leftist organisations have been central to the movement.[19] Kalra and Butt show that while Punjabi is "shunned" by elites
because of its association with the working classes, "it is precisely this
status that provides the rationale for its appeal to Left-wing groups and
parties."[20] There are, therefore, instrumental aims to Punjabi language
promotion in Pakistan, tied to a progressive political project. Such activism also exhibits strong ties to Punjabi language advocacy and cultural
production in East Punjab and the Punjabi Diaspora. This is indeed one
of the controversies with the movement in Pakistan: the perception that
pro-Punjabi activism would undermine the two-nation justification for
Pakistan and establish unwanted cross-border relationships.[21]

THE STORIES OF ZUBAIR AHMED

Zubair Ahmed (legal name, Muhammad Zubair) was born in Lahore in
1958.[22] In one of his stories, entitled 'Sweater', Ahmed describes himself
through the story's first-person narrator: after finishing high school, he
tells us, "A different kind of bird began to fly in me". That bird led the

---

[18] Alyssa Ayres, "Language, the Nation, and Symbolic Capital: The Case of Punjab," *The Journal of Asian Studies* 67, no. 3 (Aug 2008): 918–919.

[19] Virinder S. Kalra, and Waqas M. Butt, "'In One Hand a Pen, in the Other a Gun': Punjabi Language Radicalism in Punjab, Pakistan," *South Asian History and Culture* (September 2013): 4; see also 6, 15.

[20] Kalra and Butt, "In One Hand a Pen," 2.

[21] Tariq Rahman, *Language and Politics in Pakistan* (Karachi: Oxford University Press, 1996), 202–203; see also Kalra and Butt, "In One Hand a Pen," 1, 2, 7–11; Ayres, "Language, the Nation, and Symbolic Capital," 923.

[22] Mahmood Awan, "Stories That Never End," 19 January 2014. http://tns.thenews.com.pk/stories-never-end/#.V2BMGJMrJ0t. Online document accessed 14 June 2016. Naeem Sadhu, "A Storyteller from the Streets of Lahore," in *Dawn* 14 July 2015. Online document available at: http://www.dawn.com/news/1194352. Accessed 14 June 2016.

character, and Ahmed himself, to Italy. Ahmed remained there for over a year, struggling to survive. He was drawn back to Lahore, to his family, his life there and the memories within the city that sustained him. It is perhaps for this reason that he writes so poignantly about the pull of memory, of its determined hold upon us. Back in Lahore, Ahmed pursued degrees in English language teaching and English literature. He teaches English literature now at Islamia College Lahore, and has been a stalwart supporter of the Punjabi-language movement in Pakistan. He was involved in the Punjabi-language daily newspaper, called *Sajjan* or "Friend", serving as sub-editor on a volunteer basis from 1988 to 1990, and in *Kitāb Trinjan*, the all-volunteer-run Punjabi-language bookstore in Lahore, which was open from 1997 to 2009.[23] He writes Punjabi in the Shahmukhi script (the Perso-Arabic or Urdu script, as it is called in Punjabi), although he also reads Gurmukhi (the script utilised in the Indian Punjab for the language), and has published a modified version of his first book, and his second book in its entirety, in Gurmukhi. He has published two books of poetry and two books of stories in Shahmukhi, the second of which, *Kabūtar, Banere, te Galīāṅ* (2013) (*Pigeons, Ledges, and Streets*), was awarded the Dhahan Prize for Punjabi Literature in Vancouver in 2014.[24]

Overall Zubair Ahmed's stories work to construct simultaneity between past and present, a past that lives in and through the present. Things and places conjure this emergent temporal field, and we see Lahore as an enlivened landscape, shimmering with the reflections of that which was. At times our narrator seems trapped by this past, unable to fully pull away—like the narrator of his story "Rain, Doors and Windows", who cannot leave his vantage point by the window, looking out at the street and the past.[25] In this story, the narrator burns with memory; he tells us: "Hate, you see, is something you have to feed and care for, just as love is."[26] His family circumstances forced his family to

---

[23] Rahman, *Language and Politics,* 206–207; Kalra and Butt, "'In One Hand a Pen'" 2, 11.

[24] Zubair Ahmed, *Mīnh, Būhe, te Bāriyāṅ* (Lahore: Kitab Trinjan, 2001); Zubair Ahmed, *Kabūtar, Banere, te Galīāṅ* (Lahore: Naveed Hafeez Press, 2013). The author of this article assisted in the foundation of the Prize in 2012–2013 and was a founding Co-Chair of the Prize Advisory Committee in 2013–2014.

[25] Ahmed, *Mīnh, Būhe, te Bāriyāṅ,* 31–40.

[26] Throughout this essay, citation is given for the Punjabi Shahmukhi (Perso-Arabic script) published versions for those that have not yet been published in translation. The translation provided here is my own, in collaboration with Mr. Ahmed, which will be

rely on the largess of his uncle and aunt, and the resentment at their high-handed behaviour burns hard and deep within. Or, sometimes the past functions to make sense out of the present—in that same story, the present is woven out of the past, out of the questions about people and places that cannot be answered, a flow of change that destabilises and makes the world unknowable. We can call this a form of nostalgia, what London-based Punjabi language poet and critic Amarjit Chandan, with reference to Ahmed's work, has called "*puṭṭhe pairīṅ jāṇā, wāpasī dā safar*, to walk backwards, a journey back."[27] Even if we do, we must recognise the specific resonances of such a frame.

Ahmed's treatment of time and presence conforms with broader literary patterns that emerge in the representation of Partition.[28] To be clear, Partition as such is not an explicit subject within Ahmed's work: he does not tell us directly of that time. Instead, Ahmed's stories resonate with the lingering effects of Partition, with the haunting of memories of a once-shared past that impinges on the present, resonating with Menon and Bhasin's observations about the reiteration of the experience of Partition through later experiences.[29] This occurs not in the register of violence, but instead in the experience of loss, displacement and betrayal: the violence of a kind of ever-repeating structure of displacement and loss. It is the "afterlife" of Partition, such as explored in a recent volume by Anjali Gera-Roy and Nandi Bhatia, that is found here.[30] Yet it is also in keeping with a general treatment of time with reference to Partition,

included in a forthcoming book-length work: Anne Murphy with Zubair Ahmed, *Windows, Doors, and Streets: The Stories of Pakistani Punjabi-Language Writer Zubair Ahmed* (forthcoming). For another English translation of this story, which differs in significant ways from mine with Mr. Ahmed, see Datt, *Stories of the Soil*, 263–271 .

[27] Amarjit Chandan, "Vele dī Sāthī. Time's Companion," *Lakīr* 91 (2004): 75–76. Translation by the author.

[28] The effort here is to move beyond a neat delineation of "Partition literature." See discussion: Rosemary Marangoly George, "(Extra)Ordinary Violence: National Literatures, Diasporic Aesthetics, and the Politics of Gender in South Asian Partition Fiction," *Signs* 33, no. 1 (2007): 135–158; see especially 139–140.

[29] See discussion in the introduction to this volume. Ritu Menon and Kamla Bhasin, "Recovery, Rupture, Resistance: Indian State and Abduction of Women During Partition," *Economic and Political Weekly* 38, no. 17 (April 24, 1993): WS2–WS11.

[30] Anjali Gera-Roy and Nandi Bhatia, eds., *Partitioned Lives: Narratives of Home, Displacement, and Resettlement* (New Delhi: Pearson Longman, 2008), xi.

in both personal narrative and in fiction. Veena Das' important work on the narration of Partition among survivors has described how "although the Partition was of the past if seen through homogeneous units of measurable time, its continued presence in people's lives was apparent in story, gesture, and conversation. Though of the past, it did not have a feeling of pastness about it."[31] Tarun Saint's comprehensive study of Partition literature similarly foregrounds the temporal displacement at the core of such work: "Partition writings often register the persistence and circulation of [...] phantasmal images from the past in problematic ways ... [taking] the form of a splintered view or double take, looking to the past even while addressing problems in the present."[32]

In some senses, this comes as no surprise: the play of time and memory is central to fictional narrative in the most general terms. The haunting of Partition (and its "before") within Ahmed's stories, however, reflects in part also the workings of time and memory that are specific to Partition literature. We are not in the realm here of the reportage of events, and his stories are not "Partition literature" in the same way as "social realist" works that provide a documentary account.[33] Partition instead haunts these stories as a kind of remembered presence. Saint has observed that over time literature on Partition has exhibited an "emphasis on interiority and a reflexive approach to memory", with writers such as Intizar Hussain engaging multiple temporalities, and a sense of "blocked" or frozen time.[34] This has resulted in "a kind of double-seeing in which both the past and present become simultaneously visible."[35] This kind of seeing is threaded through Ahmed's work, as is a kind of locative displacement that Alok Bhalla has argued is characteristic, too, of Partition literature, where location is portrayed as "incoherent and fragmented."[36]

---

[31] Veena Das, *Life and Words: Violence and the Descent into the Ordinary* (Berkeley: University of California Press, 2006), 97.

[32] Tarun K. Saint, *Witnessing Partition: Memory, History, Fiction* (New Delhi: Routledge, 2010), 28. See also: Tarun K. Saint, "The Long Shadow of Manto's Partition Narratives: 'Fictive' Testimony to Historical Trauma," *Social Scientist* 40, no. 11/12 (2012): 53–62.

[33] Saint, *Witnessing Partition*, 88.

[34] Ibid., 128, 168, and 169.

[35] Ibid., 250.

[36] Bhalla, *Stories about the Partition of India*, 12.

The sense of loss and violence imprinted upon the present in time and place, through the erasure and simultaneous re-inscription of the past, is deeply personal in Ahmed's work, and emotionally rich; the narrator speaks to us in an intimate, confessional mode about a world that is both deeply individual and universal at the same time. In some ways, such an approach may be seen to challenge a strictly social-realist, progressive literary mandate, reflecting perhaps the recourse to an inner world described by Pakistani Urdu poet and feminist Fahmida Riaz: she attributes to Najm Hosain Syed, who has acted in a foundational role in the imagination and support of Punjabi literature in Pakistan, a kind of "mystical Marxism" that is "preoccupied with the 'reality of the self', an undefined goal that transcended the issue of democracy and human rights."[37] Riaz sees Syed's ideas as "impossible" as a result.[38]

This intersection of the personal, the emotional/spiritual and the political at work in Ahmed's work aligns with such a position, but it would be a mistake to read this as a failure to address the political in real terms, or to see it as a fringe view. It reflects, instead, the pressing cultural and intellectual concerns of Pakistani writers since 1947, as described in a range of recent work on this genre, in which, in Kamran Asdar Ali's words, "mere advocacy of the economic needs of the people is [seen as] not enough, as people also have nonmaterial and spiritual needs."[39] The "modernists" are generally said to have rejected the ideological program of the "progressive" writers, in order to pursue alternative lines of inquiry and experimentation. But they did not necessarily abandon concern for material realities. It would thus be a mistake to accept the simple binary of the modernist vs. the progressive, or

---

[37] Fahmida Riaz, *Pakistan: Literature and Society* (New Delhi: Patriot Publishers, 1986), 93. For an example of Syed's work in English, see: Najm Hosain Syed, *Recurrent Patterns in Punjabi Poetry* (Lahore: Majlis Shah Husain, 1968?)

[38] Riaz, *Pakistan*, 95–96.

[39] Kamran Asdar Ali, "Progressives and 'Perverts': Partition Stories and Pakistan's Future," *Social Text 108* 29, no. 3 (Fall 2011): 14. Also on Askari, see Aamir Mufti, "The Aura of Authenticity," in *Social Text* 18, no. 3 (2000): 93 ff.; Kamran Asdar Ali, "Communists in a Muslim Land: Cultural Debates in Pakistan's Early Years," in *Modern Asian Studies* 45, no. 3 (2011): 522 ff.; Mehr Afshan Farooqi, "Towards a Prose of Ideas: An Introduction to the Critical Thought of Muhammad Hasan Askari," *The Annual of Urdu Studies* (2004): 175–190. For more extensive discussion of this issue, see Murphy, "Writing Punjabi"; this paragraph draws on that essay.

communist vs. nationalist: as Asdar Ali points out, the "political stance of the communists was at times dangerously close to that of its own opposition, the Pakistani state and the Islamists ... they too were seeking to create a universalist politics of social identity and homogeneity and a rational society."[40] Amir Mufti's important discussion of the problematics of the recourse to the "authenticity" of religion as an alternative to the destruction associated with colonial modernity addresses this set of concerns, requiring a rethinking of the binary assumed between the two to embrace "the possibilities of living *with* this crisis [of authenticity] and coming to understand the social and ethical stakes in the struggle to live."[41] This I believe speaks to our reading of Ahmed, placing his work within the longer history of the intersection of the progressive with the psychological/personal, with complex recourse to politics, culture, and "the spiritual" (or, in Ahmed's terms, the personal as spiritual).[42] Indeed, in discussing the work of N.M. Rashed, A. Sean Pue has recently argued that the author's exploration of personal experience "may very well be Rashed's response to the devastation wrought by Partition upon the claims to identity", but that "emphasizing personal experience is not the same thing as turning from the social realm, as progressive critics frequently contend."[43] Instead, Rashed's embrace of the contingency of human experience allowed him to articulate a contingent position outside of identity itself. This allows for a new kind of progressive position. Advocacy for Punjabi today is also being reconfigured on such newly drawn lines, which are no less political: as Kalra and Butt have recently observed, adherence to party lines is not at the centre of the Punjabi language movement today.[44]

---

[40] Asdar Ali, "Progressives and 'Perverts'," 20. See also discussion of "national realism" In Mufti, *Enlightenment in the Colony*, 183 ff.

[41] Mufti, "The Aura of Authenticity," overall and 96 for quote. For related discussion of the role of religion as "other" to the colonial modern, see also Christian Novetzke, "The Subaltern Numen: Making History in the Name of God," *History of Religions* 46, no. 6 (2006): 99–126.

[42] Ahmed's work does not play with the discourse of the religious; his arena of expression encompasses the personal and emotional/spiritual without formal religious affiliation.

[43] A. Sean Pue, "Ephemeral Asia: Postition without Identity in the Modernist Urdu Poetry of N.M. Rashed," *Comparative Literature* 64, no. 1 (2012): 86.

[44] Virinder Kalra, "Campaigning for Punjabi in Sahiwal," Presentation at the meeting of the Punjab Research Group, Coventry University, 27–28 June 2014. This and the prior paragraph draw on material presented in Murphy, "Writing Punjabi."

This is the personal and political frame that undergirds Ahmed's fictive work. In his story, "Dead Man's Float" ("*Murdah Tārī*"), Ahmed opens with a portrait of the changing urban landscape that is lost to those without financial means; he could as easily be speaking of Vancouver as Lahore, where investors gobble up properties to transform them into monster houses for the rich, and all but the wealthiest families are unable to buy homes to live in.[45] He writes: "It is our tragedy that we are not allowed to live in the places where we are born and become ourselves, the dreams of which remain alive within us."[46] The old home of the story's protagonist appears through and within such changes, and he seeks out a lost world that crumbled with the house of his youth. This is a theme Ahmed returns to in other stories as well, how the landscape of Lahore—marked as it is by a past that has been erased—has no space for the old, and how people are forced out to make room for the propertied, instituting yet another layer of erasure. This continuing story of displacement, lacking the "eventness" of Partition, is no less traumatic for those who are forced out, and seems to reiterate it. Involuntarily, memory accumulates and impinges on that unfolding loss. It is a kind of latticework, joining disparate points of a city into a whole knowable only through its fracture. The narrator walks around an old neighbourhood in Lahore, now slowly being gentrified:

> Walking in the old *mohalla*, it is as if he were standing in front of her house. At that time, it appeared to be such a big house. But it was just a small house on a tiny lot. It was old, from the time before Partition, and no one had spent anything on it for many years. Mud oozed from the fissures in the walls.

> The dark night has thickened.[47]

"Dead Man's Float" meditates on the social hierarchies that persist among those thrust together in urban settings by Partition and other traumas, and on those things that divide within the Lahore landscape, from the time of Partition and moving forward. A woman appears by

---

[45] Ahmed, *Kabūtar, Banere, te Galliāṅ*, 15–22.

[46] Murphy with Ahmed, "Dead Man's," 159.

[47] Slightly modified for readability, from the translation given in Murphy with Ahmed, "Dead Man's," 165.

chance, in the narrator's old neighbourhood: "How proud she was of her beauty and status; how rich she appeared at that time." He reminisces, drenched in rain outside the house that stands where his old house stood, and is overcome with memories of his brief experience as a migrant in Italy: "That night of 29 years before, when after fleeing from the hunger of his home with some friends, lost in the greed of earning in Europe, he went to Rome and got stuck."[48] That life in Italy was fragile and difficult, at the margins of society. We might see such stories as separate from the ravages of Partition, but to do so would be to ignore the structural features of loss and privation that initiated the protagonist's visit to Italy, the sense of repeating displacement that this experience speaks to. The story revolves around the promise of a night spent in a real bed, in a house: it would have been his first in Italy. Instead, the narrator spends the night in the park, fearful of the police. It is that sense of displacement and fear that links the experience in Rome with his deep alienation at home in Lahore, denying a sense of safety that might be associated with "home".

Ahmed's "Bajwa is silent now", or, perhaps better, "Bajwa has nothing more to say", (*Bājwah huṇ gall nahīṅ kardā*), provides a compelling portrait of the way memories work, speaking and silencing at the same time.[49] Ahmed opens simply: "Bajwa arrives. I've been waiting. He sits for a while and when the mosquitoes start biting his feet, he says 'Shall we go?'"[50] It is a story of lost friendship and changing times. He recounts the story of Iffi, a vulnerable childhood friend from sixth grade:

> He stuck to me like glue. I couldn't even look after myself, yet he looked to me for shelter. The boys would pass us by, pinching his cheek hard, and he would cling yet closer; he was devoted to me. But ... I didn't really understand what his company meant. When he used to be the butt of the jokes of the other boys, I would join them sometimes. I was his friend, but I wasn't loyal.

---

[48] Murphy with Ahmed, "Dead Man's," 161.

[49] Ahmed, *Kabūtar, Banere, te Galliāṅ*, 31–38.

[50] Anne Murphy, with Zubair Ahmed, "Bajwa Has Nothing More to Say", *Pakistani Literature (Journal of the Pakistan Academy of Letters)* 18, no. 1 (2015): 86.

Then the end came. Faiqi slapped his bottom and said, while pushing me:

'Wa, what a pair!

I responded with a shallow, evasive laugh.

'You should have slapped his face'. But Iffi knew that it wasn't possible for me to pay them back in kind. After that, he didn't speak with me anymore. He flat out refused. And in 8th class, he left the school once and for all.[51]

The author relates this to the experience of his own daughter, at the same age: the betrayal of close friends, the loss of intimacies never quite regained. Overall, the story is about the loss of his friend Bajwa, with whom the author developed a close friendship as an adult. Bajwa and he were comrades in politics and in life, sharing everything:

We did everything together, all through those last days of our youth. Friendship, enmities and politics: these were all the same to us, and we faced them together. People spoke of us in the same breath. We met every day, and night would melt into day again. We were one.[52]

The narrator describes his experience of a pro-democracy demonstration after the declaration of martial law by Zia ul Haq: "It was Bajwa who freed me from the policeman with a jerk, and helped me to escape; then he too fled."[53] In the end, however, Bajwa is lost, lost to the differences that emerge between them, to the accumulation of memories of disappointment and betrayal that stand in between. The story describes the hope of the lawyer's movement in Lahore, as demonstrators took on the government, and the narrator is able to return momentarily to the political commitments of youth: "Our old lawyer friends called us to join them: they thought that finally the dice had been cast in our favor. One day we joined the procession in the hottest hour of the day. The female lawyers were wearing black glasses and holding umbrellas; everyone carried bottles of mineral water. But the vigor of the slogans was no less strong."[54] Within this longed-for promise of something more, he sees Bajwa in passing, and loses him again:

---

[51] Murphy, with Ahmed, "Bajwa", 87–88.

[52] Ibid., 91.

[53] Ibid.

[54] Murphy, with Ahmed, "Bajwa", 93.

Was it he or someone else? It appeared to be him from a distance. He was holding a huge basket of flowers and was slowly throwing them over the people passing under the bridge. He appeared thin and weak. I waved my hands, recognizing him from far away; he threw flowers over us when we passed. The flowers clung to my hair and the petals slipped in my pocket. I didn't brush them off. I dreamt of Bajwa's flowers for many days after that: I am passing under a bridge and Bajwa is throwing flowers from above.

A life has passed but the fragrance of Bajwa's flowers still hangs in the air.[55]

The narrator cannot remake that life. The politics that once offered the comfort of purpose and involvement are lost.

Ahmed's stories are thus perhaps most centrally about post-colonial politics in Pakistan and the nascent (and repeatedly thwarted) democratisation movements that haunt that history. This configuration of memory and politics is at the centre of "This Is Not a Story" ("*Akahānī*"), where Ahmed describes the fate of Bali and Mani, two impoverished inhabitants of Lahore living in the "Weaver's colony".[56] Their story begins with a sense of triumphant rebellion: the story of two lovers who cast aside conventional mores and choose each other, even after Mani's marriage to another: after Mani leaves her first husband for her chosen spouse, we are told, "They were a strange couple. Bali would come back in the evening with his rickshaw and take his rowdy gang of children to the bazaar for entertainment. They would stand outside and eat junk food there. They didn't exhibit an ounce of shame or concern for what anyone thought. Women are supposed to feel the sting of shame, but she behaved as if it was nothing."[57] But the forces of poverty and social hierarchy weigh too heavily upon them, and there is no reprieve. Bali is active in the movement against the Ayub Khan dictatorship (1958–1969), acting as a leader in the Awami [Pakistan People's] Party. The victory of the People's Party, however, led to nothing for him: "The Awami Government did come, but what was there for him? He was neither literate nor educated. Though his influence was everywhere, his

---

[55] Ibid.

[56] Ahmed, *Kabūtar, Banere, te Galliāṅ*, 87–91.

[57] Murphy, with Ahmed, *Windows, Doors, and Streets.*

place was the same. Sometimes he was able to help people who came to him, and sometimes not. He became tense and irritated. The leaders started avoiding him."

The revolutionary nature of Bali and Mani's relationship could not be sustained: "He kept driving the rickshaw. Mani was unrecognizable after giving birth to so many children. Bali started taking drugs. Their relationship remained close and warm. But outside, it was cold." Bali, in the end, got little, and paid the greatest price: "When [Zulfikar Ali] Bhutto was hanged [in 1979], Bali was the first to be arrested. Just like that. He had done nothing. He hadn't even acknowledged Bhutto's death. The Islamist party must have been watching him." As the story progresses, it is as if their bodies too are erased within the city's landscape, as its skyline changes:

> When he came out of prison, Bali had fallen fully into the hands of the addicts. He slowly transformed into a skelaton. He couldn't even drive the rickshaw anymore. Mani also became weaker and weaker.
>
> The boys were given as bonded labour to shops. The time dissolved like intoxication. The houses became bigger and streets became narrow. But Bali's house was the same. The same old rough cloth over the tin door. Tall buildings were built all around them, their tiny house folded in tight among in them.[58]

These stories thus provide a history of the post-colonial state of Pakistan as a remembrance of loss. It is this presence of loss that moves through the stories as a companion, tied to a larger absence. The simultaneity between past and present produces a past which lives in the present, and does not allow that present to proceed. Time is stalled, waiting. Things, places: these conjure this temporal flux, and we see a landscape enlivened by but also lost in time, a time once shared across religious communities, communities that are now absent. We see this in the story "Rain, Doors, and Windows", where Lahore acts again as a palimpsest, the prior names

---

[58] Ibid.

of streets and places known to few. Those that do know are trapped in a kind of eternal pause, in between the naming of the now and the then:[59]

> As a postman, Riaz knows everyone and everything in the old neighborhood. He retired after forty years of service. Since our government started changing names of the roads, neighborhoods, alleys and all, Riaz has found new work. He's the only one who knows the old names. On top of that, he knows each and every person, in every house. Even other postmen come to him for help regarding letters with old addresses like 'Arjun Road, Shivaji Street, Krishna Alley.' Now, Riaz lives alone and cooks his own food.[60]

Lahore has forgotten itself with this renaming since Partition, and memory here suggests a shared time, and a different kind of knowing. This acts as an allusion to the mixed culture of the pre-Partition world, one which has operated within progressive literature as a counter to a neatly partitioned cultural world, the "critical counter-factualism" invoked recently by Anna Bernard as an central feature of representations that engage with Partition beyond its eventness to celebrate the *before,* "to consider other forms of social and political organization that could have (or still could) come into being."[61] Yet it is not a return, and it accompanies other forms of erasure. At the same time, the narrator and Riaz do not let go.

This theme emerges as an undercurrent in other stories as well. In the story "Pigeons, Ledges, and Streets" ("*Kabūtar, banere, te Galliāṅ*"), which provides the title for his award-winning second book of stories, the narrator describes his visit to India to visit his ancestral home; the story overall functions to detail the effects of Partition, of the loss of

---

[59] On the sense of timelessness in this story, see Chandan, "Vele dī Sāthī."

[60] Ahmed, *Mīnh, Būhe, te Bāriyāṅ,* 31–40. This translation is mine (Murphy, with Ahmed, *Windows, Doors, and Streets*). For Datt's translation of this passage, see Datt, *Stories of the Soil,* 270.

[61] Anna Barnard, "Forms of Memory: Partition as Literary Paradigm," *Alif: Journal of Comparative Poetics* 30 (2010): 11. See a parallel discussion with reference to Faiz' work (Mufti, *Enlightenment in the Colony,* 224–225). For valuable discussion of alternative ways of configuring the idea of shared cultural moorings, and for more discussion of modernist/progressive cultural discourse in Pakistan, see A Sean Pue, "In the Mirror of Ghalib: Post-Colonial Reflections on Indo-Muslim Selfhood," *The Indian Economic and Social History Review* 48, no. 4 (2011): 588 ff.

family, status and moorings.[62] He opens his story by describing his aunt, and her house, which was near theirs in Batala, now in India:

> You could say that this story is about Gamay, the pigeons, the rooftop ledges, or me. But really it is the story of Maasi (Auntie) Ayshan. Not too long back I tried to visit my ancestral home in Batala, back in India, and while searching everywhere for the family home, I finally happened upon the home of Maasi Ayshan. At least I think I did. Whenever Mother used to talk about our Batala home, Maasi's house would always come up. 'Our house was on a small hill, and my brother's courtyard was on the left side of Bazaar. On the right was Maasi's.' Our homes were always mentioned in the same breath.[63]

That emerges as the story of Maasi (Auntie) Ayshan, and of all the others who collected in and around her house.

> My mother's voice doesn't leave me: 'Maasi Ayshan's house was there, opposite our house, at the other side of the street.' Searching for my own house in Batala, I think I was really searching for Maasi Ayshan's house.

> When I returned from Batala, the only survivor among my six uncles came to see pictures. Seeing one of them, and relishing the pleasure of recognizing it, he said at once, 'This street used to go straight to Maasi Ayshan's house.'[64]

This haunting of partitioned landscapes is reiterated, such that everything becomes a kind of echo-effect of this lost presence. In the same story, the narrator describes the fate of Popa, Maasi's son, after his release from jail. He had been incarcerated because of his visible and vocal support for the People's Party, which did not last long in power:

> After a year, when Popa was freed from prison, Maasi reluctantly sent him to England to stay with her other son, so that when the country finally became free again, he could come back. How many times would it take for the country to get freedom? We'd been through all this before.[65]

---

[62] Ahmed, *Kabūtar, Banere, te Galliāṅ*, 47–58.

[63] See note 57 above.

[64] Ibid.

[65] Ibid.

In this moment, we see a re-inscription of the *dāgh dāgh ujālā* or scarred daybreak of independence described by Faiz Ahmed Faiz.[66] The political turmoil and both the hope and disappointment of the political in post-colonial Pakistan are also a reiteration, an effect and ongoing experience of Partition's line.

CONCLUSION

Amarjit Chandan has asked, in the face of fictional narratives about the violence of partition, "Why fiction, when we have facts?"[67] Yet, as Pandey and others have shown, there is all too little in the way of documentary reporting on Partition, and that too is steeped in silence and partial telling.[68] In general it has been the lack of factual and full accounting of Partition violence that has encouraged the turn to fiction, as a kind of "truth telling" that provides "a mode of testimony that sought to articulate the inarticulable", a document that reveals "the changing contours of the terrain of recollection."[69] It is also the case that this "long partition" and its affective dimensions are not easily captured in narrative accounts of the time of Partition itself, as an event.[70] The place for fiction persists, both problematic and honest in its fractured representation of an unfinished whole, and in its ability to allow for new frames of understanding.[71]

Drawing on a range of published scholarship on Partition, Alex Padamsee has highlighted uncertainty or "undecidability" as a feature of Partition-related histories and representations, defined "both as a mirror of the experience of Partition and as the grounds for holding open a space for resistance against the apparently closed formal systems of the

---

[66] Mufti reads the poetry of Faiz in broad terms with reference to Partition, even more so in those poems not explicitly linked to it, as this one is (*Enlightenment in the Colony*: ch. 5).

[67] Chandan, "Punjabi Literature on Partition."

[68] Gyanendra Pandey, "Community and Violence," *Economic and Political Weekly* 32, 32 (9–15 August 1997): 2037–2039, 2041–2045. See also his major work: Gyanendra Pandey, *Remembering Partition: Violence, Nationalism, and History in India* (Cambridge: Cambridge University Press, 2001).

[69] Saint, *Witnessing Partition*, 1, 10.

[70] Vazira Fazila-Yacoobali Zamindar, *The Long Partition and the Making of Modern South Asia: Refugees, Boundaries, Histories* (New York: Columbia University Press, 2007).

[71] Barnard, "Forms of Memory," 14.

narratives of Independence."[72] As Ahmed's stories demonstrate, uncertainty and fragmentation persist into the post-Partition future where memory both comforts and troubles, and Partition acts as a spectre. Zubair Ahmed's stories allude to the landscape of Partition's effects, rather than taking it as their subject. At the same time, to write in Punjabi at all in Pakistan today is in itself to write against the grain of Partition. Punjabi's status in the post-colonial state of Pakistan, and its connections across the contentious border with India, make an engagement with Partition inescapable. We can see this in Chandan's response to Ahmed's work. He asks:

> To whom does the author speak? And further, is there anyone who listens? I listen, whether or not anyone else does. He has taken these words from my own mouth. Lahore's *Motī Darwāzā* ('Pearl Gate'),[73] Amritsar's *Lūṇmaṇḍī* (Salt market), the Panj Pir shrine of Jalandhar, my neighbourhood in Nakodar, *Ṭaṇḍanāṅ*, these all are as one: they aren't really distinct. Those people, those sayings, that language.[74]

To write in Punjabi is to speak across a border. Yes, Chandan continues, "Every person is unique; each one has a unique face, and speaks a unique language. *har jaṇā niārā hai; niāre naiṇ-nakash; har jīa koī hor bolī boldā hai.*" But this commonality of language prevails, a dream of 'Punjabiyat' or Punjabiness, illusive and yet real.

Zubair Ahmed's stories demonstrate the past's power, evoking the complex political realities of post-colonial Pakistan, as well as broader human experiences of loss and remembrance that are the legacy of Partition. Perhaps this is what it means to write in Punjabi at all in Pakistan, as a continuing memory that asserts itself from within. We see in Ahmed's stories the resonances of a larger progressive political and linguistic movement: his focus on deprivation, his embrace of the memories of pre-Partition Lahore and the names that marked it, his attention to

---

[72] Alex Padamsee, "Uncertain Partitions: 'Undecidability' and the Urdu Short Story," *Wasafiri* 23, 1 (2008): 2. This is akin to Sarkar's discussion of the structure of Partition's effect, "marked by deferral, gaps, and uncertainties" (*Mourning the Nation,* 30). See also Barnard's valuable discussion of the idea of the fragment in Partition literature (in India and beyond), along stylistic lines ("Forms of Memory," 23 ff.).

[73] This location is generally known as "Mochī Darwāzā", but Chandan uses a variant.

[74] Chandan, "Vele dī Sāthī ."

loss and to memories that both consume and evade him. Ayres has suggested that cultural production in Punjabi in some ways suggests possibilities for a new experience of the contentious border that separates the Pakistani Punjab from the Indian Punjab, an experience perhaps only possible within the creative arts and literature in a transnational mode; Salima Hashmi has expressed a similar sentiment elsewhere.[75] As Kalra and Butt remind us, however, such possibilities cannot be divorced from the material circumstances of the present. What Ahmed asks us to account for in his stories also moves beyond the physical border, to those that reside both within and beyond language, tied to the harsh material and political circumstances of today.

Zubair Ahmed structures his commentary on post-colonial Pakistan as a meditation on the experience of loss, and as a measure of the "long partition". He forces us to see a continuity across time and place within the memory of what was lost, the political betrayals of post-colonial Pakistan and the continuing economic inequalities that dominate in Pakistani life. One falls into the other. They animate the landscape of Lahore with memory, as the presence of a lost past, within and outside at the same time. To speak of such phantoms in Punjabi is to embrace a language of dissent, and to write through Partition to something that persists both beyond and within it. If Mufti is correct in seeing an "exilic consciousness" at the core of the Urdu literary, with a "unique relationship ... to the crisis of Indian national culture that is marked by the figure of the Muslim", Punjabi's place in Pakistan is configured in a similarly contingent position in relation to the very idea of a national project, a form of challenge from within.[76] Ahmed's stories call attention to the affective dimensions of that contingency, a memory that colours, wells and dissipates, but does not end.

WORKS CITED

Ahmed, Zubair. *Mīnh, Būhe, te Bāriyāṅ*. Lahore: Kitab Trinjan, 2001.
Ahmed, Zubair. *Kabūtar, Banere, te Galliāṅ*. Lahore: Naveed Hafeez Press, 2013.

---

[75] Ayres, "Language, the Nation, and Symbolic Capital," 942; Salimi Hashmi, interview with Anne Murphy, February 2014. Online document, available at: http://blogs.ubc.ca/punjabisikhstudies/research/. Accessed 22 May 2016.

[76] Mufti, *Enlightenment in the Colony*, 243, 211.

Anne Murphy, with Zubair Ahmed, trans. "Dead Man's Float." *South Asian Ensemble: A Canadian Quarterly of Literature, Arts & Culture* 7, no. 1 & 2 (Winter and Spring 2015): 158–165.

Arora, Neena, and R.K. Dhawan, eds. 2010. *Partition and Indian Literature: Voices of the Wounded Psyche, vol. 1*. New Delhi: Prestige.

Asdar Ali, Kamran. "Progressives and 'Perverts': Partition Stories and Pakistan's Future." *Social Text 108* 29, no. 3 (Fall 2011): 1–29.

——. "Communists in a Muslim Land: Cultural Debates in Pakistan's Early Years." *Modern Asian Studies* 45, no. 3 (2011): 501–534.

Awan, Mahmood. "Stories that never end" 19 January 2014. http://tns.the-news.com.pk/stories-never-end/#.V2BMGJMrJ0t. Online document. Accessed 14 June 2016.

Ayres, Alyssa. "Language, the Nation, and Symbolic Capital: The Case of Punjab." *The Journal of Asian Studies* 67, no. 3 (Aug 2008): 917–946.

Barnard, Anna. "Forms of Memory: Partition as Literary Paradigm." *Alif: Journal of Comparative Poetics* 30 (2010): 9–33.

Bhalla, Alok, ed. *Stories About the Partition of India, vols. 1–3*. New Delhi, Indus, 1994.

——. *Partition Dialogues: Memories of a Lost Home*. Delhi, Oxford University Press, 2006.

Brass, Paul. *Language, Religion, and Politics in North India*. New York: Cambridge University Press, 1974.

Chandan, Amarjit. "Punjabi Literature on Partition: Some Observations." Paper presented to the British Association of South Asian scholars conference held in Bath, England, 11–13 April 1997. Online document available at: http://amarjitchandan.tripod.com/id8.html. Accessed 24 May 2016.

——. 2004. "Vele dī Sāthī. Time's Companion." In *Lakīr* 91: 75–76.

Das, Veena. *Life and Words: Violence and the Descent into the Ordinary*. Berkeley, US: University of California Press, 2006.

Datt, Nirupama, ed. & trans. *Stories of the Soil*. New Delhi: Penguin Books India, 2010.

Didur, Jill. *Unsettling Partition: Literature, Gender, Memory*. Toronto: University of Toronto Press, 2006.

Farooqi, Mehr Afshan. "Towards a Prose of Ideas: An Introduction to the Critical Thought of Muhammad Hasan Askari." In *The Annual of Urdu Studies* 2004: 175–190.

George, Rosemary Marangoly. "(Extra)Ordinary Violence: National Literatures, Diasporic Aesthetics, and the Politics of Gender in South Asian Partition Fiction." *Signs* 33, no. 1 (2007): 135–158.

Hashmi, Salimi. Interview with Anne Murphy, February 2014. Online document, available at: http://blogs.ubc.ca/punjabisikhstudies/research/. Accessed 22 May 2016.

Jalal, Ayesha. *The Pity of Partition: Manto's Life, Times and Work Across the India–Pakistan Divide*. Princeton: Princeton University Press, 2013.

Kalra, Virinder S., and Waqas M. Butt. "'In One Hand a Pen, in the Other a Gun': Punjabi Language Radicalism in Punjab, Pakistan." In *South Asian History and Culture* (September 2013): 1–16.

Kalra, Virinder S. "Campaigning for Punjabi in Sahiwal," Presentation at the meeting of the *Punjab Research Group*, Coventry University, 27–28 June 2014.

Menon, Ritu, and Kamla Bhasin. "Recovery, Rupture, Resistance: Indian State and Abduction of Women During Partition." *Economic and Political Weekly* 38, no. 17 (April 24, 1993): WS2–WS11.

Mir, Farina. *The Social Space of Language: Vernacular Culture in British Colonial Punjab*. Berkeley: University of California Press, 2010.

Mufti, Aamir. "The Aura of Authenticity." *Social Text* 18, no. 3 (2000): 87–103.

———. *Enlightenment in the Colony: The Jewish Question and the Crisis of Postcolonial Culture*. Princeton: Princeton University Press, 2007.

Murphy, Anne. "A Diasporic Temporality: New narrative writing from Punjabi-Canada." In *Towards a Diasporic Imagination of the Present: An Eternal Sense of Homelessness*, edited by Tapati Bharadwaja, 9–30. Bangalore: Lies and Big Feet Press, 2015.

———. "Writing Punjabi Across Borders." In *South Asian History and Culture, special issue on "Scripts and Identity: The Politics of Writing Systems in South Asia,"* edited by Pushkar Sohoni and Carmen Brandt. Forthcoming.

———. "Bajwa has Nothing More to Say" *Pakistani Literature (Journal of the Pakistan Academy of Letters)* 18, no. 1 (2015): 86–93.

———. *Windows, Doors, and Streets: The Stories of Pakistani Punjabi-Language Writer Zubair Ahmed*. A book-length set of translations of the short stories of Zubair Ahmed. Forthcoming.

Novetzke, Christian. "The Subaltern Numen: Making History in the Name of God." *History of Religions* 46, no. 6 (2006): 99–126.

Oesterheld, Christina. "Urdu Literature in Pakistan: A Site for Alternative Visions and Dissent." *The Annual of Urdu Studies* 20 (2005): 79–98.

Padamsee, Alex. "Uncertain Partitions: 'Undecidability' and the Urdu Short Story." *Wasafiri* 23, no. 1 (2008): 1–5.

Pandey, Gyanendra. "Community and Violence." *Economic and Political Weekly* 32, 32 (Aug 9–15, 1997): 2037–2039+2041–2045.

———. *Remembering Partition: Violence, Nationalism, and History in India*. Cambridge: Cambridge University Press, 2001.

Pue, A. Sean. "In the Mirror of Ghalib: Post-Colonial Reflections on Indo-Muslim Selfhood." *The Indian Economic and Social History Review* 48, no. 4 (2011): 571–592.

———. "Ephemeral Asia: Postition without Identity in the Modernist Urdu Poetry of N.M. Rashed." *Comparative Literature* 64, no. 1 (2012): 73–92.

Rahman, Tariq. *A History of Pakistani Literature in English*. Lahore: Vanguard Books, 1991.

——. *Language and Politics in Pakistan*. Karachi: Oxford University Press, 1996.

——. *Language, Ideology and Power: Language-Learning Among the Muslims of Pakistan and North India*. Oxford/New York: Oxford University Press, 2002.

Rammah, Safir. "West Punjabi Poetry: From Ustad Daman to Najm Hosain Syed". In the *Journal of Punjab Studies* 13, no. 1 & 2 (2006): 215–228.

Riaz, Fahmida. *Pakistan: Literature and Society*. New Delhi: Patriot Publishers, 1986.

Roy, Anjali Gera, and Nandi Bhatia, eds. *Partitioned Lives: Narratives of Home, Displacement, and Resettlement*. New Delhi: Pearson Longman, 2008.

Sadhu, Naeem. "A Storyteller from the Streets of Lahore." *Dawn* 14 July 2015. Online document available at: http://www.dawn.com/news/1194352. Accessed 14 June 2016.

Saint, Tarun K. *Witnessing Partition: Memory, History, Fiction*. New Delhi: Routledge, 2010.

——. "The Long Shadow of Manto's Partition Narratives: 'Fictive' Testimony to Historical Trauma." *Social Scientist* 40, no. 11/12 (2012): 53–62.

Sarkar, Bhaskar. *Mourning the Nation: Indian Cinema in the Wake of Partition*. Durham: Duke University Press, 2009.

Syed, Najm Hosain. *Recurrent Patterns in Punjabi Poetry*. Lahore: Majlis Shah Husain, 1968.

Shackle, Christopher. "Pakistan." In *Language and National Identity in Asia*, 100–115, ed. Andrew Simpson. London: Oxford University Press, 2007.

Steele, Laurel. "Patriotic Pakistanis, Exiled Poets, or Unwelcome Refugees? Three Urdu Poets Write of Partition and its Aftermath." *The Indian Partition in Literature and Films: History, Politics, and Aesthetics*, 89–106, ed. Rini Bhattacharya Mehta and Debali Mookerjea-Leonard. London: Routledge, 2015.

Waterman, David. *Where Worlds Collide: Pakistani Fiction in the New Millennium*. New York: Oxford University Press, 2015.

Zamindar, Vazira Fazila-Yacoobali. *The Long Partition and the Making of Modern South Asia: Refugees, Boundaries, Histories*. New York: Columbia University Press, 2007.

CHAPTER 12

In Ruins: Cultural Amnesia at the Aam Khas Bagh

Churnjeet Mahn

This chapter offers a case study of a collaborative research project between the Indian conservation architectural firm CRCI, a designer and a visual ethnographer and academics to deliver a workshop and exhibition on heritage and memory in Sirhind, Punjab. As part of a British Council/Arts and Humanities Research Council (UK) project, the workshop was designed to bring academics and their research into communities. CRCI provided maps, charts and an index to the key sites they were looking at along the Grand Trunk Road to assemble a UNESCO World Heritage Site bid for the road. The group's work would end with an exhibition in Sirhind, in East or Indian Punjab, to be followed by an exhibition in Delhi and then London that prominently featured the Aam Khas Bagh, a Mughal-era serai that the World Monument Fund had placed on an international endangered site list that year. Definitions of heritage varied across the collaborating team, and were largely determined by our training as well as our own cultural perspectives. Part of this chapter's larger purpose is to unpick some of the ways in which heritage is made and understood in East Punjab today.

C. Mahn (✉)
University of Strathclyde, Glasgow, Scotland, UK
e-mail: churnjeet.mahn@strath.ac.uk

© The Author(s) 2018
C. Mahn and A. Murphy (eds.), *Partition and the Practice of Memory*,
https://doi.org/10.1007/978-3-319-64516-2_12

What do we take and bring back in these types of international creative collaborations between academics, NGOs and communities, when we approach "heritage" in such a mode? And what are the politics that these projects entail? Through a discussion of memory and amnesia, this chapter focuses on some of the key questions and problems which informed the design and preparation of the exhibition we created on Sirhind's heritage. Starting from an understanding of "heritage" in areas that have experienced conflict and trauma, we consider what it means to work with religious sites in a region where historical tensions between religious communities are evident in the landscape. What does a heritage project look like in a post-Partition Punjabi town where most non-Sikh historical monuments have been systematically destroyed or left decaying in favour of modern gurdwara-building projects? Working in a community setting, what was the purpose of our exhibition on Sirhind's history? Was it to restore Sirhind to significance? Or to conserve cultural memory? Was it a memorialisation of the area's Islamic heritage? What were the implications of what had been *forgotten* at Sirhind? Or to put it very bluntly, what are the challenges to restoring the Aam Khas Bagh as an important site in an Indian Sirhind evacuated of its pre-Partition Muslim population?

This chapter approaches these questions through recent critical discussions in memory studies, especially in contexts where people and the nation are tied together in violence, trauma or displacement. As Marianne Hirsch points out, "The bodily, psychic, and affective impact of trauma and its aftermath, the ways in which one trauma can recall, or reactivate, the effects of another, exceed the bounds of traditional historical archives and methodologies."[1] Sirhind represents a rich assembly of diverse faiths and communities and, like much of Punjab, vernacular Punjabi has historically been a vital language for connecting forms of communication, devotion and artistic cultures.[2] However, Sirhind has also been the site of historical conflicts between Sikh and Mughal forces and was one of the towns particularly affected by displacement at the time of Partition. The story of Sirhind and Partition is thus one that reaches back into the past, activating older stories of conflicts

---

[1] Marianne Hirsch, "The Generation of Postmemory," *Poetics Today* 28, no. 1 (2008): 104.

[2] Farina Mir, *The Social Space of Language: Vernacular Culture in British Colonial Punjab* (Berkeley and Los Angeles: University of California Press, 2010).

which persist, inform and seep into the present. This chapter identifies some of the implications of these historical triggers through identifying what "counts" as official heritage in the contemporary landscape, and then using memory as a framework for analysing a community heritage project.

BEYOND RUIN: SIRHIND AND THE AAM KHAS BAGH

I first met Sirhind through a text:

> In the Mughal period, Sirhind was situated on the Delhi-Lahore-Kabul Highway. In between Delhi and Lahore it was the largest and most prosperous city. Its prosperity was reflected in its hundreds of monuments built during the period. The popular belief that at the heyday of the Mughal empire, the city had 360 mosques, tombs, gardens and wells appears to be well-founded. The number may not have been exact but just idiomatic, it certainly implied a large number. Despite the devastation of the city during the eighteenth century, about three dozens of these medieval monuments, in various stages of preservation, are still extant in and around Sirhind.[3]

It is difficult to correlate this description to Sirhind's present landscape. The area is dominated by expanded gurdwara complexes. While there are numerous tombs to be found in the middle of farmland, many are being slowly undermined by local farmers with the hope that they will simply collapse, freeing the land for use. Some tombs are home to farm animals, and while a few mosques are active sites of worship (namely Rauza Sharif, which holds the shrine of Sheikh Ahmad Sirhandi), evidence of the depth of syncretic religious practices in the region has been materially and culturally eroded and overwritten in the wake of conflict. Sirhind is almost entirely eclipsed by its twin town of Fatehgarh Sahib, home to a network of gurdwaras associated with Guru Gobind Singh and his family.

While Sirhind was a Muslim-majority town before Partition, its evacuation and the resettlement of Sikhs from West Punjab has significantly changed its demographic. In 1710 Sirhind was largely destroyed by forces led by Banda Singh Bahadur, a disciple of the tenth Sikh Guru who died in 1708, during an agrarian uprising. By the nineteenth century, Sirhind

---

[3] For a summary of historical descriptions see, Subhash Parihar, "Historical Mosques of Sirhind," *Islamic Studies* 43, no. 3 (Autumn 2004): 481.

was described by Alexander Cunningham as lying largely in ruins.[4] As Cunningham noted in his 1871 archaeological survey trip through the region, "Even to this day every Sikh, on passing through Sarhind [*sic*], carries away a brick which he is supposed to throw in the Jumna [...] with the hope that in time this detested city will thus be utterly removed from the face of the earth."[5] The 1901 *Murray's Handbook to India* has a short entry on the area, commenting on its history, dating back to the Brahman kings of Kabul. It notes that "the great *Sarai* of the Mogul emperors is to the S.E. of the city. It is now used as a public audience-hall by the Patiala authorities, and is called the *Amkhas*."[6]

The Aam Khas Bagh is a Mughal-era serai complex dating back to the mid-late sixteenth century. The original purpose of the serais along the Delhi–Kabul Highway varied from simple accommodation for travellers to larger multi-purpose administrative centres for communication as well as encampment, with the Aam Khas Bagh being one of three locations with mixed public and royal use.[7] Excavations have revealed evidence of one of the earliest hammams in northern India, alongside a complex water network which provided running water throughout the gardens, culminating in a large water tank surrounded by grand residences. The serai is an Archaeological Survey of India-protected site and has a nominal caretaker, alongside state-appointed landscapers who tend to the historical trees in amongst more recently planted flowers and grass. As it is the largest recreational space in Sirhind, a typical day will see walkers enjoying the gardens, lovers meeting secretly in leafy enclaves, young people moving around and exploring the complex; they climb in and over ruined buildings or play impromptu games of cricket in large disused water tanks. And, occasionally, along the fringe walls collapsing into the surrounding farmland, there are conservation architects working with local builders, artisans, international consultants, heritage experts

---

[4] Subhash Parihar, *History and Architectural Remains of Sirhind: The Greatest Mughal City on the Delhi-Lahore Highway* (New Delhi: Aryan Books, 2006), 18.

[5] Alexander Cunningham, *Archaeological Survey of India*, vol. 1 (Simla: Government of India Press, 1871), 208–209.

[6] *Murray's Handbook to India* (London: John Murray), 195b.

[7] Manish Chalana, "'All the World Going and Coming': The Past and Future of the Grand Trunk Road in Punjab, India," in *Cultural Landscapes of South Asia: Studies in Heritage Conservation and Management*, ed. Kapila D. Silva and Amita Sinha, 92–110 (London and New York: Routledge, 2016), 98.

and government agencies to map and document the complex. Very few tourists make it to the Aam Khas Bagh now, although there have been facilities for them in the past, including public toilets and interpretative signs around the gardens. The toilets are now largely shut and the signage has become illegible. The Aam Khas Bagh's history and significance has receded from view as it retreats into ruins or finds itself repurposed as a pedestrian-friendly space where history and architecture is almost incidental.

Subhash Parihar has collected various narratives about the Aam Khas Bagh from chronicles, travel accounts and local anecdotes which piece together the histories of the various buildings that make up the Aam Khas Bagh.[8] These sources coalesce around a series of facts, largely drawn from a few accounts left of travel in the Mughal Empire: "Many of the sources of the history of the garden are the medieval chronicles and the accounts of contemporary European travellers. Surprisingly enough, the story that emerges from these scattered references has a remarkable continuity."[9] These narratives reinforce three points: that Sirhind is historical; that during the Mughal period it was an important location; and that its monuments have been subject to destruction (the latter appears in accounts from the late eighteenth century onwards).[10] During the period of Akbar, a smaller garden complex was present which was known as Bagh-i-Hafiz Rakhna, and was later augmented by Jahangir and Shah Jahan, both of whom took a particular interest in developing the gardens, water system and residential buildings at the serai. After its systematic attack in a range of conflicts around the Mughals and the Sikhs, the rulers of Patiala took over ownership of the complex and the serai was renamed the Aam Khas Bagh (approximately translated as "everyman's garden"). More recently, the historical residential sections of the Aam Khas Bagh have been used as government offices. The detritus from this occupation is still visible. While the Aam Khas Bagh has had a history of reuse and repurposing, its significance

---

[8] Subhash Parihar, *Some Aspects of Indo-Islamic Architecture* (New Delhi: Shakti Malik, 1999); Parihar, *History and Architectural Remains of Sirhind*.

[9] Parihar, *Some Aspects of Indo-Islamic Architecture*, 90.

[10] For overviews of historical consciousness militancy nationalism see, for example, Hamik Deol, *Religion and Nationalism in India: The Case Study of the Punjab* (London: Routledge, 2011); Purnima Dhavan, *When Sparrows Became Hawks: The Making of the Sikh Warrior Tradition, 1699–1799* (Oxford: Oxford University Press, 2011).

Fig. 12.1 Interior of the Sheesh Mahal at the Aam Khas Bagh. *Source* Copyright *A Punjabi Palimpsest—an AHRC project*

with each occupation has declined, and its material components have been in slow and visible decay for two centuries (Fig. 12.1).

An annual event does draw a crowd to the Aam Khas Bagh: the Jor Mela is a light and sound show which commemorates the martyrdom of the *sahibzadas*, Zowar and Fateh Singh. However, in recent years, the Rauza Sharif shrine has closed its doors in fear that Sikh pilgrims might mistake the mosque for the tomb of Wazir Khan, who ordered the execution of the *sahibzadas*.[11] This has been compounded by the increasing visa difficulties for pilgrims travelling from Pakistan for the annual Urs,

---

[11] Amaninder Pal, "The Tale of Closed Doors of Rauza Sharif Shrine," *The Tribune*, 28 December 2015, http://www.tribuneindia.com/news/punjab/community/the-tale-of-closed-doors-of-rauza-sharif-shrine/176083.html. Accessed 15 May 2017.

around the same time of year.[12] The disinvestment in Mughal-era heritage by the government of Punjab in order to emphasise Sikh-associated history is part of a larger project to align Sikh interests with a Punjabi national imaginary. Critics and historians of Sikh history have pointed to the ways in which Sikh religious identity has become grounded in historical moments of conflict which have been used as the foundations for sometimes competing national imaginaries for the Indian Punjabi state, an ideological agenda which reached its height in the 1980s and 1990s with the violent aftermath of Indira Gandhi's assassination.[13] Sikh political and cultural domination in Punjab has enabled policy decisions to be made which have neglected the complex and discontinuous religious and cultural history of Punjab, especially in terms of its built history, in favour of Sikh sites and monuments that draw inspiration from Mughal-era architecture but are Sikh-associated.[14]

In her analysis of the region, CRCI's director Gurmeet S. Rai highlighted the underlying principles of Sirhind's greater significance.[15] The Grand Trunk Road in its earlier iterations connected Afghanistan to Kolkata, linking it to the Silk Road. As one of the world's oldest highways in continuous use, the section of the road in Punjab has been an important point of access for trade and armies, as well as the development and circulation of ideas. From the interplay between Bhakti and Sufi saints between the thirteenth and eighteenth centuries, to the amalgamation of religious and spiritual practices across faiths, and the exchange of craft knowledge, this section of road was a vital artery for the development of Punjab in its current form. The circulating diversity

---

[12] Ketan Gupta, "3-Day Annual Urs Begins at Sirhind Shrine," *Hindustan Times*, 21 December 2014, http://www.hindustantimes.com/punjab/3-day-annual-urs-begins-at-sirhind-shrine/story-cdHt9hglyY53U90nnkWO9K.html. Accessed 15 May 2017.

[13] Khushwant Singh, *A History of the Sikhs: 1469–1838* (Oxford: Oxford University Press, 2004); Tony Ballantyne, *Between Colonialism and Diaspora: Sikh Cultural Formations in an Imperial World* (Durham: Duke University Press, 2006); and Anne Murphy, *The Materiality of the Past: History and Representation in Sikh Tradition* (Oxford: Oxford University Press, 2012).

[14] William J. Glover, "Shiny New Buildings, Rebuilding Historic Sikh Gurdwaras in Indian Punjab," *Future Anterior*, IX, no. 1 (Summer 2012): 32–47.

[15] This analysis took the form of briefings which took place throughout our design process in 2013–14 and combined Rai's own extensive fieldwork, interviewing local stakeholders, with discussions with state agencies such as Punjab Tourism and national and international heritage agencies such as UNESCO.

of faith, language and culture was tied together into the singularity of the highway, an apt metaphor for Sirhind as well as for Punjab.[16]

LINES AND FRAGMENTS OF MEMORY

Sar-i-hind, translated loosely as the frontier of India, finds an appropriate partner in Punjab Tourism's strapline: "India begins here". Sirhind represents an entry point into understanding some of the broader issues in identification faced in post-Partition communities where the significant departure of a population has left behind physical emptiness through abandoned structures as well as practices of intangible heritage, such as song or literature. Sudipta Kaviraj's formulation of "fuzzy" communities to describe the difference between pre-colonial and colonial organisation of social groups is useful for modelling how the underpinning principles of community are dynamic processes strategically named for personal, collective or administrative purposes: "Rarely, if ever, would people belong to a community which would claim to represent or exhaust all the layers of complex selfhood."[17] With the impact of colonialism being partially framed through a move to enumerated communities, it becomes clear how limiting the mobility of subjects is imperative for drawing lines and distinctions that can be felt and seen. To narrow the scope of selfhood is to constrict or prohibit access to "layers" of potential identification or to make more dense and complex forms of selfhood

---

[16] Critical studies of Punjab and India, especially in the context of colonialism, have proposed a series of models to capture some of the formations underpinning societal structures and individual identity. In her analysis of syncretic practices in nearby Malkerkotla, for example, Anne Bigelow borrows from Glenn Bowmans' description of "semantically multivocal" places to account for the co-presences of faiths and communities at religious sites: "As interactive nodes between individuals, religions, genders, classes, age groups, and so on, the bodily and discursive practices and experiences at these sites are opportunities for the public performance of community and individual identities characterized by openness and inclusiveness rather than exclusivity and hostility." Anne Bigelow, *Sharing the Sacred: Practicing Pluralism in Muslim North India* (Oxford: Oxford University Press, 2010), 431. For a further discussion see Karenjot Bhangoo Randhawa, *Civil Society in Malerkotla, Punjab: Fostering Resilience through Religion* (Lanham: Lexington Books, 2012).

[17] Sudipta Kaviraj, *The Imaginary Institution of India: Politics and Ideas* (New York: Columbia University Press, 2010), 56. See discussion in Dipesh Chakrabarty, "Modernity and Ethnicity in India," in *Multicultural States: Rethinking Difference and Identity*, ed. David Bennett (London: Routledge, 1998), 91–110.

contradictory to the point of facing social censure or impossibility.[18] To put this question another way, how is it possible to create a line of Sikh history in Sirhind/Fatehgarh Sahib entirely predicated on a history of unbroken animosity when physical evidence to the contrary permeates the landscape?

One of the most evocative metaphors for imagining these processes has been the palimpsest. Andreas Huyssen's modelling of Berlin as a palimpsest offers a useful metaphor for rendering the historical and spatial complexity of a city which itself has been carved, partitioned and subject to regimes of national forgetting and remembering in the face of conflict and trauma: "Berlin as a palimpsest implies voids, illegibilities, and erasures, but it also offers a richness of traces and memories, restorations and new constructions that will mark the city as a lived space."[19] What makes Huyssen's formulation so important is not its usefulness in thinking about the co-presence of these "voids" and "erasures" and contemporary life, but that it draws from a rich history of writing about the palimpsest as a model for understanding the relationship between individuals, communities and histories, which itself has changed in significance over time. Jawaharlal Nehru evoked the palimpsest as a metaphor for his own realisation of the nation (here, imagined as "she"), framed as an experience at once individual, collective, transhistorical and transcendental:

> It was not her wide spaces that eluded me, or even her diversity, but some depth of soul which I could not fathom, though I had occasional and tantalizing glimpses of it. She was like some ancient palimpsest on which layer upon layer of thought and reverie had been inscribed, and yet no succeeding layer had completely hidden or erased what had been written previously. All of these existed in our conscious or subconscious selves, though we may not have been aware of them, and they had gone to build up the complex and mysterious personality of India.[20]

---

[18] For an example of how contradictory subject-positions produce effects of "impossibility," see Gayatri Gopinath, *Impossible Desires: Queer Diasporas and South Asian Public Cultures* (Durham: Duke University Press, 2005).

[19] Andreas Huyssen, *Present Pasts: Urban Palimpsests and the Politics of Memory* (Stanford: Stanford University Press, 2003), 84. See also Sarah Dillon, *The Palimpsest: Literature, Criticism, Theory* (London: Continuum, 2007).

[20] Jawaharlal Nehru, *The Discovery of India* (New Delhi: Oxford University Press, 1994), 59. For a discussion of how the palimpsest metaphor is later used to visualise layered cultures/histories in Salman Rushdie's writing (apparently inspired by Nehru), see Anna Guttman, *The Nation of India in Contemporary Indian Literature* (Basingstoke: Palgrave Macmillan, 2007), 75–77.

Huyssen's "lived space" in Nehru is the imaginative action of realising the nation through layered diversity. While Huyssen identifies "erasure" as a vital aspect of how a palimpsest operates (drawing on real palimpsests, which have their top layer erased to create space for another), Nehru optimistically abstracts the palimpsest into a dynamic relationship between all the layers of the national and personal text. In this context, while the ink or marking of a layer of the palimpsest may not be visible, the pressure of the impression left by those markings is felt throughout the palimpsest. Thinking of the palimpsest as a model containing pressure offers a route into understanding hegemony within the text; in other words, what is visible or accessible in the palimpsest and how are networks of associations and connections made across it? What kind of imaginative mobility is allowed, what is disallowed? This question is sidestepped by Nehru's use of consciousness as a connection to the contemporary informed by the past. A clearer source of Nehru's observation, however, can be found in an earlier text.

Thomas De Quincey used the palimpsest as a metaphor for memory in 1845: 'What else than a natural and mighty palimpsest is the human brain? [...] Everlasting layers of ideas, images, feelings, have fallen upon your brain softly as light. Each succession has seemed to bury all that went before. And yet, in reality, not one has been extinguished.'[21] Freud, and Derrida through a reading of Freud, turned to the mystic writing pad as figures of human consciousness, with the receptive surface layer acting in concert with the invisible traces beneath.[22] Moving from Huyssen back through Nehru and Freud to De Quincey offers an illustrative range of how the palimpsest has been used to figure the relationship between individual and collective imaginaries of selfhood with psychoanalysis and nationalism being added as discursive imperatives, guaranteeing the coherency of the palimpsest. They differ in the degree to which "layers" of the palimpsest are accessible or visible to either the consciousness or the present, but they do point to the unpredictable and

---

[21] Thomas De Quincey, *Confessions of an English Opium Eater and Other Writings* (Oxford: Oxford University Press, 2013), 135–136.

[22] Jacques Derrida, *Archive Fever: A Freudian Impression* (Chicago: University of Chicago Press, 1996).

asynchronous forms of pressure and impression that the past can make in the present. Memory becomes an imaginative function of connection, reanimation or enlivening of a palimpsestic node. To think of a line in the palimpsest is to draw a connection between words or points of significance which cut across other forms of connection. To think of a fragment is to isolate something in its exceptionalism or to point to the absence around it. "Absence" and "fragments" have been crucial in the history of Partition studies, as different kinds of sources are used to piece together meaningful and representative accounts and narratives.

The debate around cultural memory and amnesia has figured heavily in Partition studies, especially in how individual and state-authorised versions of memory come together, pulling away from their original theorisations in Holocaust studies to adhere more specifically to the South Asian context.[23] Ananya Kabir identifies "post-amnesia" as the attempt to rehabilitate memories and accounts of Partition which have been suppressed or erased: "post-amnesia imagines the layering of national belonging, inevitable in the modern world, with affiliations deriving from pre-modern economic and cultural histories."[24] As a response to Marianne Hirsch's formulation of postmemory, this formulation emphasises the highly selective forms of linear narrativity that are constructed in the Indian context, a narrativity which, in the example in this chapter, translates into the articulation of a continuous and distinct Sikh history and identity that selectively erases and bypasses syncretic traditions or a shared Sikh-Muslim heritage. Kabir's layers offer another formulation for the palimpsest as a text which can be selectively read when framed by national or nationalistic discourses. It serves to explain how and why sections of the palimpsest become inaccessible.

To think of a line or fragment of memory is to question the underlying logic in its form. How is linearity or a narrative sequence constructed to forge a coherent memory across time? What is the fragment a part of? The final section of this chapter will move to a specific case study, the Aam Khas Bagh, to highlight how the metaphor of the palimpsest can offer a meaningful route into challenging "regimes of forgetting".

---

[23] The move to considering oral histories has made one of the most significant impacts; see Pippa Virdee, "Remembering Partition: Women, Oral Histories and the Partition of 1947," *Oral History* 41, no. 2: 49–62.

[24] Ananya Jahanara Kabir, *Partition's Post-Amnesias: 1947, 1971 and Modern South Asia* (New Delhi: Women Unlimited, 2013), 49.

PALIMPSESTIC PRACTICE

Heritage itself is a capacious term which in its official definitions ranges across forms of song and types of craft to buildings and monuments.[25] What binds these definitions is an act of safeguarding which demands historical rights and future continuity.[26] The right to history and the right to continuity are mutually constructed with categories of belonging and community. Sirhind offers an example of a site where the definition of heritage can change fundamentally depending on how and why a "community" and its history is imagined or remembered.[27] Earlier in this chapter, I stated that I first met Sirhind through a text. But I must have been in Sirhind many years before without realising it, as I visited Fatehgarh Sahib gurdwara, which lies a short distance from my mother's ancestral village. When I returned to Punjab and to Sirhind, the refrain I heard again and again was, "but have you been to the gurdwara—it is a historical place". Heritage and the value of history were consistently rerouted away from Sirhind to Fatehgarh Sahib.

Imagining Sirhind as a palimpsest offers a reply to the systematic erasure of Mughal-era built heritage in the area along with the cultural memories and significance of the area's Muslim population. The recurring telling of *badla* (revenge) against Mughal-era monuments in the

---

[25] For some useful contemporary debates about what "counts" as heritage see Yahana Ahmad, "The Scope and Definitions of Heritage: From Tangible to Intangible," *International Journal of Heritage Studies* 12, no. 3 (2006): 292–300; Bahar Aykan, "How Participatory Is Participatory Heritage Management? The Politics of Safeguarding the Alevi *Semah* Ritual as Intangible Heritage," *International Journal of Heritage Management* 20 (2013): 381–405.

[26] An analogue of this situation, especially in terms of visualising the displacement of a Muslim population and the consequences for built history Querycan be seen in studies of nineteenth-century Greece, where the imperative for Greek nation-building was to return to "ancient" history and civilisation as a way of de-emphasising and erasing an Islamic past. For discussions of this see Artemis Leontis, *Topographies of Hellenism: Mapping the Homeland* (London: Cornell University Press, 1995); Stathis Gourgouris, *Dream Nation: Enlightenment, Colonization, and the Institution of Modern Greece* (Stanford: Stanford University Press, 1996).

[27] See *Senses of Place: Senses of Time*, ed. G.J. Ashworth and B. Graham (Aldershot: Ashgate, 2005) and for a useful overview of the use of memory in heritage studies, Sara McDowell, "Heritage Memory and Identity," in *The Ashgate Research Companion to Heritage and Identity*, ed. Brian Graham and Peter Howard (Aldershot: Ashgate, 2008), 27–54.

region, a story often repeated by locals while we were in the Aam Khas Bagh, is just one of the micro-examples of how historical conflicts can be stitched together into an unbroken narrative of animosity and religious segregation that deliberately effaces more complex syncretic histories or practices. Forgetting the Aam Khas Bagh in material terms begins with devaluing its material history (vandalism, and disinvestment by the state), to devaluing its associational history (making Mughal heritage synonymous with Islamic heritage) and finally devaluing its material present and future (not recognising it as an important site of local heritage). But this forgetting is always enabled by the prior narrative erasure, which in turn requires its echo in the material.

We benefited from the kind cooperation of the Sri Guru Granth Sahib World University, which had selected a group of 30 students (who were from across India) interested in working on a heritage exhibition. This had been initiated as part of CRCI's initial planning: for them it was integral to involve local organisations and young people in exploring ideas of heritage. In this sense, the project was informed by Kabir's discussion of post-amnesia: in the absence of an emotional, cultural and community investment in the Aam Khas Bagh from the inhabitants of Sirhind, a way of bypassing this erasure was to find different trajectories or views into the past from young people who were not connected to Sirhind through their identity, and did not themselves carry personalised histories of the impact of Partition in the area.

The project was organised into three parts. One group was tasked with finding connective themes across Sirhind's history for a short film they would produce, another group was to explore Sirhind through a range of interviews and the third was assigned to work on developing temporary interpretive signage across the Aam Khas Bagh for a one-day exhibition showcasing the film and interviews.[28] Everyone received an introductory briefing on Sirhind's history; this emphasised the site's historical significance as a site along the Grand Trunk Road, and the range of cultural influences still evident there in the built environment. Through this facilitation, the film group also workshopped ideas around water. One of the most serious environmental risks in Sirhind is the quality of the groundwater, which has elevated levels of arsenic. Alongside

---

[28] Simran Chopra and Ioanna Mannoussaki-Adamapoulou assisted in facilitating the workshops and delivering the event in Sirhind, Delhi and London.

Fig. 12.2 Still from film showing Mughal-era bridge. *Source* Copyright *A Punjabi Palimpsest—an AHRC project*

the issues of the dropping water table, water was a theme that the group felt could connect the present with the past. While the Aam Khas Bagh's hammam, fountains and water system offered the group a plethora of footage, beyond the site they filmed the historic Mughal-era bridge along the Grand Trunk Road, one of only three bridges of the period still surviving in East Punjab (Fig. 12.2).[29]

There was no narration in the film, and only ambient noise from each location was included. Short segments from a range of sites were brought together and arranged in a triptych to disrupt a singular perspective. In Rauza Sharif and Fatehgarh Sahib, the group spent time filming pilgrims and worshippers using water before prayer. Another segment of the film emphasised the volume of worshippers moving through Fatehgarh Sahib contrasted with the relatively quiet and empty Rauza Sharif.[30] Alongside this the grand temple of Fatehgarh Sahib was filmed in contrast to abandoned tombs in the farmland surrounding Sirhind. The metaphor of water in its flow worked alongside the divided perspective of the triptych, which refused to chart sites in a strict chronology, a singular perspective, or with an authorising narrative. The overall effect of the film was to make visible some of the impressions and traces from Sirhind's past and how they persist into the present. Their recognition and placement in the sequence of a film that did not articulate the story of Sikh–Muslim historical conflict was a way of using the silence of buildings, sites and monuments as a route into a less present or less visible

[29] Part of CRCI's work involved obtaining protected status for the bridge from the government of Punjab; this was eventually awarded in 2016.

[30] This is not representative of the entire year; there are pilgrims who visit in organised tours, although these are infrequent.

history through the materiality of those places, even when they are partially in ruin or abandoned.

The group collecting interviews identified 12 people to interview; they were chosen according to religion (representatives were chosen from Fatehgarh Sahib and Rauza Sharif), social role (caretakers at the Aam Khas Bagh, shopkeepers and local "important" figures) and gender.[31] No participants were questioned about their faith although, given the demographics of the area, the majority were presumed to be lay or practising Sikhs.[32] All the chosen subjects had lived in Sirhind all their lives, and the students had a particular interest in those who had experienced Partition or were old enough to remember its immediate aftermath. The group could only find one participant to speak on Partition in the interview; this was a woman living on a farm on the outskirts of Sirhind. And while there is a significant Hindu population in the region, the group decided to foreground the Sikh–Muslim axis to highlight one kind of diversity in Sirhind's history as particularly emblematic of the area, a decision which itself de-emphasised other kinds of potential connection across gender or language. Due to constrictions of time and resources, the students only had a day of training before designing and conducting the interviews. The results demonstrate the difficulty of deviating very far from received histories of the area. In the marketplace, *badla* (revenge) and the *sahibzada*s (or sons of the tenth Guru, Gobind Singh) were a recurring topic, with consistent physical redirection to Fatehgarh Sahib as the site for authoritative information. At Rauza Sharif, a story of peaceful coexistence was consistently emphasised and discussions of Partition or Sikh–Muslim conflict were summarily dismissed as historical events that were no longer relevant. Personal memories and anecdotes followed a familiar route of peaceful coexistence with neighbours prior to Partition. The interviewee who had experienced Partition deviated from the group's expectations by identifying strongly

---

[31] While oral histories have been significant in Partition Studies, the purpose here is not to produce a comprehensive alternative view of Sirhind's history but to expose students to alternative trajectories in authorising accounts of the past. Each interview lasted approximately 20 min and was led and recorded by a student.

[32] While Sikhs are in the majority in Sirhind, making up approximately half of the population, there is a significant Hindu population (46%), with just under 3% of the population registering as Muslim according to the 2011 Indian census (http://www.census2011.co.in/data/town/800185-sirhind-fatehgarh-sahib-punjab.html).

as a Sikh while acknowledging the spiritual importance of a dilapidated Mughal-era mausoleum lying next to her farm. No interviews explicitly discussed Partition or alluded to any communal violence. These recordings were curated into the community exhibition through two routes: the groups used the interviews to write short descriptions of Sirhind's history for descriptive panels and some audio extracts were used on the day of the exhibition through an interactive panel that offered textual historical descriptions of Sirhind alongside audio recordings of local memories and accounts.

The final group focussed on designing the day-long exhibition, organising publicity and planning a route through the Aam Khas Bagh that was devised in such a way as to incorporate elements of Sirhind's larger history through the use of interpretative signage, descriptive panels and the interviews. When the day arrived, we were unsure how many people would actually come to see this experimental pop-up exhibition, but we ended up having over 400 visitors pass through the site, the vast majority of whom came for the exhibition. Collecting comments at the end, the students were continually praised for taking an interest in the history of Sirhind. When students chatted with visitors, they agreed that the Aam Khas Bagh was a historical building that had value, particularly as a potential site for weddings or for visiting as a site of leisure.

After the conclusion of the event, a smaller group of students were able to attend a conference for heritage professionals in Chandigarh to present their work. Beyond this, parts of the exhibition travelled to the UnBox Festival in Delhi (2013) and following that, to the Alchemy Festival at the Southbank Centre (London) later that year. We could, therefore, end our story here, with the positive results of historical rehabilitation and the replacing of the Aam Khas Bagh in Sirhind's landscape as a site of accrued memory and significance attached to the broader Islamic past and heritage of the area. The success of the exhibition lay in reconnecting Sirhind's population to the people and communities that had lived in the same space and around the same buildings in the past, thereby identifying new lines of connection through the layers of the palimpsest. As a discussion between an academic, an artistic practitioner, designers, architects and conservation experts, this had been our larger aim, motivated by our own cultural research and practice.

CONCLUSION

"Community" approaches to heritage, especially those involving local communities in heritage management, are themselves a new kind of orthodoxy in heritage, with such involvement being a mandatory factor in many government or international heritage plans.[33] Yet, this commitment in itself points to a crucial contradiction in heritage management. As Bahar Aykan suggests, "Prioritizing national perspectives and interests on heritage, UNESCO projects may well serve to the exclusion of alternative interpretations of heritage, especially that of the marginalized groups".[34] In a discussion of participation in community heritage that offers a summary critique of "community" in practices of heritage management, Emma Waterton and Laurajane Smith use Nancy Fraser's work on social justice to interrogate hierarchies of visibility and representation in heritage narratives[35]:

> Not only are many people overlooked as authorities capable of adjudicating their own sense of heritage, so too is their lack of access to necessary resources. They are, in effect, subordinated and impeded because they do not hold the title 'heritage expert', as well as lacking the resources assumed necessary to participate in heritage projects (Western schooling, economic means, etc.), and also potentially 'lacking' a particular vision or understanding of heritage and the accepted values that underpin this vision (universality, national and aesthetic values, etc.).[36]

Our presence in Sirhind represented a temporary intervention in coordination with an agency working in heritage and conservation. I arrived in Sirhind ready to use the palimpsest as a metaphor with which to imagine

---

[33] See Steve Watson and Emma Waterton, "Heritage and Community Engagement," *International Journal of Heritage Studies* 16, no. 1–2 (2010), 1–3, who speculate whether "the cosiness of some accounts of engagement actually mask abiding and inequitable imbalances between professionals and communities in relation to the control of resources and narratives" 2.

[34] Bahar Aykan, 383. See also Yahaya Ahmed on the specific politics around UNESCO and ICOMOS's role in communities and heritage management.

[35] Emma Waterton and Laurajane Smith, "The Recognition and Misrecognition of Community Heritage," *International Journal of Heritage Management* 16, no. 1–2 (2010), 4–15.

[36] Waterton and Smith, 10.

alternative connected histories and carried with me the status of an international education. Working with a conservation architect, I was also representing the interests of conservation—ultimately community participation in heritage in this context was a tool with which to guarantee the future of the Aam Khas Bagh in the face of neglect and disinvestment on the part of the state. In Sirhind, other organisations with competing interests and political alignments positioned themselves as the best caretakers of Sirhind's history. While creating the exhibition was an illuminating experience for the students who participated in the process, and the community exhibition at the Aam Khas Bagh allowed the site to exist in a different relief for a day, it is all too easy to neatly package a moment of community cooperation and of the rehabilitation of the past as a success, without full appreciation of the broader picture.

The process of staging this exhibition brought together a series of complex hierarchies. Firstly, there are the global politics of heritage management and the danger of communities living in the vicinity of neglected historical sites being *informed* and *educated* on their own environment outside of a framework of peace-building and reconciliation. Secondly, there is the persistent power of erasure. While we may have delivered a process designed to trigger different kinds of imaginative connection to the past, connections which questioned and critiqued dominant narratives of heritage in the area, this work becomes inert without an afterlife of continued creative engagement in that area and at the site (something that is impossible without state funding and permission). In the end, the exhibition experienced no resistance, and in an area so impacted by a history of religious conflict and the legacy of Partition, mention of 1947 itself appeared to be absent, seemingly irrelevant to the task at hand. Part of the reason the Aam Khas Bagh fails to resonate in Sirhind is because a community that could connect the site to other historical, religious and cultural sites, has now been resettled in Pakistan. The partitioning of Sirhind's community memory leaves gaps and silences that were either too painful, too distant or irrelevant to those taking part in our exhibition. Filling in these blanks, or "educating" a population about a larger Punjabi heritage that goes beyond religion, becomes impossible without raising the spectre of Partition. With memories rerouted, forgotten, or displaced, the Aam Khas Bagh finds itself a stranger in Sirhind, a beaten and weathered testimony to a Punjab divided.

WORKS CITED

Ahmad, Yahana. "The Scope and Definitions of Heritage: From Tangible to Intangible." *International Journal of Heritage Studies* 12, no. 3 (2006): 292–300.

Ashworth, G.J., and B. Graham, eds. *Senses of Place: Senses of Time.* Aldershot: Ashgate, 2005.

Aykan, Bahar. "How Participatory is Participatory Heritage Management? The Politics of Safeguarding the Alevi *Semah* Ritual as Intangible Heritage." *International Journal of Heritage Management* 20 (2013): 381–405.

Ballantyne, Tony. *Between Colonialism and Diaspora: Sikh Cultural Formations in an Imperial World.* Durham: Duke University Press, 2006.

Bhangoo Randhawa, Karenjot. *Civil Society in Malerkotla, Punjab: Fostering Resilience Through Religion.* Lanham: Lexington Books, 2012.

Bigelow, Anne. *Sharing the Sacred: Practicing Pluralism in Muslim North India.* Oxford: Oxford University Press, 2010.

Chakrabarty, Dipesh. "Modernity and Ethnicity in India." In *Multicultural States: Rethinking Difference and Identity,* ed. David Bennett. London: Routledge, 1998, 91–110.

Chalana, Manish. "'All the World Going and Coming': The Past and Future of the Grand Trunk Road in Punjab, India." In *Cultural Landscapes of South Asia: Studies in Heritage Conservation and Management,* ed. Kapila D. Silva and Amita Sinha. London and New York: Routledge, 2016, 92–110.

Cunningham, Alexander. *Archaeological Survey of India,* vol. 1. Simla: Government of India Press, 1871.

Derrida, Jacques. *Archive Fever: A Freudian Impression.* Chicago: University of Chicago Press, 1996.

Dillon, Sarah. *The Palimpsest: Literature, Criticism, Theory.* London: Continuum, 2007.

Dhavan, Purnima. *When Sparrows Became Hawks: The Making of the Sikh Warrior Tradition, 1699–1799.* Oxford: Oxford University Press, 2011.

De Quincey, Thomas. *Confessions of an English Opium Easter and Other Writings.* Oxford: Oxford University Press, 2013.

Deol, Hamik. *Religion and Nationalism in India: The Case Study of the Punjab.* London: Routledge, 2011.

Glover, William J. "Shiny New Buildings, Rebuilding Historic Sikh Gurdwaras in Indian Punjab." *Future Anterior,* IX, no. 1 (Summer 2012): 32–47.

Gopinath, Gayatri. *Impossible Desires: Queer Diasporas and South Asian Public Cultures.* Durham: Duke University Press, 2005.

Gourgouris, Stathis. *Dream Nation: Enlightenment, Colonization, and the Institution of Modern Greece.* Stanford: Stanford University Press, 1996.

Gupta, Ketan. 3 day annual Urs begins at Sirhind Shrine. *Hindustan Times,* December 21, 2014, http://www.hindustantimes.com/punjab/3-day-annual-urs-begins-at-sirhind-shrine/story-cdHt9hglyY53U90nnkWO9K.html. Last Accessed 15 May 2017.

Guttman, Anna. *The Nation of India in Contemporary Indian Literature.* Basingstoke: Palgrave, 2007.

Hirsch, Marianne. "The Generation of Postmemory." *Poetics Today* 28, no. 1 (2008): 103–128.

Huyssen, Andreas. *Present Pasts: Urban Palimpsests and the Politics of Memory.* Stanford: Stanford University Press, 2003.

Kabir, Ananya Jahanar. *Partition's Post-Amnesias: 1947, 1971 and Modern South Asia.* New Delhi: Women Unlimited, 2013.

Kaviraj, Sudipta. *The Imaginary Institution of India: Politics and Ideas.* New York: Columbia University Press, 2010.

Leontis, Artemis. *Topographies of Hellenism: Mapping the Homeland.* London: Cornell University Press, 1995.

McDowell, Sara. "Heritage Memory and Identity." In *The Ashgate Research Companion to Heritage and Identity,* ed. Brian Graham and Peter Howard, 27–54. Aldershot: Ashgate, 2008.

Mir, Farina. *The Social Space of Language: Vernacular Culture in British Colonial Punjab.* Berkeley and Los Angeles: University of California Press, 2010.

Murphy, Anne. *The Materiality of the Past: History and Representation in Sikh Tradition.* Oxford: Oxford University Press, 2012.

Murray's Handbook to India. London: John Murray, 1909.

Nehru, Jawaharlal. *The Discovery of India.* New Delhi: Oxford University Press, 1994.

Pal, Amaninder. The Tale of Closed Doors of Rauza Sharif Shrine. *The Tribune,* December 28, 2015, http://www.tribuneindia.com/news/punjab/community/the-tale-of-closed-doors-of-rauza-sharif-shrine/176083.html. Accessed 15 May 2017.

Parihar, Subhash. *History and Architectural Remains of Sirhind: The Greatest Mughal City on the Delhi-Lahore Highway.* New Delhi: Aryan Books, 2006.

Parihar, Subhash. "Historical Mosques of Sirhind." *Islamic Studies* 43, no. 3 (Autumn 2004): 481–510.

Parihar, Subhash. *Some Aspects of Indo-Islamic Architecture.* New Delhi: Shakti Malik, 1999.

Singh, Khushwant. *A History of the Sikhs: 1469–1838.* Oxford: Oxford University Press, 2004.

Virdee, Pippa. "Remembering Partition: Women, Oral Histories and the Partition of 1947." *Oral History* 41, no. 2: 49–62.

Waterton, Emma, and Laurajane Smith. "The Recognition and Misrecognition of Community Heritage." *International Journal of Heritage Management* 16, no. 1–2 (2010), 4–15.

Watson, Steve, and Emma Waterton. "Heritage and Community Engagement." *International Journal of Heritage Studies* 16, no. 1–2 (2010): 1–3.

INDEX

© TheEditor(s) (if applicable) and The Author(s) 2018
C. Mahn and A. Murphy (eds.), *Partition and the Practice of Memory*,
https://doi.org/10.1007/978-3-319-64516-2